The Architectonics of Meaning

THE ARCHITECTONICS OF MEANING

Foundations of the New Pluralism

With a new Preface

Walter Watson

The University of Chicago Press

Chicago and London

The University of Chicago Press, Chicago 60637
The University of Chicago Press, Ltd., London

© 1985, 1993 by Walter Watson

Originally published 1985
University of Chicago Press Edition 1993
Printed in the United States of America
01 00 99 98 97 96 95 94 93   6 5 4 3 2 1

ISBN 0-226-87506-7 (pbk.)

Library of Congress Cataloging-in-Publication Data

Watson, Walter, 1925–
    The architectonics of meaning : foundations of the new
pluralism / Walter Watson.
        p.   cm.
    Originally published: Albany : State University of New York
Press, 1985. With a new preface.
    Includes bibliographical references and index.
    1. Methodology.   2. Pluralism.   3. McKeon, Richard Peter,
1900–   . I. Title.
BD241.W37   1993
121′.68—dc20   93-9213
                                                          CIP

♾ The paper used in this publication meets the minimum
requirements of the American National Standard for Information
Sciences—Permanence of Paper for Printed Library Materials,
ANSI Z39.48-1984.

To Ernest C. Pollard,
An exemplary scientist and an exemplary person.

Contents

Preface to the 1993 Edition

This new edition—for which I wish to express particular thanks to Douglas Mitchell, Donald Levine, and Wayne Booth—provides an occasion for commenting on events that have occurred since the book first appeared. One of these is the publication of Richard McKeon's 1966 paper "Philosophic Semantics and Philosophic Inquiry," in Richard McKeon, *Freedom and History and Other Essays,* edited by Zahava K. McKeon (The University of Chicago Press, 1990). This paper presents McKeon's later semantic schema, which invites comparison with the archic matrix of the present book. I have undertaken such a comparison in an article that will appear in *Philosophy and Rhetoric.* I argue that the approaches of McKeon and myself are homoarchic except for a difference in method, his being rhetorical and mine resolutive. His approach is innovative and provocative and opens up new possibilities of inquiry, but ultimately it is tied to his unique genius and does not admit of a definitive formulation as a doctrine, whereas the archic matrix is independent of any individual mind, being justified by its capacity to order the materials that it treats, and is therefore suited to a wide use by many different individuals.

One example of its use is in David Dilworth's *Philosophy in World Perspective: A Comparative Hermeneutic of the Major Theories* (Yale University Press, 1989), which provides complete archic profiles of all the major philosophers, Eastern as well as Western, thus sparing the rest of us much labor. Dilworth also argues against the parity of archic modes and for the superiority of the pure modes. His view makes sense within his own mode, but perhaps he would agree that it has not been shown that the criteria he uses would be acceptable within all modes. Presumably it is possible to formulate neutral criteria, but they would take the form of ambiguous commonplaces that would not, I believe, provide grounds for universally accepted judgments of the superiority of one mode to another.

One general criticism of *The Architectonics of Meaning* deserves mention because it both shows a grasp of the central import of the book and represents a natural reaction to it. In Patricia Athay's succinct formulation, "They can't all be right!" "They" here refers to the whole range of philosophers who are customarily included in the teaching of the discipline. The reply to this requires a distinction between the generative principles of a philosophy and philosophy as a concrete expression in which the generative principles are used to order a particular set of materials. It is the principles that are ultimately defensible, not the results of their use in a particular situation. This is why philosophy is never finished, but must always be again thinking everything through from principles. There is nevertheless a heuristic advantage in working from the supposition that a philosophy is defensible even in its concrete expression, for this counters our natural tendency to dismiss as erroneous whatever does not accord with our preconceptions. Such an unqualified defense of the great philosophers was a central feature of McKeon's teaching.

The shift from philosophies as concrete expressions to their principles leaves us with stark oppositions of principle unless we return again to the use of principles in concrete cases. When this is done pluralistically, setting aside at least temporarily the endeavor to annihilate principles different from our own, the capacity of philosophies to assimilate the positive results of their opponents comes to the fore and the irreducible oppositions of principle recede into the background.

For example, the present architectonics of meaning is pluralistic, while Aristotle's architectonics of being is so nonpluralistic that Francis Bacon was led to say (*Advancement of Learning,* book II, "Calendars of Doubts") that Aristotle, as though he had been of the race of the Ottomans, thought he could not reign except the first thing he did he killed all his brethren. Yet both architectonics seek to discover causes in their full power and autonomy, and nowhere can the full power and autonomy of man the measure or of material causes or of ideal connectedness or of the finality of functioning be better seen than in the philosophies that make them primary. Whatever these philosophies justifiably attribute to the causes they favor can therefore be read back into Aristotle as consequences of his causes, and the pluralism of *The Architectonics of Meaning* and Aristotle's nonpluralism come to express the same truth.

The more one works with pluralism, the more the doctrines that at first seem opposed to each other and to one's own view become incorporated in the unity of one's own view, whatever that may be. The sense in which they can all be right thus becomes evident, although this sense varies with one's own view. The plurality of pluralisms has been discussed in my "Types of Pluralism" (*The Monist* 73 [1990]: 350–66).

Since the initial publication of this book there has been an increasing awareness of the validity of multiple points of view and an increasing attention to the great figures in the history of philosophy. These developments have been accompanied by a strong resurgence of sophistic modes of thought in the form of deconstruction, antifoundationalism, and postmodernism. The opposition between Analytic and Continental philosophy has faded away, and it seems that the principal divide in the intellectual world is now (as it has sometimes been in the past) between those for whom indeterminacies of meaning and incommensurabilities of approach preclude comprehensive rational structures and those for whom this is not the case. In this situation the present book has the value of providing an alternative to the prevailing questioning of rationality, for it shows how the welter of appar- ently irreconcilable interpretations and views can be included in a larger rationality.

Although one who has argued for the parity of archic modes can hardly condemn the principles of the new sophistic, it is still possible to argue that the principles are being used in a reductive way that fails to do justice to the positions that are being interpreted. What is needed, first, is a better understanding of the sophistic tradition as a whole. Sophistic modes are always new and fashionable and attractive to the young, and the new insights of these modes result in the dismissal of previous theories as without adequate foundation; however, though popular and central in their own time, the new modes tend to become marginalized in the subsequent histories, thus leaving space for new claims to novelty. In *Reason Papers 16* (Fall, 1991) I have attempted to place Richard Rorty's antifoundationalism in the context of the longer history of antifoundationalism and to exhibit its properties as consequences of its archic profile.

A second need can be identified by noting the superiority of Protagoras to his fellow Sophists. While all the Sophists were concerned to change beliefs, and did so by making use of beliefs that were already accepted, the ends sought by Protagoras distinguish him (if we are to believe Plato) from other Sophists such as Gorgias, who conceives rhetoric as a neutral power that can be used to attain whatever end the rhetorician desires, or Hippias, whose universal wisdom is used to enhance the esteem in which Hippias himself is held, or Euthydemus and Dionysodorus, whose eristic is used to win arguments.

The resurrected Protagoras of Plato's *Theaetetus* defines his wisdom as follows: "By a wise man I mean precisely a man who can change any one of us, when what is bad appears and is to him, and make what is good appear and be to him" (*Theaetetus* 166d, trans. Cornford). Similarly, "The wise and honest rhetoricians substitute in the community sound for unsound views of what is right. For I hold that whatever practices seem right and laudable to any particular state are so, for that state, so long as it holds by them" (ibid. 167c). It is thus clear that, according to this account, Protagoras used his wisdom to realize the ends that were sought by his clients. This is supported by the statement of Protagoras in the *Protagoras* that Hippocrates will learn from Protagoras "only what he has come to learn" (318e, trans. Guthrie), and by the method of payment Protagoras adopted (ibid. 328b–c). It also makes clear the significance of the remarkable passage in the *Theaetetus* in which Protagoras accuses Socrates of proceeding agonistically rather than dialectically:

> It is very unreasonable that one who professes a concern for virtue should be constantly guilty of unfairness in argument. Unfairness here consists in not observing the distinction between a debate (*hōs agōnizomenos tas diatribas poiētai*) and a conversation (*hōs dialegomenos tas diatribas poiētai*). A debate need not be taken seriously and one may trip up his opponent to the best of one's power, but a conversation should be taken in earnest; one should help out the other party and bring home to him only those slips and fallacies that are due to himself or to his earlier instructors." (*Theaetetus* 167e, trans. Cornford)

This serious respect for the views of the other is a point of coincidence between the dialectic of Plato and the method of Protagoras, a method which appears to have been superior to the methods of his fellow Sophists in its results, whether in education, in exhibiting the power of the art, in gaining esteem, or in winning arguments. (One might think here also of William James, or Carl Rogers.)

The point of bringing up this distinction between Protagoras and the other Sophists is to suggest that if any of those who currently operate in the sophistic mode were to follow his distinguished example and treat as the views of an author only those views that the author himself would be willing to accept, he would become a genuine pluralist, and, by bringing the power of a comprehensive rationality within the scope of his principles, rather than excluding it, he would both advance his own cause and contribute to the education of mankind.

Setauket, New York
November 17, 1992

Preface

This book presents what I take to be the most significant philosophic discovery of the present century. This is the discovery, first, of the fact of pluralism, that the truth admits of more than one valid formulation, and, secondly, of the reason for this fact in arbitrary or conventional elements inseparable from the nature of thought itself. With this discovery, the very thing that was formerly thought to be a scandal and a disgrace to philosophy, namely, that philosophers do not agree, turns out to be its great virtue, for through it are revealed essential features of all thought, present indeed everywhere, but nowhere so clearly as in philosophy.

At the present time this discovery is emerging into consciousness in many ways. In general, its consequences are recognized before the reasons for them are clear. In philosophy, it is becoming increasingly apparent that the attempt to establish the one true philosophy by refuting all other philosophies is not destined to succeed, for the refutation of all other philosophies depends on interpreting them in the terms of one's own philosophy, and this exposes one to the danger of the fallacy known technically as *ignoratio elenchi*, or ignorance of what refutation is, that is, refuting what has not been asserted. What philosopher has not had occasion to complain that his critics seem unable to read? But even as the attempt to refute all philosophies different from one's own has come to seem futile, the problems of communication across different theoretical frameworks and of how achievements made possible by one framework can be incorporated in another have acquired new interest and urgency. It is also becoming apparent that comparisons of the conclusions of different philosophies that fail to take account of the different principles on which they depend are for this reason unenlightened and unenlightening, while comparisons that do take account of such principles have a precision formerly unattainable and disclose hitherto unnoticed relationships and lines of determination in our thinking. The history of philosophy is now seen less as a museum of curiosities and errors and more as an inventory of archetypal possibilities that supply standards and resources for future inquiries. The teaching of philosophy today is in general not limited to the presentation of a single view, but at every level the student works with a multiplicity of philosophic approaches. Leading departments of philosophy are deliberately organized around some conception of this multiplicity of approaches.

Further, since the special arts and sciences are particular embodiments of philosophic principles, a pluralism at the level of philosophy implies the possibility of a similar pluralism at the level of the special arts and sciences. Differences of approach within the arts and sciences are no longer seen as differences to be settled by a simple appeal to the facts, but as differences of approach or framework or style or paradigm that determine what the facts are and that reflect ultimate philosophic differences. In every discipline today, in literary criticism through psychology and economics to physics, one encounters a new awareness of the presence and significance of fundamental differences of approach.

The implicit recognition of pluralism in many domains has led to the development of explicit theories about it. The possible approaches to a subject are schematized (if their number is considered finite), the reasons for this multiplicity are examined, and the practical interrelations of the different approaches are explored. These problems are being approached from many different directions, and already there is a pluralism of pluralisms. One hears on all sides talk of root metaphors, semantic schemata, conceptual frameworks, structuralism, paradigm shifts, language games, ontological relativity, philosophical styles, meta-philosophy, hermeneutics, and so on. The time is therefore opportune for an attempt to clarify this situation by investigating the foundations of pluralism and why they themselves assume plural forms, and for doing so in a way that will, so far as possible, make these foundations intelligible to the many people who are now encountering in one way or another their pervasive consequences.

Although the times are propitious for this endeavor, formidable difficulties remain. We are here dealing with a fundamental advance in the life of the spirit, and such an advance, as Hegal reminds us, has the negative significance of death and destruction for the self and its truth. Pluralism runs counter to habits of thought deeply engrained in both the individual and the race. The world, we think, is one, and therefore our accounts of it should agree. If two people, or two philosophies, disagree, we think that at least one of them must be wrong. All such differences are considered substantive and resoluble by an appeal to logic and the facts, and we find it difficult to become aware of arbitrary or conventional elements in thought and to appreciate their importance. For the discovery of pluralism is not the discovery of some new item to be added to our knowledge, but is rather the discovery of an unrecognized dimension present in all our knowledge.

Heavy demands are therefore placed on both the author and the reader of a book that attempts to present the foundations of the new pluralism. The discovery of pluralism is the result of the whole development of conscious thought from its first beginnings, and it can best be appreciated in the history of philosophy itself. But the history of philosophy is familiar to few people, and even those who are familiar with it have not always understood it in the way required, for if a philosophy is to become a living possibility, one must be so at home in it that one can see how to reply to the criticisms and objections that have been or might be raised against it; that is, one must understand it in its fundamental validity. But how many philosophies can one person understand in this way?

Philosophies are difficult to understand because to understand a philosophy is to understand the possibility of a reorientation of all one's thought. A philosophy re-orients all one's thought because it is in its nature concerned with what is primary and universal. This very primacy and universality, however, can also make it easy to attain at least a partial grasp of a philosophy, for its consequences can be seen anywhere. Thus all the philosophic possibilities examined in this book can be illustrated within any of the natural sciences or social sciences or arts. There is access to them through whatever domain one finds congenial. In what follows I have therefore made use of well-known examples from different special fields, although in so doing, since I am not a specialist in these fields, I cannot hope to avoid shortcomings and errors. But it is my hope that the principles I am presenting will emerge clearly enough from the diverse examples so that they can be used to remedy the shortcomings and correct the errors with which they may here be encumbered.

Even in the commonplaces of everyday thought one can find adumbrations of the great philosophic possibilities, so that one can up to a point meet the requirements Molly Bloom lays down when she asks her husband the meaning of "metempsychosis":

—Who's he when he's at home?

—Metempsychosis, he said, frowning. It's Greek: from the Greek. That means the transmigration of souls.

—O, rocks! she said. Tell us in plain words.

And the basic insight of pluralism, however unintelligible or wrongheaded it may appear at first, becomes, once attained, obvious, even trivial, and the sort of thing one somehow knew all along. But there has been a genuine advance of thought to a new level of awareness, and everything said or written in ignorance of it will be seen, by that fact alone, to belong to a bygone epoch.

My own approach to pluralism is through the work of Richard McKeon. All that I say derives from him, and yet I would not want to claim that any of it represents his views, which he in any case is perfectly capable of presenting himself. For I am well aware that there are many differences between us both in general and in detail. Perspective as an archic variable is not to be found, so far as I know, in his work, and the introduction of this variable influences the interpretation of the others and this in turn the characterization of particular authors. My concern has been neither to reproduce what McKeon has said, nor to introduce some novel view of my own, but to formulate principles that are free of arbitrary or personal elements because grounded in conditions of knowing that are the same for all.

In this project, I am indebted to many others, and in particular to three colleagues whose help has been invaluable. To Richard Wynne I am indebted for wide-ranging and sustained conversations almost every summer over a period of many years. I have consulted him on questions of terminology and formal structure, and he has made detailed and helpful suggestions with respect to the greater part of the manuscript. With Leonard Gardner I have discussed in weekly meetings during the academic year, again for a period of many years, what has become the content of this book and the application of this content to many subjects, particularly to literature, psychology, and religion. His own study of the book of Genesis is an admirable example of the value of archic analysis in interpreting a single text. And David Dilworth has criticized and developed the ideas of this book with great acumen and vigor, frequently correcting my mistakes, and has applied these ideas to a world-wide range of texts, particularly those of the Asian traditions. I am also indebted to him for organizing a faculty and graduate student seminar on this book before it was even completed, as well as to the participants in that seminar, particularly Patricia Athay and Mary Rawlinson.

I am in fact indebted to all my colleagues at Stony Brook, and I wish to mention particularly Robert Sternfeld and Harold Zyskind, to whom I owe innumerable insights derived from discussions extending over many years. Bruce Bashford in the English Department has been my principal source on pluralism in literary theory.

To my former colleagues at the New School, particularly Kenneth Telford and David Depew, I owe many fruitful discussions whose results are reflected in what follows. Edmund Leites has been most helpful both in personal discussion and in providing opportunities for presenting in speech and writing much that has gone into this book. The encouragement and advice of Patrick Heelan and Robert Neville have been of great value to me, and I must also thank Charles Sherover for his appreciative and benign insistence that I write this book.

My wife Norma, in spite of heavy professional obligations of her own, has provided helpful advice on every sort of question, as well as editorial assistance and typing.

I. Archic Variables

1. Philosophic Diversity

When philosophy is viewed as what philosophers have written, and this is the way we tend to view it today, the primary fact about it is just the fact of its diversity. A great variety of positions have been formulated, attacked, and defended. Each position has endeavored to resolve the differences and produce agreement. But the result has always been the same: the diversity has continued, although perhaps in new forms. And it is not just the Western tradition stemming from Greece and noted for its contentiousness that has been characterized by diversity of doctrine; the same is true of the Indian and Chinese traditions.[1] Nor is this diversity limited to philosophy, although it is most evident there. For all the arts and sciences make use of philosophic principles, and disagreements within the arts and sciences usually involve a philosophic component.

There is something marvelous in this state of affairs. For the world is one, and our accounts of it should therefore agree, but those who are most competent to give such an account do not agree. Those in whom philosophic differences emerge with the greatest clarity and force are the great minds of the race, those whom above all others we should expect to resolve the entire situation by disclosing the principles on which it depends. And yet it is precisely these who seem to aggravate the situation and render it insoluble. One cannot escape the impression that something is at work here which is not understood.

That the greatest wisdom should enforce the most profound and persistent diversity is paradoxical only on the supposition that the truth admits of only one valid formulation. How sure are we of this supposition? The world is not the same as its formulation in language, and perhaps the formulation in language inevitably introduces unnoticed sources of variation. The failure of all efforts to resolve philosophic diversity on the assumption that there can be only one correct philosophy suggests that we explore the opposite possibility, that the diverse philosophies only appear to be incompatible, but are not really so. We can gain some insight into what this might mean by examining instances from other domains in which apparent incompatibilities can be mistaken for real ones.

If one person asserts that a certain distance is about ten feet, and another that it is approximately three meters, it is not at once evident whether the two propositions are compatible, since they state the distance in different units. To determine whether they are compatible, we use a conversion formula to convert the two estimates into the same units. We find that 10 feet = 3.04801 meters, and conclude that the two propositions are compatible. There is a certain arbitrariness in the choice of units of length, and we cannot eliminate it because we must use some units or other. But the different units are convertible into one another, and are incompatible only in the sense that in any measurement one must use some one unit of length and not mix up the different units indiscriminately.

If one person asserts that $7+5=12$, and another that $7+5=10$, we seem to have a real incompatibility. And yet if the second person is using the duodecimal system the incompatibility disappears. For "12" in the decimal system represents the same number as "10" in the duodecimal system. Just as there is a certain arbitrariness in the choice of the unit of length in measurement, so there is a certain arbitrariness in the choice of base in a positional notation. And just as one must use some unit of length, so here one must use some base. And as we can convert measurements expressed in different units into each other, so we can convert numbers expressed in different notations into each other, and the different notations are incompatible only in the sense that in any calculation one must use some definite notation and not mix them up indiscriminately.

Suppose that one person asserts that the sum of the angles of a triangle is equal to two right angles, and another denies it. These propositions appear to be incompatible, but if the second is made in a non-Euclidean geometry, the incompatibility disappears. The difference of the two assertions is then the result of different postulates as to the number of lines parallel to a given line that can be drawn through a point not on the line. The arbitrariness in the number of parallels that can be postulated is analogous to the arbitrariness in the choice of unit of length or in the choice of base for a positional notation. Both geometrical propositions are true in the sense that they can be proved from their respective postulates. If one is to have a geometry in which the angles of a triangle have a definite sum one must use some postulate of this kind, and just as there were in the two previous examples conversion formulae which enable us to convert the results of different systems into one another, so here there are translation formulae for converting the results of one geometry into propositions in the other geometry. The two geometries are incompatible only in the sense that in proving a theorem one must work within one of them and cannot mix them up indiscriminately. Of course, if one asks which geometry is true of the physical world, and also specifies how the geometric entities such as straight lines are to be interpreted physically, then there is a real incompatibility. But this is analogous to the real incompatibility of 10 and 3 as the number of units of length in a given distance once the unit of length has been specified, or the incompatibility of 12 and 10 as the sum of $7+5$ once the base has been specified.

Again, suppose that one person asserts that during the course of a day the sun and stars revolve around the earth, and another that it is the earth that is rotating. These propositions appear to be incompatible until we reflect that any description of motion implies a body relative to which it is described. If the earth is taken as at rest, then the sun and stars move around the earth, but if the sun and stars are taken as at rest, then the earth rotates on its axis. For the purpose of describing the motion there is no reason why we must choose one reference body rather than the other; the same motion can be described either way. Even for the purpose of explaining the motion, if the principle of general relativity is correct, the motion as described from either standpoint will be explained by the same laws. There is here an arbitrariness in the choice of reference body that is analogous to the arbitrariness noted in the choice of unit of length, base for a number system, and parallel postulate. And, as in the previous cases, one must use some reference body or other to describe the motion, and there are translation formulae that enable one to convert the description from one reference body to the description from another. The Ptolemaic and Copernican hypotheses are incompatible only in the sense that one cannot adopt both at once for the description of motion, or mix them up indiscriminately. And yet at one time they were thought to be really incompatible, and the shift from one to the other figures as an important revolution in the history of thought.

When knowledge is expressed mathematically, it is comparatively easy to distinguish between real and apparent incompatibility and to identify arbitrary elements. Schrödinger, for example, was able to demonstrate the formal equivalence of his own wave mechanics and the matrix mechanics of Heisenberg. But in the case of knowledge expressed verbally it may be more difficult. Suppose that one person asserts that a government-controlled press cannot be free, and another denies it. The two propositions appear incompatible until we reflect on the meaning of "freedom." If freedom implies the freedom to choose or express alternatives, then a government-controlled press is not free. But if it is the truth that makes one free, so that one is free not when one can chose or express alternatives, but when one knows which alternatives to choose or express, then a government-controlled press can be free. There is here a certain arbitrariness in the meaning of "freedom," or rather, since this meaning is determined as part of a system of meanings, in the systems of meaning that we use to state our knowledge. And, as in the mathematical cases, one must use some system of meaning or other if one is to assert anything, and presumably translation from one system to another is possible, although hardly with the precision of conversion formulae. The two systems are incompatible only in the sense that in thinking and expressing one's meaning one must use a consistent system and not mix up the meanings indiscriminately.

Again, suppose that one person asserts that works of literary art are imitations, and another denies it. The two propositions appear incompatible until we reflect on what "imitation" means in the two cases. If "imitation" means copying, so that the better imitation is the better copy, then works of literary art are not imitations. But if "imitation" is used to distinguish artificial things having an organization and integrity of their own from the non-artificial things they resemble, then works of literary art are imitations. This case is similar to the preceding one. The arbitrariness lies in our systems of meaning, and the incompatibility only in the fact that one must use one system at a time, and not mix them up indiscriminately.

This series of examples indicates that apparent incompatibilities may be mistaken for real ones when they depend upon some arbitrary or conventional factor that is not perceived. If the apparent incompatibilities of philosophies are analogous to the apparent incompatibilities in these examples, we would expect to find in philosophic diversity the following features: (1) There is a certain arbitrariness in the nature of thought and in its expression in words that gives rise to philosophic diversity. (2) There is no way of avoiding this arbitrariness, since if one is to think or speak at all one must make some choice or other with respect to these arbitrary elements. (3) Some kind of translation or conversion from one philosophy to another is possible. (4) Different philosophies are incompatible only in the sense that one must think and speak in terms of one philosophy at a time, and not mix them up indiscriminately.

But even if all this were so, there would remain an important difference between philosophy and the other cases we have considered. For philosophy is concerned with what is primary and universal. In other fields differences of approach may be understood in ways that resolve the disagreement, but this will not be possible in philosophy because it is precisely the character of the inclusive system within which differences are to be resolved that is at stake in philosophic disagreements. The differences of number systems do not produce irresolvable disagreements in mathematics, for they are easily incorporated in a single theory of numerical notation. But in philosophy the incorporation of the diversity of philosophies into a systematic unity always presupposes a philosophy, and thus the same diversity reappears again at this meta-level. Even if the differences of philosophies correspond to apparent rather than real incompatibilities, we may still expect them to be irresolvable. There will thus be an inescapable pluralism in philosophy, and in all the arts and sciences so far as they reflect the principles that philosophy investigates. The actual situation in philosophy and the other arts and sciences does indeed correspond to this expectation, but if we are to say that it is because of the presence of arbitrary or conventional elements, we must first find such elements, and it is to this search that we now turn.

2. Ontic, Epistemic, and Semantic Epochs

Let us first look at one example of a philosophic difference to see whether it depends upon some arbitrary or conventional element. We began by noting that at the present time we tend to view philosophy as what philosophers have written. This primacy of the text is characteristic not only of philosophy today, but of all disciplines. All works of art have become texts in a broad sense of that word, and similarly social behavior and institutions, and even nature itself, have become texts for us to interpret. The pervasiveness of this concern with language and texts and interpretation indicates that we are dealing with a philosophic fact about the present epoch.

It has not always been the case that texts were thus conceived as a primary subject matter—one need only think back to the origins of the modern period in its revolt from verbalism and scholasticism. The history of philosophy exhibits a cycle of epochal shifts: from an ontic epoch concerned with that which is, or being, to an epistemic epoch concerned with how we know that which is, or knowing, to a semantic epoch concerned with the expression of what we know about that which is, or meaning, and back again to an ontic epoch concerned with being.

To illustrate what is meant, consider the period from the Greek sophists to the formulation of a Christian philosophy by St. Augustine. In the culminating phase of Hellenic philosophy, the Sophists, the Atomists, Plato, and Aristotle all were concerned with being, although being was differently conceived by each of them. For Protagoras, man measured the being of the things that are and the not-being of the things that are not; for the

Atomists, the atoms and the void, or being and not-being, were the elements of all things; Plato distinguished that which always is and has no becoming from that which is always becoming and never is; and Aristotle argued that there are several senses in which a thing may be said to be, but that which primarily is, is substance. Following the Hellenic period, in the first phase of Hellenistic philosophy, the Stoics, Epicureans, Academics, and Peripatetics all were concerned with the criterion by which we know being, although they differed as to what this criterion was. In the second phase of Hellenistic and Roman philosophy, philosophers such as Cicero, Sextus Empiricus, and Plotinus all were concerned with the different schools of philosophy and the multiple doctrines they had formulated, although they differed as to the way in which this multiplicity was to be resolved. And in formulating a Christian doctrine of bodies, minds, and God, and in distinguishing the history and destiny of the city of God from the history and destiny of the city of man, St. Augustine returned to a concern with being.

We ourselves are now in the concluding phase of a cycle which begins with the new sciences of the 17th century. Philosophers such as Francis Bacon turned from the interpretation of words to the interpretation of nature: "Man, being the servant and interpreter of Nature," says Bacon at the beginning of his *New Organon*, "can do and understand so much and so much only as he has observed in fact or in thought of the course of nature: beyond this he neither knows anything nor can do anything."[2]

Hume, however, at the beginning of his *Treatise of Human Nature*, proposes a new foundation for the system of the sciences in the principles of human nature, and this foundation is, he says, the only one upon which they can stand with any security:

> Here then is the only expedient, from which we can hope for success in our philosophical researches, to leave the tedious lingring method, which we have hitherto followed, and instead of taking now and then a castle or village on the frontier, to march up directly to the capital or center of these sciences, to human nature itself; which being once masters of, we may every where else hope for an easy victory . . . . There is no question of importance, whose decision is not compriz'd in the science of man; and there is none, which can be decided with any certainty, before we become acquainted with that science. In pretending therefore to explain the principles of human nature, we in effect propose a compleat system of the sciences, built on a foundation almost entirely new, and the only one upon which they can stand with any security.[3]

Similarly Kant, in the Preface to the second edition of the *Critique of Pure Reason*, proposes to make metaphysics scientific, and thus to put an end to the disagreements and lack of progress which have characterized it hitherto, by supposing, not that our knowledge must conform to objects, but that objects must conform to our knowledge:

> Hitherto it has been assumed that all our knowledge must conform to objects. But all attempts to extend our knowledge of objects by establishing something in regard to them *a priori*, by means of concepts, have, on this assumption, ended in failure. We must therefore make trial whether we may not have more success in the tasks of metaphysics, if we suppose that objects must conform to our knowledge . . . . We should then be proceeding precisely on the lines of Copernicus' primary hypothesis. Failing of satisfactory progress in explaining the movements of the heavenly bodies on the supposition that they all revolved round the spectator, he tried whether he might not have better success if he made the spectator to revolve and the stars to remain at rest.[4]

In the 20th century, however, philosophers have despaired of making philosophy scientific by seeking principles in the mind, and have instead turned to the meanings expressed in language. G. E. Moore, one of the first to make the linguistic turn, says in his *Autobiography*,

> I do not think that the world or the sciences would ever have suggested to me any philosophical problems. What has suggested philosophical problems to me is things which other philosophers have said about the world or the sciences. In many problems suggested in this way I have been (and still am) very keenly interested—the problems in question being mainly of two sorts, namely, first, the problem of trying to get really clear as to what on earth a given philosopher *meant* by something which he said, and, secondly, the problem of discovering what really satisfactory reasons there are for supposing that what he meant was true, or, alternatively, was false.[5]

Similarly, Rudolph Carnap concludes *The Logical Syntax of Language* by saying that philosophy will become scientific only when it is recognized and practiced as syntactical research:

> Only then will it be possible to replace traditional philosophy by a strict scientific discipline, namely, that of the logic of science as the syntax of the language of science. The step from the morass of subjectivist philosophical problems on to the firm ground of exact syntactical prob-

lems must be taken. Then only shall we have as our subject-matter
exact terms and theses that can be clearly apprehended. Then only will
there be any possibility of fruitful co-operative work on the part of the
various investigators working on the same problems—work fruitful for
the individual questions of the logic of science, for the scientific domain
which is being investigated, and for science as a whole.[6]

These changes from one epoch to another are generally accompanied by
high hopes, enthusiasm, and a certain amount of hoopla and fanfare about
Great Instaurations, Copernican Revolutions, and Linguistic Turns. There
are two reasons why this should be so. First, these changes are not merely
individual, but cultural. They affect the whole intellectual life of the epoch.
Thus to a person experiencing them they seem to offer the key to everything that is going on around him. In our own epoch, for example, in
which one finds everywhere a concern with readings, texts, and
interpretations, so that even the world has become a text to be interpreted,
it seems that a theory of interpretation is what is needed to master the
world. More than this, those who work out a new theory of being or
knowing or meaning correctly perceive in it the potentiality for a new and
secure foundation, although they may also mistakenly suppose that past
philosophic disagreements had their source in a poor choice of subject
matter. The high hopes and enthusiasm with which each epoch begins are
therefore eroded as the epoch advances and the old differences reappear in
new forms.

We can conceive the sequence in the following way. At the outset there
are only existent things to be investigated. But the investigation of existent things brings a new subject matter into existence, the knowledge of
these things, and after a sufficient time everything favors turning to the
investigation of how we know. For the investigation of the things that are
has led to a plurality of philosophies, and it seems impossible to resolve
this plurality by continuing along the same lines; rather, it seems probable
that it results from an insufficient investigation of how we know. How we
know is a new and relatively unexplored domain, and it is expected that its
investigation will end the disagreements of the past. Both Hume and Kant,
as we have seen, expected to attain certainty and agreement by founding
philosophy on principles in the human mind. After the investigation of
how we know has continued for a sufficient time, however, everything
favors turning to the expression of knowledge in what we say and do. For,
contrary to what was expected, the pluralism has reappeared, the possibilities of resolving it by investigating the mind appear to be exhausted, and
it even appears to result from a concern with what is subjective and unob-

servable. But the language we use to express our thoughts is objective and observable, and is a new and relatively unexplored domain. It is therefore expected that its investigation will put an end to the disagreements of the past. Thus Rudolph Carnap and the logical positivists expected to make philosophy scientific and to secure cooperative activity by turning from the morass of subjective problems to the clarity and definiteness of linguistic expression. But after the inquiry into meaning has been carried on for a sufficient time it too disappoints the sanguine hopes of its initiators, for the pluralism reappears, and in fact seems to result from the concern with what is merely scholastic or verbal. It is therefore expected that if we return to the realities of that which is the pluralism will finally disappear. Bacon treats the systematic disagreements of the ancients and the particular disagreements of the moderns as evidence that they both lacked a method for discovering the nature of things.[7]

This return to being is furthered by the entrance into the world of data and problems from some new source, so that the being now studied is no longer the same as the being studied in an earlier epoch. The beginnings of the principal phases of the intellectual history of the West are marked by such renewed inquiries into being. After the Hellenic inquiry into being, new data and problems arose with the advent of Christianity, with the establishment of a Christian kingdom under Charlemagne, with the recovery of Greek thought, particularly that of Aristotle, in the 12th and 13th centuries, and with the promise of the new sciences in the 17th century.[8]

3. Reciprocal Priority

What makes it possible for philosophy to change its subject matter in this way from being to knowing to meaning and back to being again? An adequate subject matter for philosophy must be all-inclusive or universal. There can be a plurality of all-inclusive or universal subject matters only if each of them includes the others. And we can see that this is the case with respect to the three principal ones that we have considered, for thoughts and words are among the things that are, and thought can be of things and words as well as itself, and words can be about things and thought as well as words. Since each subject matter includes the others, any of them can be used as a base for dealing with the others, and with all problems. Other universal subject matters are also possible; Dewey, for example, bases his philosophy on experience, where experience involves an interaction of subject and object, and things, thoughts, and words correspond to distinctions that can be made within experience. But insofar as each subject matter includes all the others, whatever can be achieved by an inquiry that takes one of them as primary can be incorporated in inquiries that take others as primary, and so the selection among them is not one that can be decided by an appeal to the facts.

The general relation among the different subject matters is one of *reciprocal priority*; that is, each is prior to the other two. The choice among the reciprocally prior alternatives, since it cannot be decided by the facts, corresponds to the arbitrary element noted earlier in the choice of units of length, base for a number system, geometric postulates, reference body for the description of motion, and systems of verbal meaning. If one is to use a universal subject matter, one must choose among the reciprocally prior alternatives, and presumably there will be modes of translation from one to another. The different subject matters are incompatible only in the sense that one must use one of them at a time, and not mix them up indiscriminately.

The apparent incompatibility of universal subject matters is in this way like the earlier examples of apparent incompatibility, and the arbitrariness from which it results depends upon reciprocally prior alternatives. The difference between universal subject matters is only one example of philosophic differences, but since philosophy is concerned with first principles, and since different principles can be first if each is prior to the others, it is reasonable to adopt the hypothesis of reciprocal priority as a guide in our inquiry into other philosophic differences.

I will begin this inquiry by locating it in the historical context just sketched. The hypothesis that reciprocal priorities underlie philosophic differences is not so very obscure or recondite, and one might wonder why it should be proposed so late in the history. We would indeed expect it to be proposed in a semantic epoch, like our own. For the world is one, but philosophies are many. If one is investigating being, or the faculties of the mind by which we know being, one does not at once encounter a diversity of universes or a diversity of faculties of knowing comparable to the diversity of philosophies that one encounters when the writings of philosophers themselves become the subject matter of philosophy. One can of course find a plurality of philosophies in epochs that investigate being or thought, but even in these the multiplicity comes to light only as philosophic doctrines are expressed in language. And in fact earlier semantic epochs were, like our own, concerned with what to make of the multiplicity of doctrines. In Cicero's dialogues, for example, the participants represent the various schools of philosophy. Isidore of Seville in the 7th century incorporates the multiple doctrines of his predecessors as the meanings of words in his encyclopaedic *Etymologies*. The Books of Sentences characteristic of the 12th century exhibit the divergent statements of different authorities on particular questions. And Pico della Mirandola in the 15th century incorporates all doctrines in his own eclecticism.

But why was it necessary to go through the cycle five times before its nature was discovered? Here we have a measure of the extent to which the path we are pursuing runs counter to our fundamental habits of thought. It requires a revolution in customary ways of thinking to suppose that philosophic differences have their source in reciprocal priorities rather than in inadequate data or faulty arguments. It seems that every other path consistent with these customary ways of thinking was tried many times before this possibility could be taken seriously. Long experience with the diversity of philosophies and with the impossibility of producing agreement by arguments for any one of them, however excellent these arguments might be, seems to be required before we at last come to realize what was, on the present hypothesis, the case from the very beginning. The whole history of philosophy would thus have been supplying the experiential base on which the discovery I am presenting rests, and it would not have been possible to make it until the accumulation of doctrines and the repetition of their principles had made the situation clear.

4. The Problem of Archic Variables

The historical context of our inquiry, then, is one in which being and knowing are approached through texts and their meanings, and we have this advantage over previous epochs of the same type, that we have a greater accumulation of texts at our disposal, and particularly all the texts written since the beginning of modern science in the 17th century, no small increment! Our problem is to use the extensive resources provided by the history of thought to see whether and how reciprocal priorities can account for the philosophic diversity that can be found in any epoch, whether that epoch is ontic or epistemic or semantic.

The reciprocally prior elements that we are seeking are within texts, for we are working in a semantic epoch and meaning is our universal subject matter. Some of the elements within texts are fundamental and some are derivative. Since we are trying to account for the full range of philosophic diversity, we are seeking the elements that are fundamental, that is, that bring with them a train of consequences but are not themselves consequences of some other element. Such fundamental internal determinants or causes of the characteristics of a text can be called its *principles*.

If the principles of different texts are reciprocally prior to one another, there must be in the different texts some common aspect or dimension with respect to which there is a reciprocal priority. For example, in the case we have already considered, the common aspect or dimension was what we have been calling their universal subject matter, whether being or knowing or meaning. I will call such a common aspect or dimension of a text a *variable*, and the different reciprocally prior principles the *values* of this variable.

It is evident that philosophic diversity is not a function of a single variable, but of multiple variables. For philosophies do not simply resemble and differ from each other as wholes, but are related in complex patterns of likeness and difference, resembling each other in some ways and differing from each other in other ways. Our problem therefore cannot be solved by a one-dimensional set of distinctions, such as those between idealism and realism, or empiricism and rationalism, or monism, dualism, and pluralism, or by distinguishing various kinds of root metaphors.

If we could combine the various traditional distinctions into a multi-dimensional typology or classification of philosophies, this would still not be what we are seeking. For while such a typology or classification would discriminate philosophies systematically from one another, it would leave the problem of their functioning or truth unresolved. But our concern from the outset is with functioning or truth, not with a typology or classification. If a typology or classification were to result from our efforts, it would only be a typology or classification of principles by virtue of which a text is potentially able to fulfill its function; for example, if it is a philosophy, to be a true philosophy.

We must therefore derive our principles from a conception of the text as functioning. Now if different principles are reciprocally prior to one another, they will be presupposed in the arguments by which they are defended and alternative principles attacked. Indeed, this is already implied in the distinctive character of philosophic controversy: each side refutes the other and remains unscathed in its own essential validity. The principles themselves must therefore be such as to be implicated in any functioning of the philosophy; it will be impossible to proceed at all without them. And if this is so, the variables of which the principles are values must be essential elements in a philosophic text, or, more generally, since philosophic differences can appear in any context, in any text. The variables we are seeking, then, are variables without which a text cannot be a text, and the principles that are the values of these variables are first principles or causes in the sense that they or their alternatives are required for any functioning of the text.

The search for such first principles or causes is a new problem for philosophy, and a fundamental one for philosophy today. And yet in another sense it is not a new problem, but simply a new form of the search for first principles and causes, the *protai archai* and *aitiai*, that has always characterized philosophy. What is new is conceiving of them as causes of the functioning of texts, and as reciprocally prior values of variables common to all texts.

In order to have a name for what we are seeking, I will call the internal variables essential to any text, whose values are causes of its functioning, and are reciprocally prior to one another, *archic variables*. The word "archic," pronounced ARK-ik, is derived from the Greek *archē,* meaning beginning or principle, and is intended to denote that which is a beginning or principle and which is leading, ruling, governing. The same root appears in the prefixes "archi-" or "arche-" or "arch-", as in "architecture," "archetype," or "archangel," and in the suffix "-archic," as in "monarchic," "anarchic," as well as in "archaic" and "archaeology." The archic variables are archic or first insofar as they cause without being caused, and are variables insofar as they assume different values in different texts. The values assumed in a particular text are the *archic elements* of that text.

We are seeking, then, the archic variables and the values they assume. All texts that are not fragmentary will have their archic elements. The word "text" is here used in a broad sense to include any expression of thought, not merely expressions of thought in words. Non-verbal expressions are also texts and will have their archic elements. The archic elements of a text may be more or less obscure and confused, however, and it will be best to seek them in texts in which they are clearest. These will be texts whose content has been most thoroughly thought through. Philosophers make it their business to think things through to their principles, but we need not limit ourselves to philosophic texts, for principles are no less evident in well thought-out texts in any field—in texts by Newton or Lincoln or Tolstoy, for example.

In investigating these texts, we must show, on the formal side, that every text must have some value for each of the archic variables, and that it must have one and only one of the possible values we discriminate. On the material side, we must show that archic variables and their values are able to introduce a scientific order into all expressions of human thought, in all traditions, on all subjects, throughout its history. At present the multiple philosophies of the world and their use in the special arts and sciences present a vast, disordered, confusing, problematic array. The test of our principles, or of any philosophic principles today, is their ability to order this whole domain.

II. Perspective

Every text is the work of an author. The author can, however, be considered as separate from the text, and we are concerned with the internal determinants of the text, and therefore with the author as presented by the text itself. The text may of course present itself as the work of an author quite different from the actual author of the text. But in any case this authorial voice will be present throughout the text as determining its approach or context or point of view or perspective. I will call the way in which the text presents its own authorship the *perspective* of the text.

Perspectives have the possibility of reciprocal priority, for each can be a perspective on all the others, a perspective on perspectives. Let us therefore take perspective as our first archic variable and as a rubric under which to investigate a first internal determinant of any text.

The varieties of authorial perspective have been investigated more fully by literary critics than by philosophers. Wayne Booth in *The Rhetoric of Fiction*, for example, is concerned with authorial perspectives, and his assertion that "though the author can to some extent choose his disguises, he can never choose to disappear"[1] corresponds to our treatment of perspective as an essential element in any text, although among the possible kinds of perspective we should leave room for one in which the author does indeed choose to disappear, and is present by being absent. The literary treatments of perspective reassure us that it is an important aspect of a text, and one that admits of variations that must be taken into account in interpreting the text. But they do not seek to identify the fundamental architectonic perspectives, that is, the set of fundamental kinds of perspective that are (1) exhaustive of the possibilities, (2) mutually exclusive in the sense that one cannot adopt two of them at the same time, and (3) mutually inclusive in the sense that each includes all the others in its own way.

1. Personal Perspectives

Each of us has first of all his own perspective. I have my perspective, you have your perspective, a third person has his perspective. These are *individual* or *personal* perspectives. Some aspects of a personal perspective may be shared by others, so that groups may have a group perspective, cultures a cultural perspective, civilizations a civilizational perspective, and mankind a human perspective. These are all *human* perspectives. Not only people, but also gods, baboons, frogs, and indeed all sentient beings, may be supposed to have their own perspectives. The distinctive perspectives of whatever may be supposed to have a perspective may be called *idiocentric* perspectives. We are people, however, and the idiocentric perspectives that are primary for us are personal perspectives. For the perspectives of creatures other than ourselves can become ours only as they enter into our own perspective, and human and group perspectives are weakened forms of personal perspectives. I will therefore call this first kind of perspective *personal* perspectives. The view that there is no escape from the limitations of one's own perspective is familiar as perspectivism—everyone sees things in his own way.

Perspectivism appears in the West as early as Xenophanes. The question that he says should be addressed to a guest when the circumstances are appropriate is fundamental to understanding personal perspectives: "Beside the fire in the winter season, reclining on a soft couch, well-fed, drinking sweet wine, nibbling chick-peas, it is meet to speak thus: 'Who and whence are you among men? How many are your years, my friend? How old were you when the Mede came?' "[2] Everyone has his own story, and the distinctive individuality of the person is also the ground for Xenophanes' ridicule of the Pythagorean doctrine of the transmigration of souls: "What he says about Pythagoras runs thus: 'Once they say he was passing by when a puppy was being whipped, and he took pity and said: "Stop, do not beat it; for it is the soul of a friend that I recognized when I heard it giving tongue." ' "[3]

We judge things in relation to us and not as they are in themselves: "If god had not made yellow honey, men would consider figs far sweeter."[4] We use our limited perspectives to form our ideas of reality as a whole, and imagine the gods to be like ourselves: "But mortals consider that the gods are born, and that they have clothes and speech and bodies like their own. The Ethiopians say that their gods are snub-nosed and black, the Thracians that theirs have light blue eyes and red hair. And if cattle and horses or lions had hands, or were able to draw with their hands and do the works that men can do, horses would draw forms of the gods like horses, and cattle like cattle, and they would make their bodies such as they each had themselves."[5] But the one god, greatest among gods and men, and identified with the whole, is in no way similar to mortals either in body or in thought.[6] The gods have not revealed all things to men from the beginning, although in time men by seeking find out better.[7] But the truth about the whole remains inaccessible to us: "No man knows, or ever will know, the truth about the gods and about everything I speak of: for even if one chanced to say the complete truth, yet oneself knows it not; but seeming is wrought over all things."[8] This "seeming" is the result of our inability to get away from ourselves and our own point of view.

For Protagoras also we each have our own perspective, but for him there is no reality over and above the way things appear to each person, and consequently what appears to each person is true for him. This difference between Xenophanes and Protagoras points to another archic variable, the kind of reality upon which we have a perspective, to which we must turn after we have completed our consideration of perspectives. For now, let us note the idiocentrism implied in the famous opening phrase of Protagoras' *On Truth*, "Man is the measure of all things." "Man" in this phrase is interpreted as the individual man by both Plato and Aristotle. Plato in the *Theaetetus* interprets Protagoras' statement by means of the example of the wind that feels cold to one person but not to another. Socrates asks, "Is it not the case that sometimes when the same wind is blowing one of us may be chilled and the other not, or one slightly and the other very chilled?" Theaetetus agrees, and Socrates continues, "Then in this case shall we say that the wind in itself is cold or not cold, or shall we agree with Protagoras that it is cold to him who is chilled and not to the other?"[9] Aristotle similarly interprets Protagoras as meaning that all opinions and appearances are true,[10] and Sextus Empiricus, interpreting the same statement, says, "He posits only what appears to each individual, and thus he introduces relativity."[11]

For the idiocentrist, all philosophies are personal views, and to present one's philosophy is to present oneself. Montaigne's *Essays* are a prime example of philosophy in this mode. Montaigne writes about a great variety of subjects (and primarily about what he has read, for he is writing in a semantic epoch), but in so doing he is always writing about himself, and his work taken as a whole is, as he tells us in his preface, a portrait of himself.[12] It is his extended reply to the question of Xenophanes.

Another sort of possibility for the personal perspective is represented by Descartes, for he seeks in his own individual existence a truth that is independent of that existence. After studying the books of others and the great book of the world, he finally made himself the object of his study, as

Montaigne had in the previous epoch, but with a view to establishing a firm and permanent structure in the sciences. His *Meditations* are an account of a process that he went through as an individual, and which he invites each of us to go through for ourselves. From the "I think, therefore I am," of Descartes it does not follow that you or I or anyone else exists, nor from your thinking that you exist does it follow that Descartes exists. Each individual must follow a process like that which Descartes went through, founded on his own "Cogito," in order to establish for himself the truths that Descartes established for Descartes. Descartes' philosophy has no validity for anyone unless he goes through such a process and grounds it in his own individual self-awareness.

Problems of perspective are much in evidence in Kierkegaard's writing, and his view of truth as inwardness or subjectivity makes it dependent on the individual. In the words of the pastor on the Jutland heath that close *EitherOr*:

> For one may have known a thing many times and acknowledged it, one may have willed a thing many times and attempted it; and yet it is only by the deep inward movements, only by the indescribable emotions of the heart, that for the first time you are convinced that what you have known belongs to you, that no power can take it from you; for only the truth which edifies is truth for you.[13]

All of Kierkegaard's writings are thoughts whose significance derives from the individuals who express them, Kierkegaard himself or his host of pseudonyms. The problem of the unity of his work is just the problem of who Kierkegaard truly is as an author, which he treats briefly in *My Activity as a Writer* and more fully in *The Point of View for My Work as an Author*, another answer to Xenophanes' question. The discerning mind, he says, will recognize that corresponding to this authorship there is an originator who, as author, "has only willed one thing."[14] On the assumption that the author is a religious author, all the works can be explained, and the so-called aesthetic works then appear as indirect communications in which the author attempts to reach his readers by beginning from where they are. The aesthetic works are written over pseudonyms because, unlike the religious works, they do not represent the position of Kierkegaard himself. Kierkegaard even contrived that his personal mode of existence should second his works. At the time *EitherOr* was published, he appeared to be living an aesthetic life:

If Copenhagen ever has been of one opinion about anybody, I venture to say that it was of one opinion about me, that I was an idler, a dawdler, a *flâneur*, a frivolous bird, intelligent, perhaps brilliant, witty, &c.—but as for "seriousness," I lacked it utterly. I represented a worldly irony, *joie de vivre*, the subtlest form of pleasure-seeking—without a trace of "seriousness and positivity;" on the other hand, I was prodigiously witty and interesting.[15]

With the publication of the *Concluding Unscientific Postscript* it was important to alter his personal mode of existence to correspond to his transition to the statement of religious problems, and at his own request he became the target of public ridicule. The audiences to which the different types of works were directed corresponded to the intentions of the author: the aesthetic works were directed to the crowd, which is the untruth, whereas his *Edifying Discourses* sought "that single individual whom with joy and gratitude I call my reader."[16] The communicator of truth, he says, can only be a single individual, and again the communication of it can only be addressed to the individual, for the truth consists precisely in that conception of life which is expressed by the individual.[17] This matter of the individual, Kierkegaard says, is the most decisive thing,[18] and the enemies of the individual, whether the System of Hegel or the institutions of Christendom, were the objects of his attack.

Nietzsche is also known for his perspectivism, and for him the desire for knowledge is the desire for the appropriation of other individuals by an all-coveting self:

> *The sigh of the search for knowledge.*—"Oh, my greed! There is no selflessness in my soul but only an all-coveting self that would like to appropriate many individuals as so many additional pairs of eyes and hands—a self that would like to bring back the whole past, too, and that will not lose anything that it could possibly possess. Oh, my greed is a flame! Oh, that I might be reborn in a hundred beings!"—Whoever does not know this sigh from firsthand experience does not know the passion of the search for knowledge.[19]

Nietzsche echoes Xenophanes on the inescapable limitations of the human intellect to its own perspectives:

> *Our new "infinite."*—How far the perspective character of existence extends or indeed whether existence has any other character than this; whether existence without interpretation, without "sense," does not

become "nonsense;" whether, on the other hand, all existence is not essentially actively engaged in *interpretation*—that cannot be decided even by the most industrious and most scrupulously conscientious analysis and self-examination of the intellect; for in the course of this analysis the human intellect cannot avoid seeing itself in its own perspectives, and *only* in these. We cannot look around our own corner: it is a hopeless curiousity that wants to know what other kinds of intellects and perspectives there *might* be; for example, whether some beings might be able to experience time backward, or alternately forward and backward (which would involve another direction of life and another concept of cause and effect). But I should think that today we are at least far from the ridiculous immodesty that would be involved in decreeing from our corner that perspectives are permitted only from this corner. Rather has the world become "infinite" for us all over again, inasmuch as we cannot reject the possibility that *it may include infinite interpretations.*[20]

Nietzsche also resembles Xenophanes in his ridicule of traditional religious conceptions that betray their origin in human perspectives. The tendency to read ourselves into the universe is found in the prejudices of philosophers: "Gradually it has become clear to me what every great philosophy so far has been: namely, the personal confession of its author and a kind of involuntary and unconscious memoir."[21] Nietzsche's own individuality, his answer to Xenophanes' question, is presented in *Ecce Homo*, and indeed in all his works.

The great American champion of personal perspectives is William James. His essay "On a Certain Blindness in Human Beings" presents what he says is the perception on which his whole individualistic philosophy is based. The blindness of which his discourse treats is that with which we all are afflicted in regard to the feelings of creatures and people different from ourselves. Neither the whole of truth nor the whole of good is revealed to any single observer, although each observer gains a partial superiority of insight from the peculiar position in which he stands.[22]

The primacy of the individual in the 20th-century semantic context of what is written or said can be exemplified by Merleau-Ponty's existential phenomenology. This professes to derive from the phenomenology of Husserl and Heidegger, neither of whom makes phenomena relative to the individual, but this is no obstacle to Merleau-Ponty, who finds the true meaning of phenomenology not in what Husserl or Heidegger may have said, but in ourselves:

We find in texts only what we put into them, and if ever any kind of history has suggested the interpretations which should be put on it, it is the history of philosophy. We shall find in ourselves, and nowhere else, the unity and true meaning of phenomenology. It is less a question of counting up quotations than of determining and expressing in concrete form this *phenomenology for ourselves* which has given a number of present-day readers the impression, on reading Husserl or Heidegger, not so much of encountering a new philosophy as of recognizing what they had been waiting for.[23]

Perhaps we should include also a representative from the sciences, lest it be supposed that idiocentrism is somehow incompatible with science. Percy W. Bridgman is a notable defender of the primacy of the individual, and one of the fundamental insights that he formulates in *The Way Things Are* is, "We never get away from ourselves. Not only do I see that I cannot get away from myself, but I see that you cannot get away from yourself."[24] "It was my original intention," he says, "to present my analysis of doings or happenings exclusively in the first person singular, the doings or happenings being doings by me or happenings to me."[25]

Let us conclude with one or two examples of personal perspectives in literary works. We have, first, Walt Whitman's "Song of Myself," which begins "I celebrate myself, and sing myself." Whitman says, "*Leaves of Grass* indeed (I cannot too often reiterate) has mainly been the outcropping of my own emotional and other personal nature—an attempt, from first to last, to put *a person*, a human being (myself, in the latter half of the Nineteenth Century, in America,) freely, fully and truly on record."[26] Or again, there is the beginning of Dostoyevsky's *Notes from Underground*, which immediately establishes a personal perspective:

I'm a sick man . . . a mean man. There's nothing attractive about me. I think there's something wrong with my liver. But, actually, I don't understand a damn thing about my sickness; I'm not even too sure what it is that's ailing me. I'm not under treatment and never have been, although I have great respect for medicine and doctors.[27]

Personal perspectives lend themselves to the presentation of extraordinary personalities.

Here then is an assortment of authors with personal perspectives: Xenophanes, Protagoras, Montaigne, Descartes, Kierkegaard, Nietzsche, William James, Merleau-Ponty, P. W. Bridgman, Walt Whitman, and Dostoyevsky. Taken together, they indicate something of the range of

possibilities represented by this approach. The particular set of authors
chosen is not essential; another set would doubtless serve as well or better.
The problem is to see the universal in the particulars. Further examples
seem unnecessary, for this kind of perspective is readily understood by
everyone. One might almost say it is the point from which we all begin.

There is an important general point to be noticed in connection with
this first archic element, however, and it is one that might have been
anticipated from the general discussion of the first chapter. This is that
there is no common doctrine or substantive content associated with this
particular kind of perspective—it suffices to think of Protagoras, Descartes,
and Kierkegaard. What is common is simply the starting-point or principle.
It is, we might say, a procedural rather than a substantive commitment.
And this must be so, if the different values for the same variable are to be
reciprocally prior to one another, and if the values for different archic
variables are to be united in a single doctrine. For any substantive content
would interfere with the reciprocal priority of the elements and with the
possibility of their combination into a coherent doctrine.

In fact, we may anticipate that once the character of the archic elements becomes clear, the differences among them will seem obvious and
even, because non-substantive, of no great importance. And we will need
to recur to the great and apparently substantive differences of philosophies in order to appreciate their importance. What difference does it
make whether we measure distances in feet or meters, or use the earth or
the sun as a reference body? The selection of a reference body does not
seem to us a matter of great theoretical importance, and we need to recur
to Galileo's *Dialogues on the Two Great Systems of the World*, and the
controversy and trial that this work provoked, to appreciate the importance that the difference between the geocentric and heliocentric systems
once had.

2. Objective Perspectives

A second kind of perspective endeavors to eliminate all that is merely
subjective and personal in order to see things objectively, as they are in
themselves. Such a perspective is an impersonal or *objective* perspective.
It is often associated with science, for it is thought that to be scientific is
to eliminate the influence of biases and prejudices and of all that is merely
personal.

An objective perspective is evident in Democritus' theory of knowledge.
The intelligible images by which we have genuine knowledge come to us
from without,[28] and they are, as I have argued elsewhere, radiations from

the divine mind which encompasses the cosmos. What is essential in both divine and human knowledge is simply the image-object relationship; if the knowledge is genuine, the individual subjectivity of the mind does not enter into it at all. In fact, identification of knowing with the existence of images of the things known seems, from other perspectives, to leave out the problem of awareness, as if the mind were only a picture book or mirror and God himself were simply the images that constitute his mind.

Such an objective perspective does not provide a ground for action. This requires in addition some non-cognitive element such as feeling or desire. Objective rationality can then tell us how feelings or desires are to be gratified. Democritus' ethics has its non-cognitive basis in the fundamental feeling of *euthumia* or cheerfulness: "It is best for men to lead a life with as much cheerfulness and as little distress as possible."[29] Cheerfulness, unlike other pleasures, cannot be excessive because it is the enjoyment of one's being, of what one objectively is.

An objective perspective is evident in Francis Bacon's *New Organon.* "I am building," he says, "in the human understanding a true model of the world, such as it is in fact, not such as a man's own reason would have it to be."[30] In order to do this he examines the various classes of idols that beset men's minds, the Idols of the Tribe, Cave, Market-place, and Theatre. The Idols of the Tribe have their foundation in human nature itself, and in the tribe or race of men. We may recall here the comments of Xenophanes and Nietzsche on the limitations of the human perspective. The Idols of the Cave are the idols of the individual man, and may be compared to the individuality of perspective noted by Montaigne, Kierkegaard, William James, and others. The Idols of the Market-place arise from the words that men use in their association with one another, and the Idols of the Theatre have immigrated into men's minds from the various dogmas of philosophies. All of the Idols must be extirpated from the understanding and replaced by Ideas of the divine, if we are to interpret, rather than anticipate, nature.

Spinoza says in *On the Improvement of the Understanding* that he wil endeavor to associate and arrange ideas so that our mind may, as far as possible, reflect subjectively the reality of nature. In order to reproduce in every respect the faithful image of nature, our mind must deduce all its ideas from the idea that represents the origin and source of the whole of nature. His *Ethics*, as contrasted with Descartes' *Meditations*, presents this impersonal order of ideas that reflects the order of nature. Man as the thinker of these ideas does not appear in the demonstrations until Part II, and the intuitive knowledge of individual existence from which Descartes began is treated, still impersonally, at the end, in Part V. The detachment from subjectivity is also evident in Spinoza's dispassionate treatment of the passions. He says at the beginning of Part III that he will consider human actions and appetites just as if he were considering lines, planes, and bodies. The non-cognitive foundation for ethics, corresponding to the feeling of well-being in Democritus, is the *conatus*, or endeavor, of each thing to persevere in its being, and this is the actual essence of the thing itself.

Newton's *Principia* resembles Spinoza's *Ethics* in being an objective and impersonal sequence of ideas, and Hume follows Bacon and Newton in his objective perspective, and, like Spinoza, applies it to moral subjects. In his *History of England* Hume sought to correct the misrepresentations of faction, and thought himself the only historian that had at once neglected present power, interest, and authority, and the cry of popular prejudices.[31] In his philosophy he observes in a detached way the ideas and passions as they appear in the mind, and in his autobiography he describes his own passions and life with a detachment one ordinarily expects only in describing objects of no particular concern to oneself. This autobiographical perspective can be contrasted with that of Montaigne, Rousseau, or Nietzsche. The disappearance of the self as subject in Hume is analogous to its disappearance in Democritus.

Hume's theory of morals is a strictly objective one, explaining why people in fact make the moral judgments that they do. It becomes a basis for action only if one adds in the regard for one's own happiness and welfare: "Having explained the moral *approbation* attending merit or virtue, there remains nothing but briefly to consider our interested *obligation* to it, and to inquire whether every man, who has any regard to his own happiness and welfare, will not best find his account in the practice of every moral duty."[32]

Darwin continues the marvelous objectivity of the English scientific tradition. At one point he comments on the difficulty of constantly bearing in mind the truth of the universal struggle for life:

> Nothing is easier than to admit in words the truth of the universal struggle for life, or more difficult—at least I have found it so—than constantly to bear this conclusion in mind. Yet unless it be thoroughly engrained in the mind, I am convinced that the whole economy of nature, with every fact on distribution, rarity, abundance, extinction, and variation, will be dimly seen or quite misunderstood. We behold the face of nature bright with gladness, we often see superabundance of food; we do not see, or we forget, that the birds which are idly singing round us mostly live on insects or seeds, and are thus constantly destroying life; or we forget how largely these songsters, or their eggs, or their nestlings, are destroyed by birds and beasts of prey; we do not

always bear in mind, that though food may be now superabundant, it is not so at all seasons of each recurring year.[33]

Darwin here observes objectively the struggle in the mind between what Freud formulates as the two principles of psychic functioning, the pleasure principle and the reality principle. The very contrast of these two principles can be taken as defining an objective perspective—we can apprehend things either as we want them to be, or as they are. The aim of scientific thought, according to Freud, "is to arrive at correspondence with reality—that is to say, with what exists outside us and independently of us."[34] He compares the work of the man of science to that of a sculptor with a clay model, who tirelessly alters his rough sketch, adds to it and takes away from it, until he has obtained a satisfactory degree of resemblance to the object he sees or imagines.[35] This corresponds to the Baconian model of the world in the mind and to the Democritean images. It is the pleasure principle, however, that draws up the program of life's purpose.

The objectivist contrast between the pleasure principle and the reality principle appears in Max Weber as the notorious distinction between fact-statements and preference-statements, or between fact and value. The objectivity of science requires *Wertfreiheit*, freedom from value judgments. "The investigator and teacher should keep unconditionally separate the establishment of empirical facts (including the "value-oriented" conduct of the empirical individual whom he is investigating) and *his* own practical evaluations, i.e., his evaluations of these facts as satisfactory or unsatisfactory (including among these facts evaluations made by the empirical persons who are the objects of investigation)."[36] Perhaps no one has more thoroughly worked out the interrelations of fact and value from an objective perspective than Max Weber. And it should be noted that although science for Weber does not itself state value judgments, values are for him involved in the decision to pursue science, and to pursue the science of a particular subject. Democritus, Hume, Freud, and the others are objectively clear about the subjective factors that determine their own pursuits.

Another general point may be noted in connection with Weber. Since the objective perspective attempts to eliminate subjectivity in order to get at the object as it is in itself, it is a perspective shared by all the sciences. Thus Max Weber's scientific sociology shares its scientific perspective with the natural sciences. Similarly, Freud asserts that psychoanalysis has no *Weltanschauung* of its own, but must accept that of science in general.[37] And Hume subtitles his *Treatise of Human Nature*, "An Attempt to Introduce the Experimental Method of Reasoning into Moral Subjects." The experimental method here means, as Hume explains, that the foundations of the science are laid on experience and observation. And Hume views his *Treatise* as putting the science of man on the same sort of footing, that is, an objective footing, as that on which Bacon and Newton had placed the sciences of natural subjects.[38]

Objective perspectives can be found not only in the natural and social sciences, but also in the arts. Here our example must be Shakespeare, who conforms to Hamlet's dictum that the end of acting is to hold, as 't were, the mirror up to nature. This is the mirroring that we have already noted in Democritus, Bacon, and Freud. The puzzles as to the personal identity of Shakespeare and whether he had a philosophy of his own are in part the result of his personal subjectivity disappearing in the objective perspective of the plays. Dramatic works of course need not have an objective perspective simply because they are dramatic, as we have seen in the case of Kierkegaard. And similarly a work written in the first person need not have a personal perspective, as we have seen in the case of Hume's autobiography. The question is what sort of an "I" it is. It is perfectly possible to observe in an objective perspective one's own thoughts and feelings and thus to have lyric poetry in an objective voice. This is what we find in Shakespeare's Sonnets. If the author says, for example, "But if the while I think on thee, dear friend, /All losses are restor'd and sorrows end,"[39] or if he says, "Two loves I have, of comfort and despair,"[40] or if he says, "For I have sworn thee fair and thought thee bright, Who art as black as hell, as dark as night,"[41] he is stating objective facts about himself and others. He can even objectively observe the distortions of his own perception: "Thou blind fool, Love, what dost thou to mine eyes, /That they behold and see not what they see?"[42] We can see already here the reciprocal priority of personal and objective perspectives: whatever distortions personal perspectives introduce can be objectively seen, but this in turn implies a personal observer who is seeing them, whose distortions can in turn be corrected, and so on, each perspective able to claim priority over the other.

Here then are some authors who share an objective perspective: Democritus, Francis Bacon, Spinoza, Newton, Hume, Darwin, Freud, Weber, and Shakespeare. As one might expect, this perspective has enjoyed great success in the development of physics, biology, psychology, and social science, when these are conceived as objective sciences. As in the case of the personal perspectives, however, although there is a common starting point or principle, there is no common doctrine, and the agreement is procedural rather than substantive.

3. Diaphanic Perspectives

One can avoid the relativity to individuals of the personal perspectives not only by seeking to eliminate subjectivity in an objective perspective, but also by subordinating one's own subjectivity to a higher and more inclusive individual perspective, and ultimately to an absolute perspective in which all other perspectives are included. Individual subjectivity can disappear not only if we become pure mirrors of the objective world, but also if we become purely transparent to an absolute perspective, such as that of an omniscient god. Since we are not gods, the author of a text is then in the position of transmitting truths that transcend his own perspective, or speaking for an author superior to himself. He is a conduit, a vehicle, a mouthpiece, a spokesman, a herald, a prophet, an interpreter, a *hermeneus*. His perspective is transmissive, oracular, revelatory, inspired, illuminationist. This kind of perspective can be called *revelatory*, but since the religious overtones of this word may result in too restricted a conception of its meaning, I will prefer *diaphanic*, or "through-showing." It should be noted that the archic elements do not derive their existence and properties from the way in which we happen to name them. They are real features of texts which are what they are regardless of how we name them, but suitable names can help us to apprehend these features as what they are. Diaphanic perspectives are familiar to us in religious revelations, but are not restricted to such revelations.

A diaphanic perspective is evident in the writings of Parmenides, both the Way of Truth and the Way of Opinion. For although Parmenides is in one sense the author, he for the most part simply transmits to us the words of the goddess:

> "Welcome, o youth, that comest to my abode on the car that bears thee, tended by immortal charioteers. It is no ill chance, but right and justice, that has sent thee forth to travel on this way. Far indeed does it lie from the beaten track of men. Meet it is that thou shouldst learn all things, as well the unshaken heart of well-rounded truth, as the opinions of mortals in which is no true belief at all . . .
> "Come now, and I will tell thee—and do thou hearken and carry my word away—the only ways of enquiry that are for thought."[43]

This type of perspective is presented as such in Plato's *Ion*. Divine possession proceeds from the Muse through Homer and his rhapsode Ion to the audiences who hear Ion, just as magnetism proceeds from the lodestone through a series of iron rings suspended from it. But all the Platonic dialogues have this same kind of perspective. They center around some real or purported source of wisdom through whom a higher truth may be revealed. The Socrates of the *Apology*, for example, transmits to the Athenians the bite of the gadfly which he received from the Delphic oracle, and is thus the voice of god in the state that accuses him of impiety.[44] What in general is the perspective of a Platonic dialogue, or of the dialogues as a whole? The speakers in the dialogue have their own perspectives, but we cannot identify the perspective of the dialogue with that of any one of them. The perspectives of the speakers are diaphanic in the sense that the perspective of the dialogue shows itself through the speakers. And if there is a perspective of the dialogues as a whole, this shows itself through the different dialogues. Can we identify this with Plato's perspective? Yes and no, for Plato too is diaphanic, and the truth revealed through him and through his dialogues is not his truth, but a truth that transcends him. Just as the individuality of the author disappears in an objective perspective as he becomes more purely objective, so here the individuality of the author is subordinated as he becomes more purely diaphanic to the truth that is revealed through him.

A similar kind of perspective is found in St. Augustine, for whom the second person of the Trinity is the light of the mind for learning all things.[45] To take one example, in his dialogue *Concerning the Teacher*, Augustine says:

> For do teachers profess that it is their thoughts which are perceived and grasped by the students, and not the sciences themselves which they convey through speaking? For who is so stupidly curious as to send his son to school in order that he may learn what the teacher thinks? But all those sciences which they profess to teach, and the science of virtue itself and wisdom, teachers explain through words. Then those who are called pupils consider within themselves whether what has been explained has been said truly; looking of course to that interior truth, according to the measure of which each is able. Thus they learn, and when the interior truth makes known to them that true things have been said, they applaud, but without knowing that instead of applauding teachers they are applauding learners, if indeed their teachers know what they are saying.[46]

We must not omit Leibniz from our discussion of perspectives, for his is a perspectival universe composed of monads each of which has its own perspective on all the other monads. The perspectives are thus in appearance idiocentric, but in reality "the only immediate object of our perceptions which exists outside of us is God, and in him alone is our light."[47] God is the sun and the light of souls, the light that lighteth every man that cometh into this world.[48] Monads are illuminated by God in different degrees. Mere monads have perception, but souls have perception that is more distinct and accompanied by memory, and rational souls or spirits have a knowledge of eternal and necessary truths and thus are images of God in thought and action: "Souls in general are the living mirrors or images of the universe of creatures, but minds or spirits are in addition images of the Divinity itself, or of the author of nature, able to know the system of the universe and to imitate something of it by architectonic samples, each mind being like a little divinity in its own department."[49] Note that the mirroring here is a perspectival mirroring, not an objective mirroring.

The characteristic diaphanic hierarchy of perspectives culminating in an absolute perspective can hardly be better exemplified than in Hegel's *Phenomenology*. The whole book is essentially a series of perspectives, for each form or shape of consciousness along the highway of despair that leads to absolute knowledge has its own perspective. There is a continual contrast between the perspective of the consciousness that is living through one of the forms of consciousness and the perspective of the "we" who view this form of consciousness from the perspective of the *Phenomenology* itself. The perspective of the *Phenomenology* is in one sense that of Hegel, but it is not that of Hegel as a single individual. In one sense Hegel is the author of the *Phenomenology*, but in another sense it is the universal individual, self-conscious Spirit, that shows itself through Hegel: Hegel, like all single individuals, is diaphanic to absolute Spirit. The task of the *Phenomenology* is to bring the single individual to the standpoint of science by traversing the series of perspectives through which the universal Spirit has passed and which culminates in the standpoint of science:

> The task of leading the individual from his uneducated standpoint to knowledge had to be seen in its universal sense, just as it was the universal individual, self-conscious Spirit, whose formative education had to be studied. As regards the relation between them, every moment, as it gains concrete form and a shape of its own, displays itself in the universal individual. The single individual is incomplete Spirit, a concrete shape in whose whole existence *one* determinateness predominates, the others being present only in blurred outline. In a Spirit that is more advanced than another, the lower concrete existence has been reduced to an inconspicuous moment; what used to be the important thing is now but a trace; its pattern is shrouded to become a mere shadowy outline. The individual whose substance is the more advanced

> Spirit runs through this past just as one who takes up a higher science goes through the preparatory studies he has long since absorbed, in order to bring their content to mind: he recalls them to the inward eye, but has no lasting interest in them. The single individual must also pass through the formative stages of universal Spirit so far as their content is concerned, but as shapes which Spirit has already left behind, as stages on a way that has been made level with toil.[50]

The individual can be diaphanic not only to the divine, but to whatever transcends his individuality, and ultimately to whatever is absolute. Thus in Schopenhauer we apprehend the universal will through the intuition of our own will, and in Bergson we apprehend the opposite extremes of materiality and life through the intuition of our own duration. The intuition of our duration, according to Bergson,

> brings us into contact with a whole continuity of durations which we must try to follow, whether downwards or upwards; in both cases we can extend ourselves indefinitely by an increasingly violent effort, in both cases we transcend ourselves. In the first we advance towards a more and more attenuated duration, the pulsations of which, being rapider than ours, and dividing our simple sensation, dilute its quality into quantity; at the limit would be pure homogeneity, that pure *repetition* by which we define materiality. Advancing in the other direction, we approach a duration which *strains*, contracts, and intensifies itself more and more; at the limit would be eternity. No longer conceptual eternity, which is an eternity of death, but an eternity of life. A living, and therefore still moving eternity in which our own particular duration would be included as the vibrations are in light; an eternity which would be the concentration of all duration, as materiality is its dispersion.[51]

Among more recent authors, none has so emphasized the diaphanic character of our perspective as has Heidegger. His account of truth as unconcealment, *alētheia*, rather than correctness, makes all genuine authors diaphanic. It is never we who speak, but always something else that speaks through us. It is not we who speak through language, for example, but language that speaks through us. In fact, it is the character of human being, or Dasein, to understand Being and thus to disclose Being. Dasein is diaphanic to Being, and Being can therefore be investigated by interrogating Dasein. In all of Heidegger's works, Being is showing itself (and concealing itself) through Dasein.

Tolstoy is an example of a literary figure who uses a diaphanic perspective. He says that readers who agree with what he has set down "should remember that if I speak the truth it is not mine but God's, and that it is only accidentally that a part of it has passed through me just as it passes through each of us when we become conscious of truth and transmit it."[52] The illumination transmitted by a diaphanic perspective has consequences for action as well as truth:

> A wise Hebrew proverb says, "The soul of man is the lamp of God." Man is a weak and miserable animal until the light of God burns in his soul. But when that light burns (and it burns only in souls enlightened by religion) man becomes the most powerful being in the world. Nor can this be otherwise, for what then acts in him is no longer *his* strength, but the strength of God.[53]

Diaphanic perspectives are prominent in the Asiatic traditions. The author of the Bhagavad Gita permits us to overhear Samjaya's report of the conversation that he overhears between Arjuna and Krishna, and in this conversation Krishna adopts a series of perspectives in which he reveals himself to Arjuna. The transmission of the revelation is comparable in effect to the transmission of possession in the *Ion*, for as Samjaya says at the end:

> And as I recall again and again that
> Most wondrous form of Hari
> Great is my amazement, O king,
> And I thrill with joy again and again.[54]

The author of the *Tao-te ching* makes his perspective that of heaven and earth, and thus they act through him. The ideal of non-action, *wu-wei*, does not imply that the sage is motionless, but that he is diaphanic to the Tao, so that he does not act on his own, but the Tao acts through him.

> Heaven is eternal and Earth everlasting.
> They can be eternal and everlasting because they
>   do not exist for themselves,
> And for this reason can exist forever.
> Therefore the sage places himself in the background,
>   but finds himself in the foreground.
> He puts himself away, and yet he always remains.
> Is it not because he has no personal interests?
> This is the reason why his personal interests
>   are fulfilled.[55]

Again, for the neo-Confucian Chu Hsi the individual mind is illuminated by the Great Ultimate. Asked whether the nature bestowed by Heaven
differs in the degree of its completeness, he replies:

> No, there is no difference in the degree of its completeness. It is like
> the light of the sun and moon. In a clear, open field, it is seen in its
> entirety. Under a mat-shed, however, some of it is hidden and obstructed
> so that part of it is visible and part of it is not. What is impure is due
> to the impurity of material force. The obstruction is due to the self,
> like the mat-shed obstructing itself. However, man possesses the princi-
> ple that can penetrate this obstruction, whereas in birds and animals,
> though they also possess this nature, it is nevertheless restricted by
> their physical structure, which creates such a degree of obstruction as
> to be impenetrable. In the case of love, for example, in tigers and
> wolves, or in the sacrificial rites in the wolf and otter, or in the
> righteousness in bees and ants, only the obstruction to a particular part
> of their nature is penetrated, just as light penetrates only a crack. As to
> the monkey, whose bodily form resembles that of man, it is the most
> intelligent among other creatures except that it cannot talk.[56]

All minds are illuminated by the same source, although different species
are diaphanic in different degrees.

Here then is a group of diaphanic texts: Parmenides, Plato, Augustine,
Leibniz, Hegel, Schopenhauer, Bergson, Heidegger, Tolstoy, the Bhagavad
Gita, Lao Tzu, and Chu Hsi. We may note the great success of this kind
of perspective in establishing the religions of the world. Although a revelatory perspective lends itself to religious uses, there is no necessary connection between such a perspective and a transcendent reality. The two seem
to be naturally suited to each other, and both are found in Parmenides,
Plato, Augustine, Leibniz, and the Bhagavad Gita. But in Hegel, Heidegger,
and Chu Hsi, there is no revelation of an ideal world transcending this
one. And in Schopenhauer, Bergson, and Lao Tzu, what is revealed is the
universal substratum of this world. A revelatory perspective does not itself
determine what is to be revealed; that evidently depends upon a second
archic variable.

4. Disciplinary Perspectives

Suppose an author does not wish to attach his text to an individual
perspective, does not think it possible to eliminate the knower from his
perspective, and questions the availability to us of a divine perspective.
Are there any other possibilities? There remains the possibility that the

knower constitutes his own perspective, but does so in a way that is valid for all knowers. This kind of perspective will result not in an infinite multiplicity of personal views, nor in the objectivist contrast between what is scientific and what depends on non-cognitive factors such as feeling, nor in a hierarchy of perspectives culminating in one absolute perspective. It will result instead in a multiplicity of independent and impersonal disciplines, and we may appropriately call it a *disciplinary* perspective. It is familiar to us in the saying that every occupation has its own perspective— the lawyer has his perspective, the doctor has his perspective, the theologian has his perspective, the scientist has his perspective, the poet has his perspective, the man-in-the-street has his perspective, and so on.

Let us seek a first example of disciplinary perspectives in the work of that great founder of disciplines, Aristotle. He distinguishes three principal disciplinary perspectives by the ends at which the disciplines aim: the theoretical perspective defined by an interest in knowing, the practical perspective defined by an interest in action, and the poetic perspective defined by an interest in making. Each interest determines its appropriate subject matter: the theoretical interest requires things that cannot be other than they are, for if they can change without our knowing it our theoretical interest will be frustrated; the practical interest requires things that can be done; and the poetic interest requires things that can be made. Each of these perspectives includes the other two in its own way and the differences among them are sometimes puzzling to those who suppose Aristotle is using the single scientific perspective of the objectivists. At the beginning of the *Ethics*, for example, Aristotle tells us that politics is the most authoritative and most architectonic of the sciences,[57] whereas at the beginning of the *Metaphysics* he tells us that wisdom is the most archical of the sciences.[58] These assertions would be inconsistent if the disciplinary perspectives were the same, but in the perspective of action politics is architectonic and governs metaphysics, whereas in the perspective of knowing metaphysics is architectonic and governs politics. And similarly in a context of emotion poetics is architectonic and orders both the theoretical pleasure of learning and the moral pleasure of *philanthropia*, humanity, to a poetic pleasure such as the catharsis of pity and fear. Or, to give some other examples, the soul and its parts are differently defined in *On the Soul* and the *Ethics*, and happiness and virtue are differently defined in the *Ethics* and the *Rhetoric*.

There are also different perspectives and sub-perspectives within the theoretical, practical, and poetic sciences. The principal theoretical perspectives are physical, mathematical, and theological, distinguished by whether things are known in matter and motion, as abstracted from matter and motion, or as existing apart from matter and motion.

The mark of the disciplinary perspective in Aristotle is the frequent appearance of the word *hē* (in Latin, *qua*), meaning *as*. For example, in distinguishing mathematics from physical mathematics, Aristotle says, "While geometry investigates physical lines but not *qua* physical, optics investigates mathematical lines, but *qua* physical, not *qua* mathematical."[59] The object itself does not determine in what context it will be investigated; the disciplinary perspective, which comes from the side of the inquirer, does this. Man, for example, can be investigated in many different disciplines: *qua* substance in metaphysics, *qua* shape in mathematics, *qua* body in physics, *qua* animal in biology, *qua* agent in ethics, *qua* citizen in politics, *qua* curable in medicine, *qua* persuadable in rhetoric, *qua* imitable in poetics.

These different perspectives are not personal, nor determined by the objects studied, nor approximations to an absolute perspective, but rather are constituted as sharable perspectives by the inquirer. Instead of the personal "I" of the idiocentrist, we have the disciplinary "we"—we physicists, we mathematicians, we poets, we philosophers, etc. And the structure of a discipline does not mirror the structure of the world, as in an objectivist perspective. There are no proofs in nature, but our disciplines can be so constituted that the conclusions they reach by argument will be true of nature. And our disciplinary perspectives do not by their limitations limit the degree of truth we can attain, but rather it is through these limitations that it is possible to attain a truth appropriate to each perspective.

Thomas Aquinas follows the Aristotelian disciplinary perspectives, but adds the science of Sacred Doctrine, that is, the science of things knowable by the light of divine revelation: "Sacred Doctrine, being one, extends to things which belong to the different philosophical sciences, because it considers in each the same formal aspect, namely, so far as they can be known through the divine light."[60] In his commentary on Aristotle's *Nicomachean Ethics*, Aquinas gives a succinct summary of four Aristotelian perspectives, including that of logic, as four ways in which reason is related to order. Each relation of reason to order constitutes an independent disciplinary perspective.

> Order, however, is related in four ways to reason. Thus, one kind of order is that which reason does not make but only investigates, such as the order of natural things. Another kind, again, is the order which reason, by investigation, makes in its own activity, for example when it orders its concepts to each other and the signs of concepts to each other, since they are significative words. A third kind, again, is the order which reason, by investigating, makes in the operations of the will. The fourth, finally, is the order which reason makes, by investigating,

in external things, in which case reason is the cause of the things, as in a box or a house.[61]

Another example of disciplinary perspectives is provided by Kant. In the Preface to the Second Edition of the *Critique of Pure Reason*, he runs through a series of branches of knowledge that have become scientific, and inquires what the condition was that made them so. In each case the answer is the same: the knowledge became scientific when the mind recognized its role in the constitution of the science. Thus mathematics became scientific with the realization that the mathematician was not to inspect what he discerned either in the figure, or in the bare concept of it, and from this, as it were, to read off its properties; but to bring out what he had himself put into the figure in the construction by which he presented it to himself. Empirical physics became scientific when reason approached nature not in the character of a pupil who listens to everything the teacher has to say, but of an appointed judge who compels the witnesses to answer questions that he has himself formulated.[62] Here again the mind is constituting the perspective within which a discipline can be established.

The counterpart in Kant of the Aristotelian distinction between theoretical, practical, and productive sciences is the distinction between the three critiques. The *Critique of Pure Reason* is concerned with the determination of cognition by the understanding, the *Critique of Practical Reason* is concerned with the determination of desire by reason, and the *Critique of Judgment* with the determination of pleasure and pain by judgment:

> As regards the faculties of the soul in general, in their higher aspect, as containing an autonomy, the understanding is that which contains the *constitutive* principles *a priori* for the *cognitive faculty* (the theoretical cognition of nature). For the *feeling of pleasure and pain* there is the judgment, independently of concepts and sensations which relate to the determination of the faculty of desire and can thus be immediately practical. For the faculty of desire there is the reason, which is practical without the mediation of any pleasure whatever.[63]

John Dewey, although he inveighs against Aristotle for the fixity of his forms (the result of an archic difference that we must subsequently investigate), nevertheless recovers his three disciplinary perspectives. Just as in Aristotle the theoretical, practical, and poetic sciences differ in their ends but each science includes the others in relation to its own end, so in Dewey any vital experience is at once emotional and intellectual and practical, but experiences can be distinguished as dominantly emotional or intellectual or practical because of the interest or purpose that initiates and controls them:

> It is not possible to divide in a vital experience the practical, emotional, and intellectual from one another and to set the properties of one over against the characteristics of the others. The emotional phase binds parts together into a single whole; "intellectual" simply names the fact that the experience has meaning; "practical" indicates that the organism is interacting with events and objects which surround it. The most elaborate philosophic or scientific inquiry and the most ambitious industrial or political enterprise has, when its different ingredients constitute an integral experience, esthetic quality . . . . Nevertheless, the experiences in question are dominantly intellectual or practical, rather than *distinctively* esthetic, because of the interest and purpose that initiate and control them . . . . In a distinctively esthetic experience, characteristics that are subdued in other experiences are dominant; those that are subordinate are controlling—namely, the characteristics in virtue of which the experience is an integrated complete experience on its own account.[64]

It is not difficult to relate Dewey's own works, in terms of their dominant interests, to those of Aristotle. Thus Dewey's *Logic* corresponds to the *Organon*, *Experience and Nature* to the *Metaphysics*, *Human Nature and Conduct* to the *Ethics*, *The Public and Its Problems* to the *Politics*, and *Art as Experience* to the *Poetics*.

In conclusion, let us return again to the literary perspectives from which this chapter began. Consider the familiar opening sentence of Jane Austen's *Pride and Prejudice*: "It is a truth universally acknowledged that a single man in possesion of a good fortune must be in want of a wife." There is a definite authorial presence in the ironic formality and exaggeration, so this is not an objective beginning such as one finds, for example, in Thomas Hardy's *Jude the Obscure*: "The schoolmaster was leaving the village, and everybody seemed sorry." But neither is the presence an idiocentric one, as in the case of "I'm a sick man." Nor do we see it as a vehicle through which to see something beyond it, as in the beginning of Melville's *Moby Dick*: "Call me Ishmael." Rather, the opening sentence defines a comic perspective on social life. There are the observed and the observers, the many who are ridiculous and the knowing few who know how to laugh at them. The author makes those with narrow or selfish views ridiculous by formulating the principle of their action as a universally acknowledged truth, and the reader immediately adopts the perspective of the author and joins her in relishing the follies of the rest of mankind. This is the constitution of a disciplinary perspective, in this case a comic one.

Several disciplinary perspectives may appear within a single work, as in James Joyce's *Ulysses*, in which each chapter has a different perspective. This multiplicity of disciplinary perspectives can be contrasted with the more usual multiplicity of personal perspectives, as in Faulkner's *The Sound and the Fury* or in the Japanese film *Rashomon*.

These, then, are some of the best-known authors who use disciplinary perspectives: Aristotle, Thomas Aquinas, Kant, Dewey, Jane Austen, and James Joyce. If personal perspectives have a characteristic success in presenting personalities, objective perspectives in the sciences, and diaphanic perspectives in religion, so the disciplinary perspectives have a characteristic success in the great architectonic philosophies.

The four kinds of perspective have been distinguished by beginning from the kind nearest and most evident to us, and identifying the others by successive negations. But the perspectives in their own nature do not require any particular order or arrangement. Any arrangement is possible, and different arrangements bring out different features of the perspectives. Let us therefore arrange the perspectives by pairs in all possible ways. Four things can be grouped in pairs in three ways, as the four suits of a deck of playing cards can be grouped by pairs as major or minor, red or black, and pointed or rounded at the top. (1) Both personal and objective perspectives begin from a distinction between subject and object, one making the subject primary, the other the object. Diaphanic and disciplinary perspectives, on the other hand, begin from a unity of subject and object, but the unity is in the one case to be attained, in the other an initial condition. (2) Both personal and diaphanic perspectives are personal, but in the one case the perspectives are merely personal and infinite in number, while in the other the personal perspective is subordinated to a higher perspective and ultimately to one absolute perspective in which all personal perspectives are included. Objective and disciplinary perspectives, on the other hand, are impersonal either because subjectivity is excluded or because it is universalized. (3) Both the personal and disciplinary perspectives are constitutive of their content, although the constitution is individual in one case, universal in the other. Objective and diaphanic perspectives, on the other hand, are non-constitutive or vanishing, subordinating themselves to the content in the one case and to a better point of view in the other.

It remains to consider whether the various perspectives are reciprocally prior to one another and hence only apparently incompatible. The ontic, epistemic, and semantic subject matters that we discussed earlier were reciprocally prior to one another because each includes the others: things include thoughts and words, thoughts can be of things and words, and words can express things and thoughts. We have already noted that perspectives can also be mutualy inclusive insofar as a perspective can be a perspective on other perspectives. They need not be like blinders that prevent one from seeing some aspect of the object; rather everything can be visible from each perspective. The situation is not like that of the blind men and the elephant, where each perspective apprehends a different part of the whole. Such a situation does not give rise to a true pluralism at all. A true pluralism arises only if each can apprehend the whole elephant.

Personal perspectives include the other perspectives and all that is seen within them, for the other perspectives are all held by particular individuals. Whatever anyone thinks can always be treated as simply his way of viewing things, and if he claims objectivity or transcendence or universality, this too is his own opinion about his own perspective, his own idiocentricity. Nietzsche thus describes in memorable phrases the diaphanic perspective as it appears from his own perspective (he is speaking of the change in Wagner under the influence of Schopenhauer): "He now became an oracle, a priest, or more than a priest—a kind of mouthpiece of the absolute, a telephone line of Transcendence. God's ventriloquist . . ."[65]

From the objectivist standpoint, all the perspectives are objective facts, and whatever is seen within them can be included in an objective account. That is, one can understand objectively why things appear as they do in the other perspectives.

From the diaphanic standpoint, all the other perspectives are diaphanic and reveal the truth more or less. The conditions that define the other perspectives are in fact precisely what prevent them from being absolute.

From the disciplinary standpoint, finally, all the perspectives are disciplinary, that is, modes of constituting inquiries into things. What is seen depends on the perspective or approach as well as on the thing itself. This is the perspective that we have adopted here in distinguishing the different perspectives. Apparent contradictions between the different perspectives are analogous to the apparent contradictions between Aristotle's sciences already referred to—the statements from different sciences appear to contradict each other until the disciplinary perspective is taken into account.

The sense in which a disciplinary perspective such as the one used here makes the other perspectives also disciplinary can be developed by treating them as determining typical organizations of the sciences. Since the number of possible idiocentric perspectives is infinite, idiocentric perspectives determine an infinite number of sciences. We cannot reject the possibility, Nietzsche says, that the world may include infinite interpretations. In

Descartes, for whom each individual mind can begin from its own existence in order to arrive at universal truths, this infinity is simply the infinite multiplicity of the same science in different individuals. Aristotle in
the context of *On Sophistical Refutations* says that "possibly the sciences
are infinite in number."[66]

If an objective perspective determines the possible sciences, there will
first of all be objective knowledge of the world as it is, then the ordering
of this knowledge to a non-cognitive end, such as we have noted in a
number of authors, and finally the logic used in both theoretical and practical knowledge. The traditional names for these three sciences are physics,
ethics, and logic. As Locke puts it,

> All that can fall within the compass of human understanding, being
> either, First, the nature of things, as they are in themselves, their relations,
> and their manner of operation; or, Secondly, that which man himself
> ought to do, as a rational and voluntary agent, for the attainment of
> any end, especially happiness; or, Thirdly, the ways and means whereby
> the knowledge of both the one and the other of these is attained and
> communicated: I think science may be divided properly into these three
> sorts.[67]

The physics-ethics-logic distinction can, however, also be given other
interpretations. Augustine relates it to the persons of the Trinity: physics
corresponds to God as the cause of subsisting, logic to the Son or *logos* as
the reason of understanding, and ethics to the Holy Spirit as the order of
living.[68] Hegel treats logic as the science of the idea in and for itself, the
philosophy of nature as the science of the idea in its otherness, and the
philosophy of mind as the science of the idea come back to itself out of
that otherness.[69] The physics-ethics-logic distinction thus serves as a com-
monplace or topic that can be given different meanings in different
philosophies, and Aristotle uses it in the context of his *Topics*:

> Of propositions and problems there are—to comprehend the matter in
> outline—three divisions: for some are ethical propositions, some are
> physical, and some are logical. Ethical propositions are such as, "Should
> one rather obey one's parents or the laws, if they disagree?" Logical are
> such as, "Is the knowledge of opposites the same or not?" Physical are
> such as, "Is the universe eternal or not?" And similarly also for problems.[70]

If diaphanic perspectives determine possible sciences, any given perspective will influence both truth and action, or theory and practice, as we

have noted in Leibniz, Tolstoy, and Lao Tzu, and there will typically be a hierarchy of cognitive states culminating in a single supreme science, at once theoretical and practical, in which all things are viewed from an absolute perspective. This can be exemplified by the Way of Opinion and the Way of Truth in Parmenides, by the hierarchy of the divided line in the *Republic*, which proceeds from imagination (*eikasia*) to belief (*pistis*) to thought (*dianoia*) to knowledge (*noesis*) or science (*epistēmē*), by the hierarchy of mere monad, soul, spirit, and God in Leibniz, by the hierarchy of forms of consciousness in Hegel's *Phenomenology*, and by the ontic and the ontological in Heidegger.

Finally, if disciplinary perspectives determine the possible sciences, there will typically be the theoretical sciences corresponding to an interest in truth, the practical sciences corresponding to an interest in action, and the productive sciences corresponding to an interest in the work of art. Or, if one prefers, there are the natural sciences and mathematics, the social and behavioral sciences, and the humanities.

In typical cases, then, idiocentric perspectives give us infinite sciences, objective perspectives give us physics, ethics, and logic, diaphanic perspectives give us hierarchies culminating in a single unified science, and disciplinary perspectives give us theoretical, practical, and poetic sciences.

Our more general result is that each kind of perspective is reciprocally prior to the others, and thus that the differences between them are archic differences that cannot be settled by an appeal to the facts. The perspectives are therefore incompatible only in the sense that one cannot adopt different perspectives at the same time or mix them indiscriminately.

III. Reality

Every text not only has a perspective, but a perspective on something. That on which any particular text has a perspective is its subject matter, and that on which texts in general have a perspective is reality. Even fictional texts are said to present a fictional reality, and this fictional reality admits of the same variations as non-fictional reality. The distinction between the reality presented by fiction and by non-fiction is therefore not essential here, but is a subsequent distinction made within one or another conception of the real.

Reality, like the author, can be considered as external to the text, but we are working in a semantic context and seeking reality as presented in the text. In a semantic context, however, all realities are realities presented in texts and it will therefore be appropriate to use the term *reality* for our second archic variable. It may seem strange to treat reality as a variable, but it must be borne in mind that this is a textual rather than an extratextual reality. If a more technical term is required, I will call the reality signified by the text the *signification* of the text.

The reality presented in a text is its interpretation of a universal subject matter such as being or knowing or meaning. In this sense the text's reality can also be called its *interpretation*. There are two senses in which a text has a universal subject matter. In the first chapter we discussed being and knowing and meaning as examples of universal subject matters. In the present chapter we are discussing the reality presented in the text, and this, as an interpretation of the first kind of universal subject matter, is also a universal subject matter. They differ because the first is an indeterminate or uninterpreted subject matter, and in order for meaning to be constituted this uninterpreted subject matter must be given a determinate interpretation as the reality presented in the text. It is because the first kind of universal subject matter is indeterminate and uninterpreted that it can function to determine a whole epochal context. Because it determines a whole epochal context, the changes in it are conspicuous. The illusory hopes that have accompanied these changes arise from the fact that the change is observed, but not the fact that the change is only a change in an uninterpreted subject matter admitting of multiple interpretations. As the epoch progresses, the multiple interpretations appear.

The reality presented in the text may be the interpretation of any universal subject matter. It may, for example, be the reality of being or of knowing or of meaning. The different kinds of reality or interpretation that we are seeking, however, should be independent of the universal subject matter of which they are an interpretation.

The kinds of reality must also be independent of the kinds of perspective discussed in the second chapter. Whatever is real must be such that it could be real to the individual, or objectively real, or transcendently real, or real for a discipline. It will then of course also be the case that each perspective could be a perspective on any reality. Although the archic variables must be formally independent in this sense, they are independent only as starting-points for the constitution of meaning. In the actual constitution of meaning, the way each starting-point is developed will depend on the other starting-points with which it is associated, so that all together become constitutive of an organic whole. One and the same kind of reality may thus look different from different perspectives.

Most of the attempts to distinguish kinds of philosophies have been based on what the philosophy takes to be real. Philosophies are said to be instances of realism or nominalism, of idealism or materialism, of existentialism or essentialism. These have been taken to be simply incompatible, because the reality presented by the text has been identified with non-textual reality, and non-textual reality is not thought to be a variable. And non-textual reality may indeed not be a variable, but as formulated in our texts it admits of differences as to what is real or really real. If there is a reciprocal priority among the realities, then each must include what the others take to be real, not in the sense of recognizing the other's reality as real in the way in which the other takes it to be real, but in a way appropriate to its own reality. Each of the realities will then include the others, and be a reality of realities.

1. Existential Realities

The reality that is nearest and most evident to us is whatever is real for us. This is reality as we encounter it, and primarily the reality of the perceived world in all its concrete variety and particularity.

As perceived, this reality is an *apparent* or *phenomenal* reality. As particular, it is an *existential* reality, for "existence" is the name we give to reality in its particularity. (The so-called existentialists need not of course be the only ones for whom reality is existential.) Abstract ideas and categories may exist as words or ideas standing for similar particulars, but as existing they too are particular. Strictly speaking, existence is limited to the present moment, for what is past we say no longer exists, and what is future does not yet exist. Existence is always more or less in flux, for in its concrete particularity it keeps changing even if parts or aspects of it remain unchanged.

Being and knowing and meaning all admit of existential interpretation. The flux of being is an ontic flux of coming-to-be and passing away, like the stream into which one cannot step twice. The flux of knowing is an epistemic flux or stream of consciousness. The flux of meaning is a semantic flux in which a text never has the same meaning twice, for meaning depends on a particular interaction of text and reader.

In Plato's *Theaetetus*, the first definition of knowledge offered by Theaetetus is that knowledge is perception. In examining this definition, Socrates treats it as an alternative formulation of Protagoras' doctrine that man is the measure of all things, and treats both formulations as founded on the view that all things are in flux. The perceiver is in flux and the perceived is in flux and perception is the momentary interaction of the two.

For Protagoras, matter in relation to us *is* what it appears to be—the reality is the appearance. In itself it is able to be all the things that appear. Sextus Empiricus gives the following account of Protagoras' view of matter:

> What he states then is this—that matter is in flux, and as it flows additions are made continuously in the place of the effluxions, and the senses are transformed and altered according to the times of life and to all the other conditions of the bodies. He says also that the "reasons" (*logoi*) of all the appearances subsist in matter so that matter, so far as depends on itself, is capable of being all those things which appear to all. And men, he says, apprehend different things at different times owing to their differing dispositions; for he who is in a natural state apprehends those things subsisting in matter which are able to appear to those in a natural state, and those who are in a non-natural state the things which can appear to those in a non-natural state. Moreover, precisely the same account applies to the variations due to age, and to the sleeping or waking state, and to each several kind of condition.[1]

The extreme partisans of the flux held that it could not be signified by words at all. Speaking of those who inferred the truth of appearances from the observation of the sensible world, Aristotle says,

Because they saw that all this world of nature is in movement, and that about that which changes no true statement can be made, they said that of course, regarding that which everywhere in every respect is changing, nothing could truly be affirmed. It was this belief that blossomed into the most extreme of the views above mentioned, that of the professed Heracliteans, such as was held by Cratylus, who finally did not think it right to say anything but only moved his finger, and criticized Heraclitus for saying that it is impossible to step twice into the same river; for *he* thought one could not do it even once.[2]

Even if one does not cease to speak, one can still endeavor to use language in ways that keep it close to the perceptual realities. Plato has made the Greek sophists notorious for their tendency to stay with the perceived particulars rather than ascend to the generality of ideal forms. And Aristotle criticizes Gorgias' method of education on the ground that it does not impart an art at all:

> For the training given by the paid professors of contentious arguments was like the treatment of the matter by Gorgias. For they used to hand out speeches to be learned by heart, some rhetorical, others in the form of question and answer, each side supposing that their arguments on either side generally fall among them. And therefore the teaching they gave their pupils was rapid but without art. For they used to suppose that they trained people by imparting to them not the art but its products, as though any one professing that he would impart a form of knowledge to obviate any pain in the feet, were then not to teach a man the art of shoe-making or the sources whence he can acquire anything of the kind, but were to present him with several kinds of shoes of all sorts: for he has helped him to meet his need, but has not imparted an art to him.[3]

This method of education is reflected in Gorgias' pupil Meno. When asked what virtue is, he replies with a whole swarm of virtues. (Aristotle in this case defends Gorgias, saying that those who enumerate the virtues in this way speak better than those who deceive themselves with universal definitions.[4]) When asked what virtue is, Meno replies:

> But there is no difficulty about it. First of all, if it is manly virtue you are after, it is easy to see that the virtue of a man consists in managing the city's affairs capably, and so that he will help his friends and injure his foes while taking care to come to no harm himself. Or if you want a woman's virtue, that is easily described. She must be a good housewife, careful with her stores and obedient to her husband.

Then there is another virtue for a child, male or female, and another for an old man, free or slave as you like, and a great many more kinds of virtue, so that no one need be at a loss to say what it is. For every act and every time of life, with reference to each separate function, there is a virtue for each one of us, and similarly, I should say, a vice.[5]

Hippias is portrayed by Plato as the sophist most impervious to the reality of universals, although his mastery over the multitude of particulars is indicated by his ability to remember fifty names after hearing them once, and his mastery over the variety of particulars is indicated by his appearance at the Olympic games:

You said that upon one occasion, when you went to the Olympic games, all that you had on your person was made by yourself. You began with your ring, which was of your own workmanship, and you said that you could engrave rings, and you had another seal which was also of your own workmanship, and a strigil and an oil flask, which you had made yourself. You said also that you had made the shoes which you had on your feet, and the cloak and the short tunic, but what appeared to us all most extraordinary, and a proof of singular art, was the girdle of your tunic, which, you said, was as fine as the most costly Persian fabric, and of your own weaving. Moreover, you told us that you had brought with you poems, epic, tragic, and dithyrambic, as well as prose writings of the most various kinds, and you said that your skill was also pre-eminent in the arts which I was just now mentioning, and in the true principles of rhythm and harmony and of orthography.[6]

In the *Greater Hippias*, Socrates, feigning to speak on behalf of a certain pertinacious fellow, says to Hippias, "He asks you not what is beautiful, but what is beauty." Hippias replies, "I understand, my good sir, and I will indeed tell him what is beauty, defying anyone to refute me. I assure you, Socrates, if I must speak the truth, that a beautiful maiden is beauty."[7] Hippias goes on to suggest that everyone thinks the same and will testify that he is right. For Hippias, and for most men, the reality of beauty is a beautiful maiden and not what Plato calls beauty itself.

Let us turn to more recent instances in which the real is identified with the perceived, or *esse* with *percipi*. Locke and others for whom reality is material had distinguished the primary qualities of bodies, which are inseparable from the body, and which include solidity, extension, figure, motion or rest, and number, from the secondary qualities of bodies, which are in truth nothing in the objects themselves but powers to produce various sensations in us by their primary qualities. Berkeley, by shifting to an existential signification, was able to eliminate matter from the world. In his *New Theory of Vision*, Berkeley treats the perceptions of distance by sight and by touch as real in their perceptual particularity, not as perceptions by two different senses of a common reality, distance. Visual perceptions are simply signs of what we can expect our tactile perceptions to be. Thus by treating extension and figure as immediate perceptual realities Berkeley made them no more objective than the secondary qualities. Berkeley's denial of the reality of matter exemplifies the kind of reciprocal priority we may expect to find among significations, for though he denies that matter is real, he in no way denies the reality of any perceptual effects that those who think matter is real suppose matter to produce. There is thus no experimental method for deciding between Locke and Berkeley on the reality of matter.

Hume looked upon Berkeley's existentialism as one of the greatest and most valuable discoveries that had been made of late years in the republic of letters,[8] and followed him in this if in nothing else. Berkeley used a diaphanic perspective, which implied the reality of spirits as well as of ideas, although no ideas can be formed of spirits. When Hume shifted to an objective perspective while retaining the existential signification, the spirits, including God and the soul, disappeared, and nothing was left but perceptions, which for Hume include impressions and ideas. Since ideas are derived from impressions, we have an easy way of determining the meaningfulness of any term:

> When we entertain, therefore, any suspicion that a philosophical term is employed without any meaning or idea (as is but too frequent), we need but enquire, *from what impression is that supposed idea derived?* And if it be impossible to assign any, this will serve to confirm our suspicion. By bringing ideas into so clear a light we may reasonably hope to remove all dispute, which may arise, concerning their nature and reality.[9]

For Ernst Mach, as for Berkeley and Hume, nature is composed of sensations as its elements: "Properly speaking, the world is not composed of 'things' as its elements, but of colors, tones, pressures, spaces, times, in short what we ordinarily call individual sensations."[10] The concepts of both common sense and science are economical devices for reproducing facts in thought in the service of practical interests. In naming things, for example, we abstract from the changes in a complex of sensations: "No inalterable thing exists. The thing is an abstraction, the name a symbol, for a compound of elements from whose changes we abstract."[11]

Einstein similarly treated sensations as the primary reality and our concepts as free creations of the mind by which we order our sensations. The development of both the special and the general theories of relativity depended on seeing science as ordering sensations having a particular existential locus in a "here" and "now." Even bodily objects and the "real world" are justified only by their connection with sense impressions:

> I believe that the first step in the setting of a "real external world" is the formation of the concept of bodily objects and of bodily objects of various kinds. Out of the multitude of our sense experiences we take, mentally and arbitrarily, certain repeatedly occurring complexes of sense impressions (partly in conjunction with sense impressions which are interpreted as signs for sense experiences of others), and we correlate to them a concept—the concept of the bodily object. Considered logically this concept is not identical with the totality of sense impressions referred to; but it is a free creation of the human (or animal) mind. On the other hand, this concept owes its meaning and its justification exclusively to the totality of the sense impressions which we associate with it.
>
> The second step is to be found in the fact that, in our thinking (which determines our expectation), we attribute to this concept of the bodily object a significance, which is to a high degree independent of the sense impressions which originally give rise to it. This is what we mean when we attribute to the bodily object "a real existence." The justification of such a setting rests exclusively on the fact that, by means of such concepts and mental relations between them, we are able to orient ourselves in the labyrinth of sense impressions.[12]

Max Weber similarly regards reality as individual and our conceptual constructs as aids in understanding this reality in its individuality. An "historical individual," like the interaction of perceiver and perceived in the Protagorean flux, reflects changes in both knower and known:

> The stream of immeasurable events flows unendingly towards eternity. The cultural problems which move men form themselves ever anew and in different colors, and the boundaries of that area in the infinite stream of concrete events which acquires meaning and significance for us, i.e., which becomes an "historical individual," are constantly subject to change.[13]

Weber's work on *The Protestant Ethic and the Spirit of Capitalism*, for example, is concerned with a particular historical individual. Concept-construction is justified by its contribution to understanding concrete historical events and patterns: "Nothing should be more sharply emphasized than the proposition that the knowledge of the cultural significance of concrete historical events and patterns is exclusively and solely the final end which, among other means, concept-construction and the criticism of constructs also seek to serve."[14] Weber's ideal types do not have the reality of Platonic forms or of Aristotelian essences, but are instrumental only. An ideal type, according to Weber,

> is a conceptual construct (*Gedankenbild*) which is neither historical reality nor even the "true" reality. It is even less fitted to serve as a schema under which a real situation or action is to be subsumed as one instance. It has the significance of a purely ideal limiting concept with which the real situation or action is compared and surveyed for the explication of certain of its significant components.[15]

Another device for ordering the particularity of perceived things is Ludwig Wittgenstein's "family resemblances." His account of games recalls Meno's account of the virtues:

> 66. Consider for example the proceedings that we call "games". I mean board-games, card-games, ball-games Olympic games, and so on. What is common to them all?—Don't say: "There *must* be something common, or they would not be called 'games' "—but *look and see* whether there is anything common to all. —For if you look at them you will not see something that is common to *all*, but similarities, relationships, and a whole series of them at that. To repeat: don't think, but look!—Look for example at boards-games, with their multifarious relationships. Now pass to card-games; here you find many correspondences with the first group, but many common features drop out, and others appear. When we pass next to ball-games, much that is common is retained, but much is lost.—Are they all 'amusing'? Compare chess with noughts and crosses. Or is there always winning and losing, or competition between players? Think of patience. In ball games there is winning and losing; but when a child throws his ball at the wall and catches it again, this feature has disappeared. Look at the parts played by skill and luck; and at the difference between skill in chess and skill in tennis. Think now of games like ring-a-ring-a-roses; here is the element of amusement, but how many other characteristic features have disappeared! And we can go through the many, many other groups of games in the same way; can see how similarities crop up and disappear.
> And the result of this examination is: we see a complicated network of similarities overlapping and criss-crossing: sometimes overall similarities, sometimes similarities of detail.

67. I can think of no better expression to characterize these similarities than "family resemblances."[16]

The Buddhist theory of reality as composed of momentary dharmas is another example of existential signification. The succession of dharmas is like the flux of the *Theaetetus*, and in the *Milindapañha* the sage Nāgasena compares it to the succession of flames of a single fire:

> "It is as if, your majesty, a man were to light a light;—would it shine all night?"
> "Assuredly, bhante, it would shine all night."
> "Pray, your majesty, is the flame of the first watch the same as the flame of the middle watch?"
> "Nay, verily, bhante."
> "Is the flame of the middle watch the same as the flame of the last watch?"
> "Nay, verily, bhante."
> "Pray, then, your majesty, was there one light in the first watch, another light in the middle watch, and a third light in the last watch?"
> "Nay, verily, bhante. Through connection with that first light there was light all night."
> "In exactly the same way, your majesty, do the elements of being (*dharmas*) join one another in serial succession: one element perishes, another arises, succeeding each other as it were instantaneously. Therefore neither as the same nor as a different person do you arrive at your latest aggregation of consciousness."[17]

Just as for Mach neither the body nor the ego are permanent, but relative stability is marked by language, so Nāgasena argues that the name of a person or a thing is "but a way of counting, a term, an appellation, a convenient designation, a mere name."[18] Liberation from suffering comes through the realization of the emptiness of dharmas.

The identification of appearance and reality in this tradition is evident in Nāgārjuna's identification of samsara and nirvana:

> There is no difference at all
> Between nirvana and samsara.
> There is no difference at all
> Between samsara and nirvana.[19]

Existential signification is congenial to art in its concern with perceptible particulars. It has often been noted that Shakespeare's characters have the reality of real individuals, that is, that he attains the end Hamlet assigns to acting, which is not only to mirror nature, but to mirror an existential nature: "to hold, as 't were, the mirror up to nature; to show virtue her own feature, scorn her own image, and the very age and body of the time his form and pressure."[20]

The flux of the *Theaetetus*, the transiency of perceptible things, pervades the Sonnets: "From fairest creatures we desire increase./That thereby beauty's rose might never die;" "When forty winters shall beseige thy brow;" "When I do count the clock that tells the time;" "When I consider everything that grows/Holds in perfection but a little moment;" "But wherefore do not you a mightier way/Make war upon this bloody tyrant Time;" "When to the sessions of sweet silent thought/I summon up remembrance of things past;" "Not marble, nor the gilded monuments/Of princes shall outlive this powerful rhyme;" "Like as the waves make towards the pebbled shore,/So do our minutes hasten to their end;" "Since brass, nor stone, nor earth, nor boundless sea,/But sad mortality o'er-sways their power;" "Thus is his cheek the map of days outworn;" "That time of year thou mayest in me behold;" "Thy glass will show thee how thy beauties wear;" "To me, fair friend, you never can be old;" "No, Time, thou shalt not boast that I do change."

Shakespeare uses the sound, rhythm, and sense of the language to give to thoughts and feelings an existential reality. Such a use of language is an alternative to Cratylus' pointing. And, paradoxically, the universality of his works results from this individuation. Here already we can see the priority of existential reality to all other realities. Everything can be presented in individual form.

Let these, then, suffice as examples of existentialists in our sense of the term: Protagoras, Gorgias, Hippias, Berkeley, Hume, Mach, Einstein, Max Weber, Wittgenstein, Nāgasena, Nāgārjuna, and Shakespeare.

2. Substrative Realities

It may be held that reality as encountered or perceived by us is *not* the reality, since as encountered or perceived it involves a contribution from ourselves as well as from the object. What is really real is the object as it is in itself, apart from its effect on us. Primary qualities, which are really in the object, must be distinguished from secondary qualities, which are nothing in the objects themselves but the power to produce effects in us by their primary qualities. Existential reality lies in the effects on us; this second kind of reality lies in that which has the power to produce such effects. The world as it appears is the manifestation of this underlying reality. The contrast between the two realities is familiar as the contrast between the two tables with which Sir Arthur Eddington begins *The Nature of the Physical World*: there is the familiar, solid, perceptual table, and the table of physics, composed of sub-atomic particles in motion and occupying only a small fraction of the total volume.[21]

This second kind of reality can be called a *material* reality, or, following Duns Scotus, an *entitative* reality, or a *substrative* reality. The latter term has the advantage of an evident meaning and a link with the Greek "*hupokeimenon*," that which underlies, which was translated by the Latin "*substratum*."

Being and knowing and meaning all admit of a substrative interpretation, for the world may be the manifestation of an underlying substance, the content of consciousness may be the manifestation of unconscious or material forces, and the manifest meanings of texts may at once conceal and reveal subtexts and latent meanings.

The doctrine that the real is material or substrative is found at the very beginning of Western philosophy. The early Ionian thinkers figure in our histories, which derive principally from Aristotle, as having held that water (Thales) or air (Anaximenes) or the indeterminate (Anaximander) was the substratum of all things, and the Pythagoreans too treat their numbers as material realities underlying the phenomena. This view was given its culminating expression in the post-sophistic period by Protagoras' fellow-citizen Democritus. Democritus agrees with Protagoras' account of perception as an interaction of perceiver and perceived and for this very reason denies that it gives us knowledge of reality, that is, of things as they are in themselves. "We apprehend in reality nothing true, but changing according to the condition of the body and of the things that impinge on it and resist it."[22] Perception is bastard rather than legitimate knowledge because it is the offspring of this mixed parentage. (The same metaphor of perception as the offspring of two parents is used by Plato in relation to the midwifery of the *Theaetetus*.[23]) "There are two forms of cognition, legitimate and bastard. To the bastard belong all these: sight, hearing, smell, taste, touch. The other is legitimate and distinct from these."[24] Reality is not found in sense perception but in the atoms and void: "By convention sweet, by convention bitter, by convention hot, by convention cold, by convention color, but in reality atoms and void."[25]

This doctrine was continued in the ancient period by Epicurus and Lucretius. The first great triumph of substrative signification in the modern period was in the work of Newton.

At the beginning of the *Principia*, in the scholium to the Definitions, Newton distinguishes between absolute and relative time, space, place, and motion:

I do not define time, space, place, and motion, as being well known to all. Only I must observe, that the common people conceive those quantities under no other notions but from the relation they bear to sensible objects. And thence arise certain prejudices, for the removing of which it will be convenient to distinguish them into absolute and relative, true and apparent, mathematical and common.

I. Absolute, true, and mathematical time, of itself, and from its own nature, flows equably without relation to anything external, and by another name is called duration: relative, apparent, and common time, is some sensible and external (whether accurate or unequable) measure of duration by the means of motion, which is commonly used instead of true time; such as an hour, a day, a month, a year.

II. Absolute space, in its own nature, without relation to anything external, remains always similar and immovable. Relative space is some movable dimension or measure of the absolute spaces; which our senses determine by its position to bodies; and which is commonly taken for immovable space; such is the dimension of a subterraneous, an aerial, or celestial space, determined by its position in respect of the earth . . . .

III. Place is a part of space which a body takes up, and is according to the space, either absolute or relative . . . .

IV. Absolute motion is the translation of a body from one absolute place into another; and relative motion, the translation from one relative place into another.[26]

In philosophical disquisitions, Newton says, we ought to abstract from our senses, and consider things themselves, distinct from what are only sensible measures of them.[27] Those defile the purity of mathematical and philosophical truths, who confound real quantities with their relations and sensible measures. It is indeed, he says, a matter of great difficulty to discover, and effectually to distinguish, the true motions of particular bodies from the apparent, but the end of the whole *Principia* is to obtain the true motions from their causes, effects, and apparent differences, and the converse: "But how we are to obtain the true motions from their causes, effects, and apparent differences, and the converse, shall be explained more at large in the following treatise. For to this end it was that I composed it."[28]

The absolute, true, and mathematical space and time are the real space and time which underlie all the apparent spaces and times. The whole achievement of the *Principia* depends on this distinction, for the relative or apparent motions do not conform to the axioms or laws of motion or to the law of gravitation. As it happens, these laws do not enable us to distinguish empirically between rest and uniform motion in absolute space; empirically, only absolute accelerations are determinable. And if we cannot identify empirically a state of absolute rest, neither can we determine empirically the absolute simultaneity of spatially separated events, for the apparent simultaneity is relative to the motion of the observer. Thus neither absolute space nor one universal time can be identified empirically, and, from the standpoint of an existential signification, this means that they are unreal. As we have seen, Einstein made use of an existential signification in his development of the special theory of relativity. But for Newton, a substrative signification had the advantage of putting aside such relativistic considerations and enabling him to develop what we now call classical mechanics, which in turn made the discovery of relativistic mechanics possible. This is one illustration of how archic differences complement each other in the historical development of a science.

It should also be noted that Newton's absolute space, time, and motion are mathematical. This means that mathematics is not a science of transcendent realities or of abstract quantity or of the consequences of hypotheses, but a science of physical realities. Geometry, for example, is a physical science founded on the drawing of straight lines and circles. If one objects that existential lines and circles, those actually drawn, lack the perfect accuracy of geometry, Newton's reply is that "the errors are not in the art, but in the artificers. He that works with less accuracy is an imperfect mechanic; and if any could work with perfect accuracy, he would be the most perfect mechanic of all, for the description of right lines and circles, upon which geometry is founded, belongs to mechanics."[29] Newton's title, *The Mathematical Principles of Natural Philosophy*, does not imply that mathematical principles are external to nature, but rather that the real is mathematical, that is, that true space, time, and motion are themselves mathematical. Newton's scientific achievement thus depends on the distinction between the true and the apparent and discloses the true in its mathematical character.

Material or substrative signification has been used not only in physics, but also in the human sciences. Machiavelli compares his *Discourses* to the exploration of unknown seas and continents, and says he is opening a new route not yet followed by anyone. The novelty lies in treating ancient history not as existentially unique, "as though heaven, the sun, the elements, and men had changed the order of their motion and power, and were different from what they were in ancient times,"[30] but rather as relevant to contemporary politics. The reason for this relevance lies in the sameness of the desires and passions of men:

> Whoever considers the past and the present will readily observe that all cities and all peoples are and ever have been animated by the same desires and the same passions; so that it is easy, by diligent study of the past, to foresee what is likely to happen in the future in any republic, and to apply those remedies that were used by the ancients, or, not finding any that were employed by them, to devise new ones from the similarity of the events. But as such considerations are neglected or not understood by most of those who read, or, if understood by these, are unknown by those who govern, it follows that the same troubles generally recur in all republics.[31]

The three more recent materialistic interpreters of man, Marx, Nietzsche, and Freud, are all working in an epistemic epoch, and consequently are concerned to account for consciousness by the substratum that determines it. For Marx it is the conditions of material production which are decisive in determining man's consciousness. The point is made with rhetorical force in the *Communist Manifesto*:

> Does it require deep intuition to comprehend that man's ideas, views, and conceptions, in one word, man's consciousness, changes with every change in the conditions of his material existence, in his social relations and in his social life?
> What else does the history of ideas prove, than that intellectual production changes its character in proportion as material production is changed? The ruling ideas of each age have ever been the ideas of its ruling class.[32]

The distinction between the science which knows the real and opinions which are based on the phenomena becomes in Marx a distinction between a true or scientific consciousness and an illusory or ideological consciousness. In his Preface to *A Contribution to the Critique of Political Economy*, Marx contrasts the economic foundation, which involves the forces and relations of production, and to which there corresponds a scientific consciousness, with the social, political, and spiritual superstructure, to which there corresponds an ideological consciousness:

> With the change of the economic foundation the entire immense superstructure is more or less rapidly transformed. In considering such transformations the distinction should always be made between the material transformation of the economic conditions of production, which can be determined with the precision of natural science, and the legal, political, religious, aesthetic, or philosophic—in short, ideological—forms in which

men become conscious of this conflict and fight it out. Just as our opinion of an individual is not based on what he thinks of himself, so can we not judge such a period of transformation by its own consciousness; on the contrary, this consciousness must rather be explained from the contradictions of material life, from the existing conflict between the social forces of production and the relations of production.[33]

Nietzsche also accounts for consciousness by means of the material realities that underlie it. Nietzsche surmises that consciousness has developed only under the pressure of the need for communication; that from the start it was needed and useful only between human beings (particularly between those who commanded and those who obeyed); and that it also developed only in proportion to the degree of this utility. Nietzsche explains conscious meanings as arising out of the need for communication, and hence as superficial: "Man, like every living being, thinks continually without knowing it; the thinking that rises to *consciousness* is only the smallest part of all this—the most superficial and worst part—for only this conscious thinking *takes the form of words, which is to say signs of communication*, and this fact uncovers the origin of consciousness."[34] The world of which we become conscious is only a surface-and sign-world: "Owing to the nature of *animal consciousness*, the world of which we can become conscious is only a surface-and sign-world, a world that is made common and meaner; whatever becomes conscious becomes by the same token shallow, thin, relatively stupid, general, sign, herd signal; all becoming conscious involves a great and thorough corruption, falsification, reduction to superficialities, and generalization."[35]

In *Beyond Good and Evil* Nietzsche treats thinking as reflecting physiological demands for the preservation of a certain type of life:

> After having looked long enough between the philosopher's lines and fingers, I say to myself: by far the greater part of conscious thinking must still be included among instinctive activities, and that goes even for philosophical thinking. We have to relearn here, as one has had to relearn about heredity and what is "innate." As the act of birth deserves no consideration in the whole process and procedure of heredity, so "being conscious" is not in any decisive sense the *opposite* of what is instinctive: most of the conscious thinking of a philosopher is secretly guided and forced into certain channels by his instincts.
>
> Behind all logic and its seeming sovereignty of movement, too, there stand valuations or, more clearly, physiological demands for the preservation of a certain type of life. For example, that the definite should be worth more than the indefinite, and mere appearance worth less than

"truth"—such estimates might be, in spite of their regulative importance for *us*, nevertheless mere foreground estimates, a certain kind of
niaiserie which may be necessary for the preservation of just such beings
as we are. Supposing, that is, that not just man is the "measure of
things"—[36]

The concluding reference to Protagoras indicates an archic difference from
him: our thinking and evaluations are not measuring reality; rather it is
the substrative reality of our instincts and physiological demands that is
measuring our measurings.

For Freud, as for Marx and Nietzsche, the content of consciousness is
not itself the primary reality, but is derivative from the realities that underlie it. In a succession of works that even today are still being assimilated
Freud revealed to consciousness the unconscious reality underlying neu-
rotic symptoms, dreams, errors, jokes, totemism and taboo, religion, works
of art, the uneasiness in culture, and the biblical account of Moses. His
work is by now so familiar that quotation is hardly necessary, but let me
cite one example, the contrast between the apparent and the real content
of dreams: "My theory is not based on a consideration of the manifest
content of dreams but refers to the thoughts which are shown by the
work of interpretation to lie behind dreams. We must make a contrast
between the *manifest* and the *latent* content of dreams."[37]

Tolstoy, working in this same epistemic epoch, provides a literary example of a substrative reality. In his writings a superficial and false consciousness of ourselves and the world is contrasted with an awareness of the
things that really matter. Ivan Ilych, for example, in the face of death
comes to see the falsity of his easy, pleasant, decorous life:

> He lay on his back and began to pass his life in review in quite a new
> way. In the morning when he saw first his footman, then his wife,
> then his daughter, and then the doctor, their every word and move-
> ment confirmed to him the awful truth that had been revealed to him
> during the night. In them he saw himself—all that for which he had
> lived—and saw clearly that it was not real at all, but a terrible and
> huge deception which had hidden both life and death.[38]

In conclusion, let us note an example of substrative reality from outside
the Western tradition. The contrast between the appearances and the underlying reality of the Tao is evident in Lao Tzu:

The Tao which is bright appears to be dark.
The Tao which goes forward appears to fall backward.
The Tao which is level appears uneven.
Great virtue appears like a valley (hollow).
Great purity appears like disgrace.
Far-reaching virtue appears as if insufficient.
Solid virtue appears as if unsteady.
True substance appears to be changeable.
The great square has no corners.
The great implement (or talent) is slow to finish (or mature).
Great music sounds faint.
Great form has no shape.
Tao is hidden and nameless.
Yet it is Tao alone that skillfully provides for all
    and brings them to perfection.[39]

Here then is a group of materialists to place alongside the earlier group of existentialists: Democritus, Epicurus, Lucretius, Newton, Machiavelli, Marx, Nietzsche, Freud, Tolstoy, and Lao Tzu. With names such as these on one side, and names such as Einstein, Max Weber, Wittgenstein, Nāgārjuna, and Shakespeare on the other, who can suppose that one of these groups must be simply wrong? Our initial thought that the greatest wisdom enforces the most profound pluralism seems sufficiently confirmed even in this single comparison.

3. Noumenal Realities

One can deny that the appearances are themselves the realities not only by treating them as manifestations of an underlying reality, but also by treating them as intimations of a transcendent reality. Perceived reality, it may be held, is unreal insofar as it is transient and imperfect, substrative reality is unreal insofar as it is a reduced and limited reality, and what is really real is perfect and imperishable. Such a reality is transcendent or supersensible or ideal or intelligible or noumenal. Both Plato and Kant use the term "noumena," things perceived by the mind, for this reality. Plato opposes noumena to horomena, or things seen,[40] and Kant opposes noumena to phenomena, or appearances.[41] I will call this transcendent reality an *ideal* or *noumenal* reality. Any kind of transcendent reality will be called noumenal, whether we can know it or not. For Plato, for example, noumena are knowable by us, for Kant they are not. Noumanal realities are familiar in doctrines that this world is not all that there is, but derives its significance from its relation to a higher order of things.

Being and knowing and meaning all admit of noumenal interpretation. An eternal and unchanging realm of being may be contrasted with the flux of becoming, a spiritual consciousness may be contrasted with a mundane consciousness, and texts may have anagogical as well as literal meanings.

Noumenal reality enters Western thought at that great moment when Parmenides was taken by the daughters of the sun through the gates of the ways of night and day and instructed by the goddess in the way of truth, as contrasted with the way of seeming. "For the same thing is real for thinking and for being. (*To gar auto noein estin te kai einai*)."[42] Parmenidean being is without internal differentiation, like the Democritean atoms of being, but, since it is one and not many, it cannot be construed as the material substratum of the universe, for then the universe would simply be one material atom and there would be no perceived reality.

The fullest development of noumenal reality in Greek thought is found in the writings of Plato. It is indeed so generally recognized and so pervasive in his writings that it seems hardly necessary to give examples, and, moreover, its use in Plato is so various that a few examples cannot do it justice. Let me simply cite Aristotle's account of the origin of the Platonic doctrine of ideas, and then give a single example from the *Republic*. Aristotle says that Plato

> having in his youth first become familiar with Cratylus and with the Heraclitean doctrines (that all sensible things are ever in a state of flux and there is no knowledge about them), these views he held even in later years. Socrates, however, was busying himself about ethical matters and neglecting the world of nature as a whole but seeking the universal in these ethical matters, and fixed thought for the first time on definitions; Plato accepted his teaching, but held that the problem applied not to sensible things but to entities of another kind—for this reason, that the common definition could not be a definition of any sensible thing, as they were always changing. Things of this other sort, then, he called Ideas, and sensible things, he said, were all named after these, and in virtue of a relation to these; for the many existed by participation in the Ideas that have the same name as they.[43]

In the educational system of the *Republic* the requirements for a knowledge of the really real things are adumbrated. The student proceeds through a hierarchy of images and realities, from the mythic reality of music to the physical reality of gymnastic to the hypothetical reality of mathematics and finally to the really real reality disclosed by dialectic.

A similar hierarchy appears in Plotinus. The ideas are in the Intelligence and are apprehended by the soul, which makes images of them in sensible things. The hierarchy is summarized in relation to beauty as follows:

> First off, beauty is the Good. From the Good, The Intelligence draws
> its beauty directly. The Soul is, because of The Intelligence, beautiful.
> Other beauties, those of action or of behavior, come from the imprint
> upon them of The Soul, which is author, too, of bodily beauty. A
> divine entity and a part, as it were, of Beauty, The Soul renders beauti-
> ful to the fullness of their capacity all things it touches or controls.[44]

Augustine found that of all the philosophers, none approximated more
peculiarly to the Christians than the Platonists, and the whole Christian
tradition has tended to adopt a noumenal signification. The hierarchy from
bodies to souls to the intelligible forms and God can be seen in Augustine's
discussion of the physics of the Platonists:

> We call sensible those things which can be sensed by the sight and
> touch of the body, intelligible that which can be understood by the
> perception of the mind. For there is no bodily beauty, whether in the
> repose of the body, such as figure, or in the motion, such as song, of
> which the mind does not judge. This it obviously could not do if this
> species were not better in it, without the distension of bulk, without
> the rumbling of voice, without extension of place or time. But likewise
> if it were not mutable there, one would not judge better than another
> concerning the sensible species; the cleverer better than the stupider,
> the more learned than the less learned, the more experienced than the
> less experienced, and even the same individual person, when he improves,
> better later than earlier. But that which is susceptible of more and less
> is doubtless mutable. Wherefore these men, clever and learned and
> experienced in these things, easily inferred that the first species is not
> in those things in which it is shown to be mutable. Since therefore in
> the presence of these both body and soul would possess species more or
> less, but if they could lack species entirely they would be absolutely
> nothing, they saw that there is something in which the first species is
> immutable and incomparable, and there they believed, most rightly, is
> the principle of things, which was not made and from which all things
> were made.[45]

The distinction between the sensible and the supersensible, or between
phenomena and noumena, is also of fundamental importance in Kant, but
the two are differently related than in the authors so far considered. Nature
as an object of sense can be known theoretically, but there is no such
knowledge of the supersensible. As moral agents, however, we can act in
accordance with a supersensible determination of the will by the moral

law. And the great gulf separating phenomena and noumena, or the realms
of nature and of freedom, is bridged by the judgment seeking a purposiveness
in nature that would accord with the determination of nature by reason.

The promises and warnings of the Koran also refer to an unseen reality,
and to the extent that this reality is accessible only through revelation and
not through reason, mankind is divided into the true believers and the
infidels, the one destined for reward, the other for punishment:

> No doubt is there about this Book: It is a guidance to the God-fearing,
> Who believe in the unseen, who observe prayer, and out of what we
> have bestowed on them, expend *for God*;
> And who believe in what hath been sent down to thee, and in what
> hath been sent down before thee, and full faith have they in the life
> to come:
> These are guided by their Lord; and with these it shall be well.
> As to the infidels, alike is it to them whether thou warn them or
> warn them not—they will not believe:
> Their hearts and their ears hath God sealed up; and over their eyes
> is a covering. For them, a severe chastisement![46]

Only when the infidels encounter the unseen reality, will they agree with
the believers on the truth of the Prophet's words ("our Lord" and "your
Lord" are the same Lord):

> And the inmates of Paradise shall cry to the inmates of the fire,
> "Now have we found what our Lord promised us to be true. Have ye
> too found what your Lord promised you to be true?" And they shall
> answer, "Yes."[47]

The arts can in a manner represent the unseen world to the senses. In
El Greco's "The Burial of Count Orgaz," for example, the lower half of
the painting represents the visible scene and the upper half the higher
reality. And in his portraits of saints the noumenal reality shines through
the sensible. In the paintings of Francis Bacon, on the other hand, it is the
substrative reality that breaks through into visible form.

Let these suffice as examples of noumenal signification: Parmenides,
Plato, Plotinus, Augustine, Kant, The Koran, and El Greco.

4. Essential Realities

If it is held that what is real for us is not the real, because it is relative to us; that the substratum is not the real, because it is a substratum and therefore lacks the reality of what emerges from it; and that ideal forms are not real, because they are ideal and therefore lack the reality that they would have if they were actualized, does any other possibility remain? There remains the possibility that each thing is real as what it is. A statue, for example, is not a real man, but it is a real statue. Since what each thing is is its *essence*, this kind of reality can be called *essential* reality.

Essences are like existential realities insofar as they are real in particular individuals, but they differ from them because as essences they are general rather than particular. The definition or formulation of an essence is general in the sense that it can apply to many particulars, even if in fact it applies to only one. Existentially, every man is different from every other, and is a different man at every moment of his life, but, essentially, different men are all men, and a man remains a man through all the changes of his life. Essences are like substrata, since they are what things are apart from their changing appearances, but the essence is not the substratum. A man is not a body but a living body. Essences are like noumena, since they do not come to be and pass away, but noumena are real apart from the individuals that may happen to be exemplifying them, whereas essences are real in the individuals whose essence they are.

Essential realities are familiar in the view that there are real kinds of things. Being and knowing and meaning all admit of essential interpretation, for being may consist of substances, knowing of essential forms of consciousness or thought, and texts of essential meanings.

Essential reality goes back in the West at least to Socrates, and in China at least to Confucius. Both Socrates and Confucius sought real and not merely apparent virtues, and virtues that would be real in individuals, not apart from them. In speaking of Socrates, I am speaking of an essential Socrates, not of an existential Socrates or an ideal Socrates. For our distinction of the kinds of realities makes it easy to distinguish different versions of the real Socrates. A real existential Socrates is given to us by Xenophon; this is Socrates as Xenophon encountered him. The Platonic Socrates is a real Socrates in the sense of an ideal Socrates, and Plato makes no claim that the historical Socrates said all that Plato attributes to him. A real essential Socrates is characterized by Aristotle in the way we have already noted: "Socrates, however, was busying himself about ethical matters and neglecting the world of nature as a whole but seeking the universal in these ethical matters, and fixed thought for the first time on definitions."[48]

Aristotle continues the Socratic essentialism, beginning his *On Sophistical Refutations* with the essentialist distinction between appearance and reality:

> That some reasonings are really reasonings, but that others seem to be, but are not really, reasonings, is obvious. For, as this happens in other spheres through a certain likeness, so it happens also in arguments. For some people possess good physical condition, while others have merely the appearance of it, by blowing themselves out and dressing themselves up like the tribal choruses; again, some people are beautiful because of their beauty, while others have the appearance of beauty because they trick themselves out. So too with inanimate things; for some of these are really silver and some gold, while others are not but only appear to our senses to be so; for example, objects made of litharge or tin appear to be silver, and yellow-coloured objects appear to be gold. In the same way also reasoning and refutation are sometimes real and sometimes not, but appear to be real owing to men's inexperience; for the inexperienced are like those who view things from a distance.[49]

Just as a foundation for an existential interpretation of being as being for us is found in Protagoras' statement that man is the measure of all things, of the being of the things that are and the not-being of the things that are not, so a foundation for an essential interpretation of being as what each thing is, is found in Aristotle's argument against Protagoras in the *Metaphysics* in which he defends the so-called law of contradiction. The law of contradiction asserts "that the same attribute cannot at the same time belong and not belong to the same subject and in the same respect."[50] It is the precondition for meaningful discourse in the essentialist mode, and hence it cannot be proved directly without begging the question. It can be shown, however, to be presupposed in any statement having an essential signification: "The starting-point for all such arguments is not the demand that our opponent shall say either that something is or that it is not (for this one might perhaps take to be a begging of the question), but that he shall say something that is *significant* both for himself and for another; for this is necessary, if he really is to say anything."[51] Of course, in an archic sense the question is still begged, since an essential meaning is attributed to the opponent's words. Aristotle argues that if a word has such a meaning, then it will not be true to say that anything both is and is not what that word means. For if "to be" and "man" have definite meanings, then "to be a man" will not *mean* the same as "not to be a man," and if these meanings are not the same, then it will not *be* the same to be a man and not to be a man, and if these are not the same, then it will not be *true* to say that the same thing both is and is not a man.

Aristotle's sciences are all investigations of some essential reality, the reality for example of nature, or the soul, or the good for man, or tragedy, or wisdom, or the art of persuasion. The adaptation of the science to the reality it is formulating is seen in the contrast between the rough, outline universals of ethics, the precise universals of mathematics, and the topical universals of rhetoric:

> Our discussion will be adequate if it has as much clearness as the subject-matter admits of for precision is not to be sought for alike in all discussions, any more than in all the products of the crafts. Now fine and just actions, which political science investigates, admit of much variety and fluctuation of opinion, so that they may be thought to exist only by convention, and not by nature. And goods also give rise to a similar fluctuation because they bring harm to many people; for before now men have been undone by reason of their wealth, and others by reason of their courage. We must be content, then, in speaking of such subjects and with such premises to indicate the truth roughly and in outline, and in speaking about things which are only for the most part true and with premises of the same kind to reach conclusions that are no better. In the same spirit, therefore, should each type of statement be *received*; for it is the mark of an educated man to look for precision in each class of things just so far as the nature of the subject admits; it is evidently equally foolish to accept probable reasoning from a mathematician and to demand from a rhetorician scientific proofs.[52]

As an example of essential reality in a later scientific work, consider William Harvey's *Exercitatio Anatomica de Motu Cordis et Sanguinis in Animalibus*. The title already suggests that Harvey is investigating the motion of the heart and blood in animals as an essential reality. The essential or universal character of this subject matter is clear at the beginning of his anatomical investigation in Chapter II:

> In the first place, when the chest of a living animal is opened, and the capsule surrounding the heart is cut away, one may see that the heart alternates in movement and rest. There is a time when it moves, and a time when it is quiet.
> This is more easily seen in the hearts of cold-blooded animals, as toads, snakes, frogs, snails, shell-fish, crustaceans, and fish. It is also more apparent in other animals as the dog and pig, if one carefully observes the heart as it moves more slowly when about to die. The

movements then become slower and weaker and the pauses longer, so that it is easy to see what the motion really is and how made.[53]

The heart signified by this text is not a particular heart, nor an unperceived heart underlying the appearances, nor an ideal heart, but simply the heart, the heart as a determinate kind of thing, as having an essence. And the alternation of motion and rest characterizes this heart, and hence all particular hearts, although it may be seen more clearly in some species than in others, and more clearly in a given species when the heart is slowed by the approach of death. But these are accidental differences; in its essence the motion is the same.

Descartes presents an unusual essentialism, for he takes the Augustinian noumenal hierarchy of body, mind, and God, and assigns to each an essential reality. He is thus supposed to have bifurcated nature, or established a pernicious dualism of mind and body. Actually, however, to treat the mind and body as separate substances does not imply for Descartes that they are not intimately united or that they do not influence each other in many ways, but only that each kind of substance has its own essential autonomy. The mind, although it is continually influenced by the body, has the power to determine the truth of its own judgments, and thus to form itself, whatever the effects of the body on it. And the body, although it can be moved and altered by the mind, can only be moved and altered in accordance with the laws of its own nature. In this sense each is what it is independently of the other.

Hegel provides an example of essentialism on a grand scale. Both his *Phenomenology* and his *Encyclopaedia* give us a parade of essential forms. Neither sequence is an existential history of forms as they happen to have occurred, nor is it on the other hand a set of ideal forms that are real apart from their actualization in history. What is rational is actual, and what is actual is rational, as Hegel says more than once.[54] History and science together, comprehended history, form the actuality, truth, and certainty of the throne of absolute Spirit, as Hegel says at the conclusion of the *Phenomenology*:

> The *goal*, Absolute Knowing, or Spirit that knows itself as Spirit, has for its path the recollection of the Spirits as they are in themselves and as they accomplish the organization of their realm. Their preservation, regarded from the side of their free existence appearing in the form of contingency, is History; but regarded from the side of their comprehended organization, it is the Science of Knowing in the sphere of appearance: the two together, comprehended History, form alike the inwardizing

and the Calvary of absolute Spirit, the actuality, truth, and certainty of
his throne, without which he would be lifeless and alone. Only

> from the chalice of this realm of spirits
> foams forth for Him his own infinitude.[55]

Similarly, although the content of logic "shows forth God as he is in his
eternal essence before the creation of Nature and of a Finite Spirit,"[56] the
essence becomes actual only as it externalizes itself in nature and returns
to itself in mind. The Hegelian essences lack the reality of the Platonic
Ideas, and are rather, like the Aristotelian essences, the reality of the
phenomenal world. And yet they are ordered in a dialectical sequence very
different from the Aristotelian organization of independent sciences. This
difference is a striking example of the need for a third archic variable
concerned with order or structure or method of a text, a variable that we
will take up in the next chapter.

Husserl is well-known for his doctrine of essences. Their nature and
their varying degrees of universality are indicated in the following passage
from *Ideas*:

> Now when we stated that every fact could be "essentially" other than it
> is, we were already expressing thereby that it belongs to the meaning
> of everything contingent that it should have essential being and there-
> with an Eidos to be apprehended in all its purity; and this Eidos comes
> under essential truths of varying degrees of universality. An individual
> object is not simply and quite generally an individual, a "this-there"
> something unique; but being constituted thus and thus "in itself" it
> has its own proper mode of being, its own supply of essential predica-
> bles which must qualify it (qua "Being as it is in itself"), if other sec-
> ondary relative determinations are to qualify it also. Thus, for example,
> every tone in and for itself has an essential nature, and at the limit the
> universal meaning-essence "tone in general," or rather the acoustic in
> general—understood in the pure sense of a phase or aspect intuitively
> derivable from the individual tone (either in its singleness, or through
> comparison with others as a "common element").[57]

In his later investigation of the life-world, Husserl asks how the life-world,
after the epochē of the objective sciences, can become the subject matter
of a science. What appears to be true is relative to the life-world: "When
we are thrown into an alien social sphere, that of the Negroes in the
Congo, Chinese peasants, etc., we discover that their truths, the facts that
for them are fixed, generally verified or verifiable, are by no means the

same as ours."⁵⁸ These differences can indeed be overcome by objective science, but since this has been put in epochē

> we have the embarrassment of wondering what else can be undertaken scientifically, as something that can be established once and for all and for everyone.
>
> But this embarrassment disappears as soon as we consider that the life-world does have, in all its relative features, a *general structure*. This general structure, to which everything that exists relatively is bound, is not itself relative. We can attend to it in its generality and, with sufficient care, fix it once and for all in a way equally accessible to all."⁵⁹

The different life-worlds have, as life-worlds, a common general structure and thus can be investigated scientifically.

The sequence of German-speaking materialists, Marx, Nietzsche, and Freud, is paralleled by the sequence of German essentialist phenomenologists, Hegel, Husserl, and Heidegger. Heidegger follows Husserl in the search for essences, if in nothing else. Heidegger seeks, for example, the essences of Dasein, truth, art, technology, science, and nihilism. These are all phenomenal essences, not Ideas that transcend the phenomena. *Being and Time* is about Dasein in the same sense in which William Harvey's book is about the heart. At the beginning of *Being and Time* Heidegger distinguishes different meanings of "phenomenon" in a way that corresponds to the distinctions we have been making here. There is first the essentialist form of the distinction between the real and the seeming:

> Thus we must *keep in mind* that the expression "*phenomenon*" signifies *that which shows itself in itself*, the manifest. Accordingly the *phainomena* or "phenomena" are the totality of what lies in the light of day or can be brought to the light—what the Greeks sometimes identified simply with *ta onta* (entities). Now an entity can show itself from itself in many ways, depending in each case on the kind of access we have to it. Indeed it is even possible for an entity to show itself as something which in itself it is not. When it shows itself in this way, it "looks like something or other." This kind of showing-itself is what we call "*seeming*" [*Scheinen*].⁶⁰

The phenomena by which substrative or noumenal realities would show themselves are, in Heidegger's terms, not "seemings" but "appearances" (*Erscheinungen*).

Alfred North Whitehead's "eternal objects" represent another variation of essentialism. The eternal objects lack the reality of Platonic Ideas for they are deficient in actuality, like the logical forms of Hegel before the creation of the world. Eternal objects are pure potentials for the specific determination of fact, or forms of definiteness. They can be described only in terms of their potentiality for ingression into the becoming of actual entities, and their analysis only discloses other eternal objects. If one denies reality to the eternal objects, Whitehead's philosophy becomes an existentialism. The essentialist character of his philosophical project, however, is evident even in the opening sentences of *Process and Reality*:

> Speculative Philosophy is the endeavour to frame a coherent, logical, necessary system of general ideas in terms of which every element of our experience can be interpreted. By this notion of "interpretation" I mean that everything of which we are conscious, as enjoyed, perceived, willed, or thought, shall have the character of a particular instance of the general scheme.[61]

Everything of which we are conscious is not left in its existential uniqueness, nor treated as an appearance of something else, but is treated as an instance of the general scheme, like the individual heart in Harvey, or like historical events in Hegel.

Let us conclude with one or two examples from the arts. The heroic figures of Michelangelo are splendid presentations of essences. Psychic essences are presented through the bodies of which they are the actualization: we see the soul through the body. The perfection and almost superhuman qualities of these figures have led some to assert that they represent a Platonic or noumenal reality. But these essences are real in individuals, not apart from them, and remain inseparable from their physical embodiment. The perspective indeed is revelatory, showing us a perfection that is not found in experience. But it is the perfection of psychic states that we do experience, the full realization of an essential possibility. Because the essence is fully realized, the work seems to *be* the subject it represents, and there seems to be no need for other representations.

Landscape painting, to take another kind of example, exhibits the reality of the landscape. But this reality may be an existential reality, as it was for the Impressionists, or a substantive or noumenal reality that shows itself through the landscape (think of El Greco's view of Toledo), or, finally, the painting may present the essential reality of the landscape. Constable's paintings do this: they exhibit nature as man's home. This essence is in the landscape itself, not brought to it by the painter, and the multiple versions of the same scene are attempts to find the point of view from which the essence can best be seen, comparable in Harvey to the conditions under which the motion of the heart can best be seen. A mill, or locks on a river, or men working in and with nature, or a boy drinking from a stream, or a great estate, or even the Salisbury cathedral all exhibit the essential unity of man and nature. The great spire of Salisbury cathedral becomes the side of a triangle whose base is the earth and whose hypotenuse is formed by the pointing arm of the Sunday stroller in the foreground. The cathedral thus does not point beyond nature, as it would in a noumenal landscape, but is grounded in nature and celebrates the noumenal as one phase of man's life in nature.

James Joyce provides a remarkable example of essential signification in literature. The meanings in his works depend on essential similarities cutting across wide differences in existential context. A day in Dublin re-enacts the events of the *Odyssey*, and the night of *Finnegans Wake* evokes resonating similarities that run through the whole of human history. The neologisms function to relate poetically the multiple recurrences of these essential similarities: the same roturns. In fact, Joyce's essentialism is the literary counterpart of the philosophical doctrine being presented here: both seek recurrent essences in the history of human thought and use Hellenic texts as paradigmatic.

The essential possibility of essentialism can be seen, then, in Confucius, Socrates, Aristotle, William Harvey, Descartes, Hegel, Husserl, Heidegger, Whitehead, Michelangelo, Constable, and James Joyce.

This completes the identification of four essential possibilities as to what is real. Grouping them in pairs, we find that (1) both existential and substrative realities are individual, the infinite individuals in the one case and the infinite individuations of a common substratum in the other. Both noumenal and essential realities, on the other hand, are general, but the generality lies in the one case in the one ideal individual apart from the many, and in the other in the many individuals themselves. (2) Both existential and noumenal realities separate the changing from the unchanging, but the one finds the real in the changing, the other in the unchanging. Both substrative and essential realities, on the other hand, can persist through change, but as substratum in the one case and as essence in the other. (3) Finally, for both existential and essential realities, reality is found in the appearances, but as the appearances themselves in the one case and as that which appears in the other. For both substrative and noumenal realities, on the other hand, reality lies behind the appearances, underlying them in the one case and transcending them in the other.

It remains to consider whether the different realities are reciprocally prior to one another in the sense that the reality of each includes the reality of all.

Existential reality includes all reality in its existential occurrence. We have already noted that although Berkeley denies the reality of matter, whatever perceptible effects matter may be supposed to produce fall within Berkeley's reality. Noumenal reality, if it has any reality at all, is similarly real in its existential manifestation. William James' *Varieties of Religious Experience* treats noumena in their existential occurrence. And whatever essential similarities there may be can be treated as similarities in existence; Hume's theory of causation, for example, refers to all the objects similar to a given object, and Russell treats numbers as classes of classes similar to a given class.

Material reality includes all reality as derivative from itself. It does not deny that appearances are what they are, but explains them by the material realities that produce them. Similarly, noumenal realities may be unreal as such, but real reasons can be given for their being taken as real, and thoughts have at least the reality of physiological processes in the brain. Marx, Nietzsche, and Freud all deny reality to noumena, but are at pains to account for the belief that they are real. And essential similarities, to the extent that they do exist, are the consequence of the material of which things are composed. Newton writes, for example, "There is a power of gravity pertaining to all bodies, proportional to the several quantities of matter which they contain."[62]

Noumenal reality in its nature includes the reality of all that is less perfect. Appearances, material things, and essences are all real in their derivation from noumenal realities.

Essential realities, finally, include all realities as what they are. Appearances are real as appearances, matter is real as matter, and noumena are real as noumena, although this last need not imply an existence outside the mind. Hegel, for example, can treat the inverted world as an essential form of consciousness.

Since each kind of reality thus includes the others, the decision among them is not determinable empirically, and, while they are mutually incompatible in any one use, they are not incompatible in the sense that only one is true or right.

IV. Method

Every text is not only a perspective on a reality, but says something about the reality from this perspective. What it says about the reality will have some kind of order or structure or form or connectedness or argument or method. The need to distinguish different ways of ordering the real appeared already in the contrast between the dialectical ordering of essences in Hegel and their ordering in independent sciences in Aristotle. As before, our concern is not with an order of the real external to the text, but with the order of the real as presented in the text. The way in which the text orders the real can be called its *method*, from the Greek *methodos*, derived from *meta*, following, plus *hodos*, way, a following-way, pursuit.

Method is the most manifest of the archic variables. Differences of method are easy to see. One has only to think, for example, of the differences between the mathematical method of Spinoza or Bertrand Russell, the aphoristic method of Heraclitus or Nietzsche, and the dialectical method of Plato or Hegel. And method has been the subject of much explicit investigation, as in Descartes' *Discourse on Method* or Peirce's *Search for a Method*.

This awareness of method has been accompanied by an awareness of the plurality of methods. Often a single author or text will use many methods. Consider for example the plethora of methods in Kant's *Critique of Pure Reason*. There is a transcendental logic, which includes an analytic and a dialectic. The analytic includes among other things a discovery and a deduction. The dialectic includes paralogisms and antinomies. The transcendental doctrine of method includes a discipline and a canon, not to mention an architectonic and a history. What then is the method of the *Critique*? Is it analytical or dialectical, a method of discovery or a method of proof, a discipline or a canon? Evidently it is all of these. We saw earlier that each archic perspective could be a perspective on perspectives, and each reality a reality of realities. In the case of method, this possibility of reciprocal priority lies on the surface, and the discovery of pluralism has proceded furthest with respect to methods. Methods order parts in a whole, and thus can order the different methods as parts in a whole that includes them all. Method in the archic sense is not so much a single method as an architectonic method governing the whole range of methods and their relation to each other: it is a method of methods.

It will be well to repeat in this context the point noted earlier, that philosophies do not differ from each other because each has a part of the whole, but because they have different ways of appropriating the whole. It might be urged that the distinctions I am making fail to distinguish philosophies from one another because every philosopher uses, or might use, all the different kinds of perspective, reality, method, etc. But that every philosopher uses, or might use, all the different kinds of perspective, reality, method, etc., is precisely what I am asserting. Philosophies differ not in the presence or absence of certain elements, but in their relative priority in the whole that includes them all.

Method is the third of our archic variables, and the problem of its relation to the preceding ones becomes more complex. On the one hand, method must be formally independent of perspective and signification in the sense that each kind of method can be combined with any perspective and any signification, but, on the other hand, since the variables are organically related to each other, what a method is in any particular case will depend on the perspective and signification. The relation of the method to the author will depend on the perspective. A personal perspective discloses a personal order, an objective perspective an objective order, a diaphanic perspective a transcendent order, and a disciplinary perspective a discipli-nary order. Again, a method orders something, but what it orders will depend on the signification. An existential signification makes possible an order of existences, a substrative signification an order of the substratum, a noumenal signification an order of noumena, and an essential significa-tion an order of essences.

When the first two variables are combined, they yield a more determi-nate specification of what the method must do. A personal perspective and an existential signification, for example, as in Protagoras or Sartre, will require a method for ordering individually perceived existences. An objective perspective and a substrative signification, as in Democritus or Freud, will require a method for ordering objectively the material substratum. A diaphanic perspective and a noumenal signification, as in Plato or Leibniz, will require a method of revealing the noumenal order. A disciplinary perspective and an essential signification, as in Aristotle or Husserl, will require a method for ordering essences within a discipline. And similarly for the other possible combinations.

1. Agonistic Methods

The method that is nearest and most evident to us is our own method, whatever method we use. And we use whatever method works for us. Such a method is in competition with the methods of others and with other methods that we might use. The method that is architectonic here is one of struggle or strife or conflict or contention or contest or competition or debate. The validity of a method is tested by its success in winning against the competition.

It is not only ourselves who may be engaged in struggles—gods and animals and plants and inanimate things may all be engaged in their own struggles, and the whole universe may be a gigantic agon. These struggles affect us so far as they relate to our own struggles. The view that our life is a struggle is familiar in many forms—looking out for Number One, the survival of the fittest, it's dog eat dog, it's a jungle out there, etc.

This first kind of method can be named for the fact that validity is a matter of success, and called pragmatic or realistic or operational or rhetorical. Or it can be named for the fact that it involves a contest between antagonists, and this way of naming it is more suitable for our purposes because it indicates how this method orders the real. It can then be called paradoxical or antilogistic or eristic or agonistic. Of these the most general term is *agonistic*, from the Greek *agon*. An *agon* was initially a gathering, but since the Greeks, a highly agonistic people, gathered for the purpose of contests, the *agon* came to mean the contest itself. It was first applied to athletic contests, such as the Olympic or Pythian games, and was extended to musical and dramatic competitions. Protagoras appears to have used the phrase "*agōnes logōn*," contests of words, debates, for the activity that he practised and taught, and the phrase is found in Gorgias.[1] Agon in its widest sense refers to all forms of struggle or endeavor; Antiphon even refers to marriage as an agon, and an agon in which one is unlikely to succeed.[2] Gorgias also uses the word "agonism": "Our agonism requires two-fold virtue: boldness to confront the danger, and wisdom to know the blow."[3] Agony, finally, derives its name from an internal agon.

The first of the long list of firsts with which Diogenes Laertius credits Protagoras is that he was the first to say that there are two arguments on every subject, opposed to one another, and that he used them in questioning, being the first to do so.[4] The implication is that if there is only a single argument on a given subject, the possibilities of reason have not been fully realized, and the argument is so far imperfect. Diogenes also says that Protagoras was the first to institute contests of words (*agōnes logōn*) and to supply the disputants with sophisms.[5] He wrote down opposing arguments in the two books of his *Antilogies*.[6] The work is lost, but we have an example of the form in the *Dissoi Logoi*, or Double Arguments, of a later date, and also in the tetralogies of Antiphon, which present arguments on both sides of imaginary trials.[7] This method of opposing arguments to one another was also the method of scepticism in Sextus Empiricus. "Scepticism," he says, "is the power of setting in opposition things perceived (phenomena) and things thought (noumena) in any way whatever, from which we attain, through equipollence in the oppositions of facts and arguments, first, suspension of judgment (epochē), and then imperturbability (ataraxia)."[8] His ten tropes of scepticism are ten general ways of opposing phenomena to phenomena, or noumena to noumena, or phenomena to noumena.

The agonistic method, as we have said, is not limited to verbal oppositions, however, and before Protagoras it appears as a struggle in things themselves. Heraclitus, for example, in attacking Homer, Hesiod, Pythagoras, Xenophanes, his fellow citizens of Ephesus, and almost everyone else, is practising an agonistic method founded in the nature of things. Things exist only so far as they embody a tension of opposites: "Things taken together are whole and not whole, something which is being brought together and brought apart, which is in tune and out of tune; out of all things there comes a unity, and out of a unity all things."[9] (The unity that holds together the opposites without reconciling them is not a consequence of the method, but of our fourth archic variable which we will treat under the head of principle.) It is through war that things become what they are: "War is the father of all and king of all, and some he shows as gods, others as men; some he makes slaves, others free."[10] "Heraclitus rebukes the author of the line, 'Would that strife might be destroyed from among gods and men': for there would be no musical scale unless high and low existed, nor living creatures without female and male, which are opposites."[11] Goods exist not in the cessation of strife, but only through strife: "Disease makes health pleasant and good, hunger satiety, weariness rest."[12]

Again, in Empedocles' cosmic cycle there is a never-ending agon or contest between love and strife, the one uniting, the other separating, the four elements.

Agonistic methods have been applied to all domains, and even to love itself. Ovid in his *Art of Love* equips men with weapons in Books I and II, and then women in Book III:

> I have just armed the Greeks against the Amazons; now, Penthesilea, it remains for me to arm thee against the Greeks, thee and thy valiant troop. Fight with equal resources and let the victory go to the side

favored by beloved Dione and the boy who flies over the whole world. It was not right to expose you, all defenseless as you were, to the attacks of a well-armed foe. Victory, my men, at such a price as that would be a disgrace.[13]

Finally, in *Love's Cure*, he arms both men and women against love itself. A similar antilogistic method is used by Andreas Capellanus in *The Art of Courtly Love*, for he provides model dialogues between men and women differentiated according to their social rank, and then in Book III, on the Rejection of Love, he, like Ovid, provides arguments against love: "Read this little book, then, not as one seeking to take up the life of a lover, but that, invigorated by the theory and trained to excite the minds of women to love, you may, by refraining from so doing, win an eternal recompense and thereby deserve a greater reward from God."[14]

Galileo and Milton in the 17th century use agonistic methods not to produce a suspension of judgment, but to reach the truth. In both the *Dialogue on the Two Great Systems of the World* and the *Discourses and Demonstrations concerning Two New Sciences*, Galileo presents his arguments in the form of a dialogue between opposed views, and the reader is left in no doubt as to which side gets the better of the argument. The same sort of method is followed by Einstein. Since there is no inductive method for arriving at the fundamental concepts of physics, but they are rather free inventions of the mind, no theory formulates the nature of reality, but there are rather alternative theories which compete with one another, and are judged according to two sorts of criteria, ability to order our sense perceptions, and internal simplicity. Thus the whole history of science becomes an agon in which different theories successively hold the field, and then are replaced by better ones. Einstein sees the central agon of his own time, after his overthrow of the Newtonian foundations, as one between field theory on the one hand and quantum mechanics on the other.

Milton is the grand example of a Christian agonist. His *Areopagitica* gives an agonistic defense of the agonistic method. The true wayfaring, or warfaring, Christian must know vice as Andreas Capellanus' lover must know love, not so that he may practice it but so that he may be fully exposed to its temptations and yet resist it:

As therefore the state of man now is; what wisdome can there be to choose, what continence to forbeare without the knowledge of evill? He that can apprehend and consider vice with all her baits and seeming pleasures, and yet abstain, and yet distinguish, and yet prefer that

which is truly better, he is the true warfaring Christian. I cannot praise
a fugitive and cloister'd vertue, unexercis'd & unbreath'd, that never
sallies out and sees her adversary, but slinks out of the race, where that
immortall garland is to be run for, not without dust and heat. Assuredly
we bring not innocence into the world, we bring impurity much rather:
that which purifies us is triall, and triall is by what is contrary.[15]

Various agonisms appear in Milton's poetry. "L'Allegro" and "Il Penseroso"
constitute a lyric antilogy. *Paradise Lost* presents a noumenal Adversary
whose efforts bring man into the cosmic agon. The role of Satan in *Paradise
Lost*, as compared to his absence in Genesis, is a mark of the shift to an
agonistic method. And Milton appropriately entitles his tragedy *Samson
Agonistes*, Samson the Agonist.

The application of the agonistic method to politics has led to the theory
of preserving liberty through the opposition of conflicting parties. Machiavelli,
like Heraclitus, criticizes those who oppose strife, and finds the origin of
Roman liberty in the opposition of nobles and people:

I maintain that those who blame the quarrels of the Senate and the
people of Rome condemn that which was the very origin of liberty, and
that they were probably more impressed by the cries and noise which
these disturbances occasioned in the public places, than by the good
effect which they produced; and that they do not consider that in every
republic there are two parties, that of the nobles and that of the people;
and all the laws that are favorable to liberty result from the opposition
of these parties to each other, as may easily be seen from the events
that occurred in Rome.[16]

Similarly, the Constitution of the United States seeks to secure liberty
and the common good through competing interests. Montesquieu had argued
that liberty depends on separating legislative, executive, and judicial powers:

When the legislative and executive powers are united in the same
person, or in the same body of magistrates, there can be no liberty;
because apprehensions may arise, lest the same monarch or senate should
enact tyrannical laws, to execute them in a tyrannical manner.

Again, there is no liberty, if the judiciary power be not separated
from the legislative and executive. Were it joined with the legislative,
the life and liberty of the subject would be exposed to arbitrary control;
for the judge would be then the legislator. Were it joined to the executive power, the judge might behave with violence and oppression.[17]

Madison argues that this separation of powers can be maintained by so contriving the interior structure of government that the powers act as checks and balances on one another:

> To what expedient then shall we finally resort for maintaining in practice the necessary partition of power among the several departments, as laid down in the constitution? The only answer that can be given is, that as all these exterior provisions are found to be inadequate, the defect must be supplied, by so contriving the interior structure of the government, as that its several constituent parts may, by their mutual relations, be the means of keeping each other in their proper places.[18]

In the 20th century, Freud has given us an agonistic psychology. Neuroses, dreams, errors, jokes, taboos, religion, civilization—all are understood as the outcome of conflicting forces. Civilization, for example, is the struggle between Eros and Death as it works itself out in the human species:

> And now, I think, the meaning of the evolution of civilization is no longer obscure to us. It must present the struggle between Eros and Death, between the instinct of life and the instinct of destruction, as it works itself out in the human species. This struggle is what all life essentially consists of, and the evolution of civilization may therefore be simply described as the struggle for life of the human species. And it is this battle of the giants that our nurse-maids try to appease with their lullaby about Heaven.[19]

Our list of agonistic authors is already rather long: Protagoras, Antiphon, Sextus Empiricus, Heraclitus, Empedocles, Ovid, Andreas Capellanus, Galileo, Einstein, Milton, Machiavelli, Madison, and Freud. There are also many examples of agonistic works in the arts. I have mentioned Milton, but others who use an agon to order their works include Homer, Euripides, Aristophanes, Shakespeare, Dostoyevsky, Beethoven, and Verdi. Each of Shakespeare's plays is an agon, ending in death if it is a tragedy and in marriage if it is a comedy. These outcomes correspond to the victory of Thanatos or Eros in Empedocles or Freud, but these are not Shakespeare's agonists. There are existential agonists in Shakespeare, substrative agonists in Freud, noumenal agonists in Milton, and essential agonists in Madison.

Agonistic methods have enjoyed great success in all that concerns man. Man has his origin in an evolutionary agon, his psyche is the battleground of conflicting forces, he orders his economic and political relations agonistically, his sports become contests, and the greatest artists exhibit man engaged in agons which he either wins or loses. If man destroys himself, it will be because he has lost the struggle against his own agonistic nature.

Agonistic methods pervade the mass media in America. A television program, for example, involves multiple agons. There is first the competition of the sponsor with his rivals for the sale of their respective products. In order to succeed in this agon the sponsor seeks a TV show that will attract viewers, and so there is a competition of TV shows for viewers and ratings. And in order to attract viewers TV shows are themselves ordered by agons: there is a sports agon, or a dramatic agon, or an audience participation agon for prizes, or an agon between experts on topics of current interest, or news of agons such as presidential races or international conflicts. The agonistic method is here indeed the method nearest and most evident to us.

2. Logistic Methods

The validity of an argument or method need not be determined by its success. Invalid arguments may be persuasive, or valid arguments unpersuasive. The problem of validity, it may be held, is whether a conclusion realy does follow from the premises, not whether someone thinks it does. Method here is fundamentally concerned with an antecedent determining something else as its consequent, with premises determining a conclusion, for example. If rules or canons of validity can be formulated, then validity can be determined by conformity to these rules or canons. It is especially in mathematics and mathematical logic that such a method is familiar. Since the premises are a part of the whole science, and since they determine the theorems that follow from them, the parts are here determining the whole.

This method has a number of related features from which it can be named. Insofar as it proceeds from elements to a whole constructed out of them it is compositive or constructive or combinatorial. Or it may have two moments, analysis to discover the elements and synthesis to combine them. Insofar as everything is done in accordance with a rule or canon, it is a formal or canonic method. The Greek word *kanon* means a straight rod, rule, or standard, and both Democritus and Epicurus called their logical works a canon. Insofar as the method is calculative or computational, it can be called logistic, if we are willing to ignore the interference from the military meaning of this word.

We lack the three books of Democritus' *On Reasonings, or the Canon*, but their counterpart in the fundamental ordering of the atomistic *kosmoi* or universes is clear enough from the fragments and testimonia that do survive. There is first of all the great fragment of Leucippus: "Nothing comes to be at random, but all things according to reason and by necessity."[20] The combination of "out of reason" (*ek logou*) and "by necessity" (*hup'anagkēs*) does not mean that the necessity is for a rational end, but only that it can be formulated and known. Democritus specified what this necessity is: "Necessity for Democritus is the resistance, motion, and impact of matter."[21] "Resistance" (*antitupia*) corresponds to the fact that the atoms are full or hard and exclude one another, motion (*phora*) to the fact that they are in motion, and impact (*plēgē*) to the fact that they bump into one another. If the laws of impact are such that the conditions before impact determine the result of the impact, then all things happen by necessity, for all things are in reality atoms and the void. If the laws of impact are invariant under time reversal, or are such that the antecedents can also be inferred from the consequents, then all events throughout infinite space and through infinite time are necessarily determined by the conditions at any one time. This is a logistic order of being, as distinguished from an order of thought or expression, understood from an objectivist perspective, as it is in itself, and characterizing the material substratum. Just as the Protagorean antilogies between existential agonists can serve as an archetypal example of the agonistic method, so the wholly determined objective material universe of Democritus can serve as an archetypal example of the logistic method.

The other side of the logistic method, the necessary relations of ideas or propositions that correspond to the necessary relations of things, can be seen in the great galaxy of 17th century logicists: Descartes, Hobbes, Spinoza, Leibniz, Newton, and Locke. The nature of the method emerges clearly in Descartes' *Discourse on Method* and *Rules for the Direction of the Understanding*. In Rule IV Descartes explains what he means by method: "By method, then, I understand certain and simple rules, such that if a man follows them exactly, he will never suppose anything false to be true, and, spending no useless mental effort, but gradually and steadily increasing his knowledge, will arrive at the true knowledge of all those things to which his powers are adequate."[22] What the method consists in is stated in rule V: "All method consists in the order and disposition of those things toward which our mental vision must be directed if we are to discover any truth. And we follow this method exactly if we reduce involved and obscure propositions step by step to simpler ones, and then attempt to ascend by the same steps from the intuition of all those that are entirely simple to the cognition of all the others."[23]

Hobbes conceives reasoning to be an addition or subtraction: "When a man *Reasoneth*, hee does nothing else but conceive a summe totall, from *Addition* of parcels; or conceive a Remainder, from *Substraction* of one summe from another: which (if it be done by Words,) is conceiving of the consequence of the names of all the parts, to the name of the whole; or from the names of the whole and one part, to the name of the other part."[24]

The logistic form of Spinoza's *Ethics* is apparent, for it is written *in more geometrico*, beginning from definitions, axioms, and postulates, and proving propositions from them step by step. The same necessity is found in things, for in nature there is nothing contingent, but all things are determined from the necessity of the divine nature to exist and act in a certain manner.[25]

Leibniz's idea of a combinatorial art or universal characteristic, although never carried out, furnishes another example of a logistic method. All truths of reason are connected by means of identities that can be stated in definitions, and a suitable way of presenting all concepts symbolically in terms of their composition from elementary concepts would facilitate reasoning in the same way that mathematical notation facilitates calculation. In cases of disagreement, one could simply say, "Sir, let us calculate."[26] This art would apply directly only to necessary truths, since contingent truths, although also identities, require an infinite number of steps to reduce them to identities.

> Every truth is either original or derivative. Original truths are those for which no reason can be given; such are identities or immediate truths, which affirm the same thing of itself or deny its contrary of its contrary. There are in turn two genera of derivative truths, for some can be reduced to primary truths; the others can be reduced in an infinite progression. The former are necessary; the latter, contingent. A necessary proposition is one whose contrary implies a contradiction; such are all identities and all derivative truths reducible to identities. To this genus belong the truths said to be of metaphysical or geometrical necessity.[27]

Newton's *Principia* is another evident example of the logistic method, and one which had a decisive influence on the development of science for two hundred years. The approach resembles that of Democritus, except that the phenomena are explained by forces of attraction and repulsion between the particles of bodies rather than by the laws of their impact. The necesssities in nature correspond to necessities in the propositional proofs. The propositions of Books I and II are proved from the axioms or laws of motion, and even the great induction of the law of gravitation at the beginning of Book III is safeguarded as a canonic procedure by the Rules of Reasoning in Philosophy which precede it. In the famous words of Newton's Preface,

> I offer this work as the mathematical principles of philosophy, for the whole burden of philosophy seems to consist in this—from the phenomena of motions to investigate the forces of nature, and then from these forces to demonstrate the other phenomena; and to this end the general propositions in the first and second Books are directed. In the third Book I give an example of this in the explication of the System of the World; for by the propositions mathematically demonstrated in the former Books, in the third I derive from the celestial phenomena the forces of gravity with which bodies tend to the sun and the several planets. Then from these forces, by other propositions which are also mathematical, I deduce the motions of the planets, the comets, the moon, and the sea. I wish we could derive the rest of the phenomena of Nature by the same kind of reasoning from mechanical principles, for I am induced by many reasons to suspect that they may all depend upon certain forces by which the particles of bodies, by some causes hitherto unknown, are either mutually impelled towards one another, and cohere in regular figures, or are repelled and recede from one another. These forces being unknown, philosophers have hitherto attempted the search of Nature in vain; but I hope the principles here laid down will afford some light either to this or some truer method of philosophy.[28]

Hume followed Newton's method in seeking the principles determining the necessary connection of phenomena, but, as we have seen, his reality is existential rather than substrative, so his laws of necessary connection are laws connecting impressions themselves. His world is a Democritean world in which atoms in the void have been replaced by perceptions in our minds. (The mind apart from perceptions has a reality comparable to that of the void.) There is no intrinsic reason why impressions should follow a necessary sequence of antecedent and consequent, but Hume shows that we expect them to do so as a result of past conjunctions of similar impressions, and that they conform to our expectation. Even the voluntary actions of men, and the reports of miracles, present no exceptions to the universal reign of the necessary connection of antecedent and consequent.

There is indeed in Hume a sceptical agon between the natural tendency to believe in the causal connectedness of the world and our inability to find any justification for this belief, but this agon and its outcome are also determined by causal necessity. Here we see one way in which the logistic method can swallow up agonistic:

> Nature is always too strong for principle. And though a Pyrrhonian may throw himself or others into a momentary amazement and confusion by his profound reasonings; the first and most trivial event in life will put to flight all his doubts and scruples, and leave him the same, in every point of action and speculation, with the philosophers of every other sect, or with those who never concerned themselves in any philosophical researches. When he awakes from his dream, he will be the first to join in the laugh against himself, and to confess, that all his objections are mere amusement, and can have no other tendency than to show the whimsical condition of mankind, who must act and reason and believe; though they are not able, by their most diligent enquiry, to satisfy themselves concerning the foundation of these operations, or to remove the objections, which may be raised against them.[29]

A similar incorporation of agonistic within logistic is found in Adam Smith, Malthus, and Darwin. Adam Smith's system of natural liberty leaves every man perfectly free to pursue his own interest in his own way, as long as he does not violate the laws of justice, and to bring both his industry and capital into competition with those of other men. The outcome of this competition, however, is a logistic consequence of the factors entering into it, as can be illustrated by the calculation, with which the *Wealth of Nations* begins, of the advantages of the division of labor in the manufacture of pins.

For Malthus, the tendency of population to increase geometrically while the means of subsistence can at best increase arithmetically leads to an opposition between the tendency of population to increase and the checks of moral restraint, vice, and misery. But the outcome of this opposition is again a determinate consequence of the factors involved.

Darwin viewed his account of the struggle for existence as the application of the doctrine of Malthus to the whole animal and vegetable kingdoms. We do not know, says Darwin, all the checks to population and how they operate, but the result is a necessary consequence of the antecedents. This is clear in the following example, in which the struggle for existence results in the re-establishment of the initial proportions of certain trees:

> When we look at the plants and bushes clothing an entangled bank, we are tempted to attribute their proportional numbers and kinds to what we call chance. But how false a view is this! Every one has heard that when an American forest is cut down, a very different vegetation springs

up; but it has been observed that the trees now growing on the ancient Indian mounds, in the Southern United States, display the same beautiful diversity and proportion of kinds as in the surrounding virgin forests. What a struggle between the several kinds of trees must have here gone on during long centuries, each annually scattering its seed by the thousand; what war between insect and insect—between insects, snails, and other animals with birds and beasts of prey—all striving to increase, and all feeding on each other or on the trees or their seeds and seedlings, or on the other plants which first clothed the ground and thus checked the growth of the trees! Throw up a handful of feathers, and all must fall to the ground according to definite laws; but how simple is this problem compared to the action and reaction of the innumerable plants and animals which have determined, in the course of centuries, the proportional numbers and kinds of trees now growing on the old Indian ruins![30]

The second *Principia Mathematica*, that of Whitehead and Russell, follows the same kind of method as its namesake, although its content is limited to logic and mathematics. All of its propositions except the primitive propositions are proved from and by means of the primitive propositions.

The great contemporary triumph of the logistic method is the computer. Corresponding to the full and the empty of Democritus we have the 1 and 0 of the binary system. Even that great early success of the logistic method, the reduction of speech to a sum of letters or *stoicheia*, has been carried further by the imperatives of the method, and in the dot-matrix printer each letter becomes a sum of dots and blanks. Both the combinatorial and rule-governed characteristics of the logistic method are evident in the computer. Apart from malfunctions, the computer simply does what it is programmed to do. It follows the rules, and if it does not do what we want it to do, it is because we have not given it the right instructions. The programming of computers to do more and more complex tasks is the extension of the logistic method to an ever-increasing domain.

In the social sciences one cannot expect the precision of mathematics, and yet the fundamental structure of the method, the determination of a consequence by an antecedent, can still order a text. Thus in *The Protestant Ethic and the Spirit of Capitalism* Max Weber shows how Protestant ascetism was secularized in modern capitalism:

> One of the fundamental elements of the spirit of modern capitalism, and not only of that but of all modern culture: rational conduct on the basis of the idea of the calling, was born—that is what this discussion has sought to demonstrate—from the spirit of Christian asceticism.

One has only to re-read the passage from Franklin, quoted at the beginning of this essay, in order to see that the essential elements of the attitude which was there called the spirit of capitalism are the same as what we have just shown to be the content of the Puritan worldly asceticism, only without the religious basis, which by Franklin's time had died away.[31]

The lives of individuals in a logistic system may be determined by an inexorable necessity like that of mathematics. In Weber's famous metaphor, the light cloak of care for external goods has become in our time an iron cage:

> The Puritan wanted to work in a calling; we are forced to do so. For when asceticism was carried out of monastic cells into everyday life, and began to dominate worldly morality, it did its part in building the tremendous cosmos of the modern economic order. This order is now bound to the technical and economic conditions of machine production which to-day determine the lives of all individuals who are born into this mechanism, not only those directly concerned with economic acquisition, with irresistible force. Perhaps it will so determine them until the last ton of fossilized coal is burnt. In Baxter's view the care for external goods should only lie on the shoulders of the "saint like a light cloak, which can be thrown aside at any moment." But fate decreed that the cloak should become an iron cage.[32]

Similar iron cages can also be found in fiction. One might think, for example, of Thomas Hardy's *Jude the Obscure*, or *Tess of the d'Urbervilles*. The formal rigor of the canonic method need not be oppressive, however: perhaps one can hear it also in the music of Bach or Mozart.

Let these suffice as examples of the logicists: Democritus, Epicurus, Descartes, Hobbes, Spinoza, Leibniz, Newton, Hume, Adam Smith, Malthus, Darwin, Bertrand Russell, Max Weber, Thomas Hardy, Bach, and Mozart.

3. Dialectical Methods

One can avoid making validity simply a matter of success not only by using what is laid down at the beginning to validate what comes after it, but also by using what comes after it to validate what was laid down at the beginning. Instead of the parts determining the whole, the whole then determines the parts. The beginning is tested by its relation to a larger context. Such self-transcending methods that find the truth in the whole have, since Plato, been called *dialectical*. One of their familiar forms is the view that science progresses through the unification of theories that were initially separate—terrestrial and celestial mechanics, electromagnetism and optics, optics and mechanics, quantum mechanics and field theory, and so on until all knowledge is unified.

Dialectic is opposed to agonistic, for it succeeds not when one maintains his position against the other, but when one loses and transcends his position in interaction with the other. Agonistic works by single negations which set positions in opposition to each other, whereas dialectic works by double negations which negate the otherness of the other and thus unite the opposites. In agonistic, one is only right *against* the other, for otherwise one's position is untested, whereas in dialectic one is only right *with* the other, for otherwise one's position remains inadequate and partial. Dialectic is also opposed to logistic, for logistic begins from what is fixed and definite and pursues the consequences of this, whereas dialectic proceeds in the opposite direction toward that of which the fixed and definite is itself a consequence.

"Dialectic" is Plato's word, coming from "*dialegesthai*," to talk with, and his works take the form of dialogues. They also include the speeches of deliberative rhetoric in the *Phaedrus*, judicial rhetoric in the *Apology*, and epideictic rhetoric in the *Symposium*, as well as the likely story of the *Timaeus*. Although Plato distinguishes dialectic from rhetoric, he also distinguishes dialectical rhetoric from rhetorical rhetoric, and dialectical rhetoric exhibits the same dependence of part on whole that characterizes his dialectic. Thus in the *Phaedrus*, in which dialectic and rhetoric are like the right and left halves of an organism, dialectical rhetoric organizes the disordered commonplaces of rhetorical rhetoric into a likeness of the soul's own ideal.

In dialectic proper, the dialectician asks questions and another answers them. The dialectician must work with whatever answer he gets, and therefore the method of the dialogue depends on both questioner and answerer. Since there are unlimited others, there can be no system of the dialogues. All things may be part of a single system, but it is beyond our knowledge. We each encounter the real in our own way, and these various encounters do not constitute a single method or system. The dialogues are philosophical fragments, each establishing an order in a limited domain. The order of each dialogue is dialectical in endeavoring to preserve and transcend the standpoint of the other.

In the *Theaetetus*, for example, Socrates accepts the Protagorean world of the flux, and he himself therefore becomes a midwife, but in such a world knowledge cannot be found, since, as we learn in the *Sophist*, motion and rest do not communicate.

In the *Gorgias*, Socrates adopts the flamboyant paradoxicality of Gorgias, defending his position against the opposition of all the world, but in so doing he practises an art of justice which punishes rather than entertains its audience.

In the *Protagoras*, the method becomes a Protagorean agon in which both agonists argue both sides of an antilogy on whether virtue can be taught. The agon proceeds through three phases until it reaches the point where it can be decided by an art of measurement. In the first part, in which Socrates asks and Protagoras answers, Protagoras presents an agonistic conception of wisdom as man's weapon in the struggle for existence. In the second part, in which the agonists reverse roles, Socrates adopts the Protagorean conception by attributing the power of Sparta to its wisdom, and showing how this agonistic conception of wisdom is required to interpret a poem by Simonides. In the third and decisive round of this contest for the wisdom championship of the world, the concern is no longer with wisdom as an agonistic weapon, nor with the agon of wise men, but with the wisdom itself which the wise man possesses, and it is found that what goes on in his own mind is also an agon, a contest between competing alternatives, and this he is able to resolve by an art of measurement.

In the *Apology*, Socrates works within the convictions of the Athenians. He argues that his manner of speaking is justified by Athenian custom, that he has spent his life in obedience to what they recognize as the highest religious authority, that in defying the Athenians he is staying where he is placed by his commander and thus exhibiting the courage they admire, that his refusal to bring in his wife and children is in accord with the oaths of the jurors, and so on. But at the same time he presents himself as the unity of what are conventionally considered opposites: wisdom and ignorance, clever speech and plain speech, doubt and belief, teacher and learner, statesman and private person, innovation and tradition, irony and sincerity, arrogance and humility, accusation and defense, winning and losing, and so on. All conventional beliefs depend on such distinctions and thus become, in relation to him, self-contradictory. This is the bite of the gadfly. In the perfect state, the function of the philosopher is to know the principle by which all contradictions are resolved, and apply it to the state. But in the actual state of Athens the function of the philosopher is to move it toward the ideal by stinging it with its own contradictions.

In the *Crito*, Crito, the personal friend of Socrates, conceives his obligations and those of Socrates in personal terms, as obligations to one's friends and one's family and oneself, and these all seem to require that Socrates escape from prison. Socrates accepts the personal orientation of his friend, but by personifying the laws of Athens makes clear that there is another obligation in the situation, and that by following it all the other obligations will be met.

These examples indicate the flexibility of the Platonic dialectic. In one sense, each dialogue has its own method, and there is no common method. But in the sense determined by the archic variables, it is always the same method.

Logistic structures that depend on fixed starting-points can serve as preparation for dialectical arguments that transcend their starting-points. In the *Republic, dianoia*, or thought, at the third level of the divided line serves as a prelude to the hymn of dialectic at the fourth level. Dianoia proceeds from hypotheses to conclusions using visible forms as images, and is exemplified by geometry and the other mathematical arts. Dialectic also proceeds from hypotheses, but in the opposite direction, using them as stepping stones or springboards toward what is not hypothetical. The rulers of the *Republic* are to study mathematics for ten years, from 20 to 30, before going on to practical experience and dialectic. That this mathematical training is not quite the same as it would be in logistic, however, is indicated by the emphasis on the community and relationship of the mathematical disciplines with one another: "The various studies acquired without any particular order by the children in their education must be integrated into an overview (*synopsis*) which reveals the kinship of these studies with one another and with the nature of that which is."[33] The unifying power of dialectic is reflected in this synoptic mathematics, as it was earlier in the *Republic* in the poetic or mythic world unified by the goodness of God.

Similar subordinate functions for logistic within dialectic can be seen in the hierarchy of positive sciences in Auguste Comte which prepare the way for the system of positive polity, and in Whitehead's distinction between Speculation, which, like dialectic, is not confined to any fixed framework, and Scholarship, which works within a fixed frame.

> The note of Hellenism is delight, speculation, discoursive literature: the note of Hellenistic Alexandria is concentration, thoroughness, investigation of the special types of order appertaining to special topics . . . .
> The difference between the two, namely the Hellenic and the Hellenistic types of mentality, may be roughly described as that between speculation and scholarship. For progress, both are necessary. But, in fact, on the stage of history they are apt to appear as antagonists. Speculation, by entertaining alternative theories, is superficially sceptical, disturbing to established modes of prejudice. But it obtains its urge from a deep ultimate faith, that through and through the nature of things is penetrable by reason. Scholarship, by its strict attention to

accepted methodologies, is superficially conservative of belief. But its tone of mind leans toward a fundamental negation. For scholars the reasonable topics in the world are penned in isolated regions, *this* subject-matter or *that* subject-matter. Your thorough-going scholar resents the airy speculation which connects his own patch of knowledge with that of his neighbor. He finds his fundamental concepts interpreted, twisted, modified. He has ceased to be king of his own castle, by reason of speculations of uncomfortable generality, violating the very grammar of his thoughts.[34]

Agonistic has many functions within dialectic. In the *Apology*, for example, as in the sceptical agonistic, it functions to stimulate inquiry. It has an important and characteristic role in the *Phaedo*, where the sharp attacks of Cebes that seem to utterly destroy the argument force it to higher levels at which it is consolidated and confirmed. The difference between agonists and dialecticians offers a continual challenge to both, the agonist seeking either to convert or destroy the dialectician, and the dialectician seeking to sublate the agonist:

> He drew a circle that shut me out—
> Heretic, rebel, a thing to flout.
> But Love and I had the wit to win:
> We drew a circle that took him in![35]

The encounter of Plato and the Sophists is one episode in a continuing agon, or dialogue, between agonistic and dialectic. The Pythagoreans were the great practitioners of dialectic prior to Plato, and they provoked attacks not only from their immediate neighbors at Croton but from Xenophanes, Heraclitus, the Eleatics, and Empedocles. The Manichean view of the antagonism between good and evil is antagonistic to the Augustinian view of evil as a privation of good, but Augustine found his encounter with the Manicheans providential and illustrative of the good order of the world. The tensions and contrasts of Michelangelo are balanced by the harmonies and symmetries of Raphael. Michelangelo's Vatican *Pieta* contrasts the agelessness of the Virgin with the aging and death of her Child; the *David* shows that agonist at the moment of confrontation with his formidable antagonist; and it is no accident that it was a fellow agonist, and one specializing in intra-psychic agony, Freud, who solved the riddle of the *Moses* statue by showing that it represents the victory of law over passion. Raphael, however, gives to Plato and Aristotle complementary upward and downward gestures in the so-called *School of Athens* and unites them under three great arches, and the ordered whole of philosophy itself occupies only one wall of the Stanza della Segnatura, and is complemented on the other three walls by the harmony of noumena and phenomena in poetic inspiration, in civil and ecclesiastical law, and in theology with its heavenly and earthly levels. The agonistic politics of Madison and the United States Constitution have been balanced by the dialectical economics and politics of Marx, an agon and a dialogue that still continue. The agonistic struggle for existence in Darwinian evolution evoked an opposite in the dialectical evolution of Bergson. Lincoln's dialectical conception of a house divided against itself unable to stand was opposed by Douglas' agonistic conception of local sovereignty within the constitutional frame. Freud's agonistic conception of the relation between the instincts of life and of death has been countered by Norman O. Brown's dialectical conception of their relation: "We need," he says, "instead of an instinctual dualism an instinctual dialectic . . . . The difference between a dualism of the instincts and a dialectical unity of the instincts is small and elusive; but slight shades of difference at this fundamental level can have large consequences."[36]

The dialectics of Plato and Augustine are noumenal dialectics; the fundamental order that the dialectic discloses is supersensible and eternal. Hegel's method is also dialectical in the sense that it transcends the given in the direction of a unity of opposites, but it belongs to an epistemic rather than an ontic epoch, so that its fundamental terms are derived from knowing rather than being. It is a dialectic in which subject and object are united in absolute knowledge. Further, it is an essentialist rather than a noumenal interpretation of knowing. The dialectical processes by which the Idea alienates itself in nature and returns to itself in mind are not an image of an unchanging noumenal reality, but are the order of the experienced world itself. The dialectical incorporation of agonistic reaches in Hegel a point at which an agonistic struggle is a phase or moment of all dialectical advance.

This is also true in Marx, who took his dialectical method from Hegel. In fact, in some Marxists the agonistic moment seems almost to have taken over the method altogether, and the ultimate unity of the classless society becomes a future phase unrelated to the present. Marx's dialectic, as contrasted with Hegel's, is a materialist rather than an essentialist dialectic. Its elements are not forms of consciousness, but economic classes whose relations are reflected in our consciousness. "In my view," says Marx, "the ideal is nothing other than the material when it has been transposed and translated inside the human head."[37]

Sartre's dialectic is an existential dialectic in a period in which Marxism is an existential and totalizing presence. His dialectic must therefore seek

to unite itself with Marxism. What Marxism lacks, and what existentialism can supply, according to Sartre, is the human dimension. This lack of
the human dimension has two aspects corresponding to the two archic
variables in which Marxism differs from existentialism. First, the signification of Marxism is material rather than existential, and Sartre's synthesis
therefore requires that the meaning of objects be the meaning they have
for individuals, and not be reduced to their inert materiality. Speaking of
dialectic, Sartre says,

> It surpasses by conserving, but the terms of the surpassed contradic-
> tion cannot account for either the transcending itself or the subse-
> quent synthesis; on the contrary, it is the synthesis which clarifies
> them and which enables us to understand them. For us the basic con-
> tradiction is only one of the factors which delimit and structure the
> field of possibles; it is the choice which must be interrogated if one
> wants to explain them in their detail, to reveal their singularity (that
> is, the particular aspect in which *in this case* generality is presented),
> and to understand how they have been lived. It is the work or the act
> of the individual which reveals to us the secret of his conditioning.
> Flaubert by his choice of writing discloses to us the meaning of his
> childish fear of death—not the reverse. By misunderstanding these
> principles, contemporary Marxism has prevented itself from understand-
> ing meanings and values. For it is as absurd to reduce the meaning of
> an object to the pure inert materiality of that object itself as to want to
> deduce the law from the fact.[38]

Second, Marxism has an objective rather than a personal perspective,
and Sartre's synthesis therefore requires that the inquirer not be elimi-
nated from his investigation as he is by Marxism:

> It is *inside* the movement of Marxist thought that we discover a flaw
> of such a sort that despite itself Marxism tends to eliminate the questioner
> from his investigation and to make of the questioned the object of an
> absolute Knowledge.[39]

Once this double lack in Marxism has been remedied, that is, once Marxism has acquired the archic profile of Sartre, the dialectical and existential
unity of the two will become the foundation for all inquiry:

> From the day that Marxist thought will have taken on the human
> dimension (that is, the existential project) as the foundation of anthro-

pological Knowledge, existentialism will no longer have any reason for being. Absorbed, surpassed and conserved by the totalizing movement of philosophy, it will cease to be a particular inquiry and will become the foundation of all inquiry.[40]

Dialecticians in uniting themselves with others by transcending their own standpoint can negate everything but their own archic elements, for these ground the process and validity of the unification itself.

We have, then, a noumenal dialectic in Plato, an essentialist dialectic in Hegel, a materialist dialectic in Marx, and an existential dialectic in Sartre. Other dialecticians whom we have mentioned include Pythagoras, Augustine, Raphael, Comte, Lincoln, Bergson, Whitehead, and Norman O. Brown.

4. Problematic Methods

If we reject the view that any method is valid if it works, and also the views that validity resides in a determination of the whole by the parts, as in logistic, or in a determination of the parts by the whole, as in dialectic, one possibility remains, that validity resides in the reciprocal determination of parts by the whole and of the whole by its parts, or of matter by form and form by matter. What is laid down at the beginning determines the validity of what follows from it, and at the same time what follows from it determines the validity of the beginning. Such a method will unite forms or conceptions on the one hand with materials or data on the other. What is initially indeterminate becomes, through the method, an organized whole. This method is familiar as the view that the true theory is the one that accounts for all the facts.

This fourth possible method is distinguished from agonistic because success is consequent on the right kind of order rather than the right kind of order being consequent on success. It is distinguished from logistic because the elements of the whole are indeterminate until they are organized in the method, rather than being initially determinate so that the method can pursue their consequences. Its wholes are organic rather than mechanical. This method is distinguished from dialectic because the whole is what it is as the unity of its parts, as a unity of form and matter, rather than being what it is as a part of some larger whole. Its wholes are complete rather than partial.

An appropriate name for this method is *analytic* from the Greek *analysis*, loosening up, disentangling, or resolution, and this is the name given to it in its first formulation, by Aristotle. This term illustrates the tendency of each method to appropriate the terms of the others, for it has been appropriated by all the methods. The logicists Descartes and Newton, for example, the dialectician Comte, and the agonist Freud all distinguish analysis and synthesis within their methods. There is also a large and influencial group of contemporary philosophers, predominantly logicists but including some agonists, who use the term as a general name for their method and call themselves "analysts" and their philosophy "analytic philosophy." Logistic analysis proceeds from wholes to parts, but analysis in the sense which concerns us here proceeds from problems to solutions, and a problem with respect to the parts may be resolved by the principle of the whole. "Analysis" as a name for an architectonic method originally refers to this second conception, and it is in this sense that I will use it here.

Analysis is inquiry, so this method can also be called the method of *inquiry*. Inquiry resolves problems, and so the method can also be called the *problematic* method, and this term has the advantage of being less ambiguous than the others. It should be noted, to avoid misunderstanding, that the fundamental order of a subject matter, an order that is discovered by inquiry and exhibited or demonstrated in the science of that subject matter, need not coincide with the order of inquiry by which it happened to be discovered. That is, the order of inquiry is one thing, the order discovered by inquiry another, and it is the latter which is fundamental.

The conjugate relation of principles and facts in the analytic method is clearly seen in Aristotle's *Posterior Analytics*. A scientific order proceeds from causes to that of which they are causes, it is an order of the facts, it is discovered by inquiry, and it is validated when apprehended as the order of the whole. The general theory of science in the *Posterior Analytics* is exemplified in every one of Aristotle's sciences, although, since the scientific order is an order of a particular subject matter, the order or method of each science is different from that of every other. The reciprocal relation between the basic definition of a science and the properties that follow from it is made explicit in relation to the problem of defining the soul:

> It seems not only useful for the discovery of the causes of the derived properties of substances to be acquainted with the essential nature of those substances (as in mathematics it is useful for the understanding of the property of the equality of the interior angles of a triangle to two right angles to know the essential nature of the straight and the curved or of the line and the plane) but also conversely, for the knowledge of the essential nature of a substance is largely promoted by an acquaintance with its properties: for, when we are able to give an account conformable to experience of all or most of the properties of a substance,

we shall be in the most favorable position to say something worth saying about the essential nature of that subject; in all demonstration a definition of the essence is required as a starting-point, so that definitions which do not enable us to discover the derived properties, or which fail to facilitate even a conjecture about them, must obviously, one and all, be dialectical and futile.[41]

The sciences characteristically begin from a definition of their subject—the definition of science in the *Posterior Analytics*, of wisdom in the *Metaphysics*, of nature in the *Physics*, of the soul in *On the Soul*, of happiness in the *Ethics*, of tragedy in the *Poetics*, of rhetoric in the *Rhetoric*, and so on. The initial definition delimits the whole, but the whole remains indeterminate insofar as the meanings of the component terms are not explicated. Happiness, for example, is defined as virtuous activity, but if one does not know what virtue is one does not know what the definition means. It is only as the various virtues, moral and intellectual, are defined that the concept of happiness acquires determinate content. The successive definitions are linked syllogistically in a demonstrative sequence, but each step in the development of the sequence organizes additional facts. The whole is thus made determinate as the parts are incorporated in it. The student of ethics or of any other subject is in a position to assess the validity of the principle not at the outset but only when he understands its capacity to order the whole of that subject. Aristotle's account of induction has been criticized as offering no formal procedure for arriving at inductive truths, and logicists such as Newton, Mill, and Carnap have endeavored to supply this lack, but from the standpoint of analysis such a procedure cannot be given because the data from which it would proceed become determinate only as they are incorporated in the whole.

One way in which the analytic method can incorporate the other methods is exemplified by the last four works of Aristotle's *Organon*. The *Prior Analytics* gives a formal theory of the syllogism, and the definition of the syllogism corresponds to what is essential in the logistic method: "Reasoning (*syllogismos*) is a discourse (*logos*) in which, certain things being posited, something other than what is laid down follows by necessity from the being of these things."[42] The *Posterior Analytics* deals with science, or reasoning in which the premises are true and primary. The establishment of the scientific order of a subject matter is not however a process in which the order results necessarily from premises laid down at the outset. It requires, as we have seen, a conjugate determination of syllogistic form and factual content. The *Topics* deals with dialectic in the sense of reasoning from accepted opinions (*ta endoxa*). It resembles Plato's dialectic in beginning from what people think, and in being able to test opinions for their coherence and consistency. True opinions are consistent, but consistent opinions are not necessarily true. Therefore dialectic is for Aristotle ancillary to the establishment of truth. *On Sophistical Refutations*, as its title suggests, is written agonistically, showing how to identify and refute fallacious reasoning.

The scientific treatises of Aristotle exhibit the way in which these different kinds of argument are related in particular sciences. Formal syllogistic structures are established, but, since they must be true of things, they are established by inquiry into their successive connections. The opinions of others are examined dialectically at points where they can contribute to this inquiry, and particularly in relation to the first principles of the sciences. Fallacious arguments advanced by others are refuted as the occasion requires.

When Kant said that Aristotle's logic appeared to be a closed and completed body of doctrine, he was referring to the formal theory of the *Prior Analytics*, and this formal logic has much the same relation to Kant's sciences that it has to Aristotle's. A science, as distinguished from a mere aggregate of knowledge, has the unity of a system, and a system requires an idea determining the end and form of the whole. The multiple methods in each of Kant's critiques are determined by this idea of the whole. It corresponds to the initial definition of the subject genus in Aristotle's sciences. Kant describes it as follows:

> By a system I understand the unity of the manifold modes of knowledge under one idea. This idea is the concept provided by reason—of the form of a whole—in so far as the concept determines *a priori* not only the scope of its manifold content, but also the positions which the parts occupy relatively to one another.[43]

The discovery of the idea of the whole requires familiarity with the parts. The conjugate relation of whole and parts is well presented in the Preface to the *Critique of Practical Reason*:

> When we have to study a particular faculty of the human mind in its sources, its content, and its limits; then from the nature of human knowledge we must begin with its *parts*, with an accurate and complete exposition of them; complete, namely, so far as is possible in the present state of our knowledge of its elements. But there is another thing to be attended to which is of a more philosophical and *architectonic* character, namely, to grasp correctly the *idea of the whole*, and from thence to get a view of all those parts as mutually related by the aid of

pure reason, and by means of their derivation from the concept of the whole. This is only possible through the most intimate acquaintance with the system.[44]

Not only is knowledge organized by ideas to form sciences, but knowledge itself is already a unity of concepts as form with intuitions as matter, and intuitions are a unity of the forms of intuition with the matter of sensation. There is thus a three-layered structure of form and matter: the matter of sensation united by the forms of intuition gives empirical intuitions, intuitions united by the concepts of the understanding give knowledge, and knowledge united by the ideas of reason gives the systematic unity of a science. The reciprocal dependence of form and matter in knowledge, at the middle level, is evident in the much-quoted saying, "Thoughts without content are empty, intuitions without concepts are blind."[45] The *Metaphysical Foundations of Natural Science* gives content to the principles of pure understanding in the *Critique* by applying them to the concept of matter. Similarly, in the practical sphere, *The Metaphysic of Morals* gives content to the empty form of the moral law by applying it to objects of the will. Everywhere the form orders the matter and the matter gives content to the form.

In working out the unities of form and matter there is room for a variety of subordinate methods. The sceptical method is used in the antinomies of pure reason, but it is not used for the purpose of deciding in favor of one side or the other, or for undermining certainty, but to discover the point of misunderstanding. Kant describes the sceptical method as follows:

> This method of watching, or rather provoking, a conflict of assertions, not for the purpose of deciding in favour of one or other side, but of investigating whether the object of controversy is not perhaps a deceptive appearance which each vainly strives to grasp, and in regard to which, even if there were no opposition to be overcome, neither can arrive at any result,—this procedure, I say, may be entitled the *sceptical method*. It is altogether different from *scepticism*—a principle of technical and scientific ignorance, which undermines the foundations of all knowledge, and strives in all possible ways to destroy its reliability and steadfastness. For the sceptical method aims at certainty. It seeks to discover the point of misunderstanding in the case of disputes which are sincerely and competently conducted by both sides.[46]

The conjugate relation of ideas to facts is also apparent in William Whewell's account of the methods of scientific discovery.

It has already been stated that Knowledge requires us to possess both Facts and Ideas;—that every step in our knowledge consists in applying the Ideas and Conceptions furnished by our minds to the Facts which observation and experiment offer to us. When our Conceptions are clear and distinct, when our Facts are certain and sufficiently numerous, and when the Conceptions, being suited to the nature of the Facts, are applied to them so as to produce an exact and universal accordance we attain knowledge of a precise and comprehensive kind, which we may term *Science*.[47]

There is not for Whewell as for Kant a transcendental deduction of the applicability of our concepts to the facts; it requires rather the genius or sagacity of the discoverer to hit upon the conception that will colligate the facts. Whewell's extended debate with John Stuart Mill on induction is, in one of its aspects, a contrast between Mill's canonic conception of induction as a procedure to be carried on in accordance with his canons of experimental inquiry and Whewell's problematic conception of induction that requires the sagacity of the discoverer to find the form that will fit the matter. Whewell founded his own *Philosophy of the Inductive Sciences* upon his *History of the Inductive Sciences*, and was able to renovate Bacon's *New Organon* by extracting from the past progress of science the elements of an effectual and substantial method of scientific discovery: "Bacon could only divine how sciences might be constructed; we can trace, in their history, how their construction has taken place."[48]

Dewey is similarly concerned to inquire into inquiry, but the wholes ordered by his problematic method are neither genera of being, as in Aristotle, nor determined by ideas, as in Kant and Whewell, but rather situations, situations that involve both subject and object. In *Logic: The Theory of Inquiry* Dewey defines inquiry as follows: "Inquiry is the controlled or directed transformation of an indeterminate situation into one that is so determinate in its constituent distinctions and relations as to convert the elements of the original situation into a unified whole."[49] This transformation is effected through the institution of facts and ideas as material and procedural means: "Perceptual and conceptual materials are instituted in functional correlativity with each other, in such a manner that the former locates and describes the problem while the latter represents a possible method of solution."[50]

Agonistic struggles function within Dewey's method much as they did in Kant's; the problem is not to engage in the conflict but to resolve it by ascertaining its cause. Dewey thus takes the conflict between traditional and progressive education as a starting point for *Experience and Education*:

All social movements involve conflicts which are reflected intellectu-ally in controversies. It would not be a sign of health if such an impor-tant social interest as education were not also an arena of struggles, practical and theoretical. But for theory, at least for the theory that forms a philosophy of education, the practical conflicts and the contro-versies that are conducted upon the level of these conflicts, only set a problem. It is the business of an intelligent theory of education to ascertain the causes for the conflicts that exist and then, instead of taking one side or the other, to indicate a plan of operations proceeding from a level deeper and more inclusive than is represented by the prac-tices and ideas of the contending parties.[51]

An example of the analytic method in the sciences is provided by Mendeleev's papers presenting his discovery of the periodic table of the chemical elements. At the outset, there was no known systematic order of the elements, although they were classified according to various principles: metallic or nonmetallic character, relation to hydrogen and oxygen, elec-trochemical order, and valence. Mendeleev rejects these as possible bases for a system of the elements, and finds the beginning of a system only in the natural groups:

> Only in respect to certain *groups of elements* is there no doubt that they form a single whole, that they present a natural series of similar manifestations of matter. These are the groups: the halogens, the alkaline-earth metals, the nitrogen and, in part sulfur group, the congeners of platinum, the congeners of cerium, and a few others.[52]

No one had found a system that accounted for the natural groups, for Lenssen's attempt to do so subordinated the natural groups to the formal principle of triplicity. Mendeleev selects atomic weight as a principle because it is quantitative and therefore leaves little room for arbitrariness and because it remains invariant in the different states and compounds of the elements. Arranging the elements according to this principle, Mendeleev notes a periodic recurrence in their properties and finds he can derive the natural groups from these periodic recurrences: "A comparison of the already known groups of simple bodies with respect to the weight of their atoms leads to the conclusion that the method of arranging the elements accord-ing to their atomic weights does not contradict the natural similarity that exists among the elements, but, on the contrary points directly to it."[53] He then proceeds to develop the system of the elements by which the entire domain is ordered. There was an exception to his periodic law in the relative positions of tellurium and iodine, and he concludes that this is an example of a case in which the atomic weight of an element may be revised if its analogues are known. For this method the parts must conform to the principle of the whole; in this particular case they did not, as it turned out, and it was necessary to base the table on atomic number rather than atomic weight.

Our problem of ordering diverse philosophies may be compared to Mendeleev's problem of ordering the diverse chemical elements. Sufficient data about the elements or about possible philosophies have accumulated so that an ordering becomes possible. There are initially principles that provide partial orderings of the diverse elements or philosophies, but no system of the whole. The disagreements of philosophers are analogous to the different properties of the elements, and they are used, as Kant used the antinomies, not with a view to deciding between them, or in support of scepticism, but to discover the point of misunderstanding. There is no necessary path leading from the particular philosophies or elements to the system; rather, the characteristics or traits that are systematically relevant appear as they are ordered. It is only when the system is seen as a whole that it can be adequately judged. This was in fact a principal motivation for writing this book, since on most occasions when its distinctions are used the whole system cannot be developed and the parts therefore cannot be clearly understood.

Analysis can also be used to order works of fiction. The plots are then plots of discovery, proceeding from an unsettled or indeterminate situation to its resolution through a discovery of how all the elements fit together. The classic example, made classic partly because of its citation by Aristotle, is Sophocles' *Oedipus Rex*. The initial situation is unsettled because of the plague whose cause is unknown, and it is resolved by Oedipus the riddle-solver solving the riddle of himself.

The narrator in Edgar Allan Poe's "The Murders in the Rue Morgue" distinguishes the faculty of analysis or resolution from that of calculation, and subordinates calculation to analysis: "The faculty of re-solution is possibly much invigorated by mathematical study, and especially by that highest branch of it which, unjustly, and merely on account of its retrograde operations, has been called, as if *par excellence*, analysis. Yet to calculate is not in itself to analyze."[54] The narrator illustrates analysis by the process by which a skillful whist player determines the distribution of cards in a particular deal:

> But it is in matters beyond the limits of mere rule that the skill of the analyst is evinced. He makes, in silence, a host of observations and

inferences. So, perhaps, do his companions; and the difference in the extent of the information obtained, lies not so much in the validity of the inference as in the quality of the observation. The necessary knowledge is that of *what* to observe. Our player confines himself not at all; nor, because the game is the object, does he reject deductions from things external to the game. He examines the countenance of his partner, comparing it carefully with that of each of his opponents. He considers the mode of assorting the cards in each hand; often counting trump by trump, and honor by honor, through the glances bestowed by their holders upon each. He notes every variation of face as the play progresses, gathering a fund of thought from the differences in the expression of certainty, of surprise, of triumph, or chagrin. From the manner of gathering up a trick he judges whether the person taking it, can make another in the suit. He recognizes what is played through feint, by the manner with which it is thrown upon the table. A casual or inadvertent word; the accidental dropping or turning of a card, with the accompanying anxiety or carelessness in regard to its concealment; the counting of the tricks, with the order of their arrangement; embarrassment, hesitation, eagerness, or trepidation—all afford, to his apparently intuitive perception, indications of the true state of affairs. The first two or three rounds having been played, he is in full possession of the contents of each hand, and thenceforward puts down his cards with as absolute a precision of purpose as if the rest of the party had turned outward the faces of their own.[55]

This describes the method by which Dupin solves the murders in the Rue Morgue. More generally, however, it is the method of Dupin in the other stories in which he figures (it may be contrasted with the logistic method of Sherlock Holmes), and the method used by Poe to order all his short stories. All the details in the stories are brought together in the unity of the whole, which we often discover only at the end.

The same method is used on a larger scale in the fiction of Henry James. The reality in James is existential, and the misunderstandings and discoveries in his works are the misunderstandings and discoveries of the character of individuals by one another. Cultural differences are important because they provide possibilities for such misunderstandings and discoveries. His fiction is ordered by the progressive discovery of characters by each other and by the reader.

The analytic or problematic method is represented, then, by Aristotle, Kant, Whewell, Dewey, Mendeleev, Sophocles, Poe, and Henry James.

Our four kinds of method can be grouped in pairs as follows: (1) Agonistic and logistic methods are meroscopic in the sense that the parts are primary, producing the whole either by their respective endeavors to determine the whole themselves or by respectively remaining what they are.

Dialectical and analytic methods, on the other hand, are synoptic or holoscopic in the sense that the whole determines the parts either directly or reciprocally. (2) Agonistic and dialectical methods are two-voiced, working with divergent claims to organize the whole, agonistic testing the voices against each other and dialectic uniting them with each other. Logistic and analytic methods, on the other hand, are single-voiced, working toward a determinate whole, but the one begins from what is determinate, the other from what is indeterminate. (3) Agonistic and analytic methods close off intermediate wholes, either because of external forces or because of their own internal unity, whereas logistic and dialectic methods extend toward ultimates, the one toward least parts and the other toward an all-inclusive whole.

The ways in which the different methods are reciprocally prior to one another have been indicated in the preceding inquiry and can be summarized here. We have particularly noted the ways in which agonistic struggles are incorporated in the works of authors who use other methods: the contest between Socrates and Protagoras in Plato, the moment of conflict in Hegel, the class struggle in Marx, sceptical conflicts in Hume, competition in Adam Smith, the struggle for existence in Malthus and Darwin, sceptical antinomies in Kant, and controversies in Dewey. The agonistic method can in turn incorporate all the others by relating them to each other agonistically. Any method that claims to achieve anything enters into the contest of methods. The logistic method explains why the conflicts of agonistic, the unifications of dialectic, and the resolutions of analytic eventuate as they do. It incorporates the other methods by formalizing them. Whatever is valid in any method is susceptible of logistic formulation. Dialectic lives on other methods, swallowing them whole and transcending them. And analytic methods incorporate all the others as making their distinctive contributions to analysis: agonistic helps us to discover points of misunderstanding, logistic provides a formal structure that we use in ordering the data, and dialectic provides a test for the coherence and consistency of our views.

Each kind of method is thus architectonic, ordering all the methods. The differences of method, like the differences of perspective and signification, are differences of priority within a system of reciprocal priorities. The different methods are therefore only procedurally and not substantively incompatible: one can use only one kind of method at a time, but, since each can incorporate the others, it is not the case that there is only one which is true or right or valid.

V. Principle

Every text is not only an argument by an author about a subject matter, it is also for the sake of some end or purpose or function. An end or purpose or function may be external to the text, however, and here as throughout we are working in a semantic context and seeking causes internal to the text. An end or purpose or function is present in the text so far as the text has within it something that causes it to function, a principle of its functioning. Such internal principles of functioning can be called *principles* in a distinctive sense. All the archic variables are principles in the sense that they function as firsts or beginnings, but only principles are principles in the sense that it is their nature to be firsts or beginnings. A principle can be either relatively or absolutely first; that is, it can cause functioning and itself be caused, or it can be an uncaused cause of a functioning, a first principle. God, if He is a principle at all, is ordinarily a first principle.

Principles then cause texts to function, and without a principle a text cannot function. A text without a principle would be like Adam before God breathed into his nostrils the breath of life. Imagine, for example, a geometry that lacks definitions, axioms, and postulates. There may be an ordered set of statements about geometrical figures, but without principles there can be no proofs, and without proofs a geometry is not functioning as a geometry. Or imagine an ethics that fails to supply any reason for action. There may be an ordered set of statements about action, but unless there is some reason for action the text cannot function as an ethics. Or imagine a tragedy that lacks any engagement of feeling. There may be an ordered sequence of actions and events, but without feeling the text cannot function as a tragedy. On the other hand, if to the perspective, signification, and method of a text, a principle is added, the text becomes a functioning whole, as Adam became a living soul. And since these four variables suffice to produce a functioning whole, there is no need for any more. Each of them is necessary, and all together are sufficient. There are these four and no others.

The perspective and signification and method and principle of a text may or may not be formulated as such within the text itself, but they are all in evidence throughout the text. All of the text has the perspective of the text, all that it signifies belongs to the signification of the text, all of the text is ordered by its method, and the principle causes a functioning to which all of the text contributes. The meaning of single sentences or even of single terms (the Zen "Ho!", to use David Dilworth's example) therefore depends on all four variables, and often the entire archic profile of a text or author can be seen in a single sentence or term. As one example, consider the couplet of Shakespeare's Sonnet 15:

> And, all in war with Time for love of you,
> As he takes from you, I engraft you new.

The functioning, the engrafting new, is caused by the "I," the poet; the method is agonistic, a war of the poet with Time motivated by love; the reality is the existential reality of the flux, in which the beloved is simultaneously taken from and engrafted new, and the whole is observed with an objective eye.

Principles are in one sense dependent on their epochal context and on the other archic variables, but as principles they are independent of all these. Principles can be sought in things or in the mind which knows things or in the expressions of the mind which knows things. Different perspectives require principles related in different ways to the author: Personal perspectives require principles that are one's own. Objective perspectives require principles that are independent of the author. Diaphanic perspectives require principles that transcend the author. Disciplinary perspectives require principles appropriate to disciplinary interests. Different realities correspond to different ways in which principles can be real: principles may be existential acts or material atoms or noumenal ideas or essential definitions. And different methods require principles to function in different ways: Agonistic methods require that principles be powers of the agonists. Logistic methods require that principles determine consequences. Dialectical methods require that principles unify the opposites with which they are working. Analytic methods require that principles order organic wholes.

At the same time, however, and in spite of all these differences, each kind of principle must be one and the same kind of thing, able to perform by virtue of what it is the different functions required by the different kinds of methods ordering different subject matters from different perspectives. And its nature as a principle, as we have said, is to be a cause of a functioning. The different kinds of principles will therefore correspond to the different ways in which something can be such a cause. First principles are prime candidates for reciprocal priority, for as uncaused causes of functioning, each kind will cause the functioning of all the other kinds without being caused by them. They will all be principles of principles.

1. Creative Principles

The principles that are nearest and most evident to us are our own principles, whatever principles we have. These principles are ours because we have made them ours, and the power we have of adopting principles is itself a principle, since it is a cause of the activity or functioning that results from their adoption. This power that we ourselves have of causing activity or functioning is what is usually meant by free will. It is an arbitrary power by which an activity or functioning that was not there before comes into existence.

We may suppose similar principles to exist in other things. God, for example, may be supposed to have the same kind of arbitrary creative power. In this case He is a first principle, since He creates without being created, and we are principles but not first principles, since we create but are also created. Other animals may also initiate behavior arbitrarily, as in B. F. Skinner's operant behavior, and inanimate things may also act spontaneously, as in the Epicurean swerve of the atoms. And according to Thales all things are full of gods.

Such initiating powers can be called arbitrary or actional or creative principles. Action may be thought to be the consequence of antecedents, however, while creativity implies the coming into being of something not explainable by its antecedents. And if the principle is called creative rather than arbitrary it emphasizes the positive result rather than the negative absence of determination. I will therefore call this first kind of principles *creative* principles.

The great beginning of creative principles in the Western tradition is in the book of Genesis. The God of Genesis is a creator who creates heaven and earth, and man in his own image. To be created in the image of God means in this context to be also a creator, with the freedom to obey or disobey the commands of the creator who created him. With the creation of man, creativity becomes part of the creation itself. In Genesis the two kinds of creators, God and man, use their creative powers to establish an harmonious dialectical order. One way of establishing an harmonious order would be for the secondary creator, man, to act in accordance with the plan of the primary creator, God. Man, however, is not content with this subordinate position and uses his freedom in a way that frustrates God's initial plan. Left to his own devices, man is inventive and occasionally good, but predominantly evil and unable to establish an harmonious order. God, in the flood, reverses his work of creation and so wipes out the evil that man has done, and makes a fresh beginning in the recognition that the imagination of man's heart is evil from his youth. His new plan calls for one family to become the means by which all the families of the earth shall be blessed. The sequence from Abraham through Jacob to Joseph provides a paradigm for a moral advance by which the primal fratricide of Abel by Cain is superseded by its opposite, the willingness of Judah to lay down his life for his brother Benjamin. The creative principles make the story a progressive history with an open future. What that future will be depends upon the conjoint activity of the two kinds of creators, God and man.[1]

Both kinds of creators, God and man, are given visual representation by Michelangelo in the Sistine ceiling. Michelangelo worked in a semantic epoch and was concerned with the interpretation of texts, and his archic elements are well-suited to the interpretation of Genesis, for, except for the method, they are the same as those of Genesis. Both Genesis and the Sistine ceiling are revelations of the essential creativity of God and man.

Creative principles tend to predominate in the religions that have sprung from Genesis. The Koran in some passages seems to exalt the arbitrary power of God to the point of excluding the freedom given to man: "God will mislead whom He pleaseth, and whom He pleaseth He will place upon the straight path."[2] If it seems unjust that God should punish those whom He has been pleased to mislead, and reward those whom He has been pleased to put on the straight path, it should be remembered that punishments and rewards are also dependent on God's good pleasure: "Whom He pleaseth will He forgive, and whom He pleaseth will He punish; for God is All-powerful."[3]

The classical Christian account of God as creator and man as having free choice of the will is provided by St. Augustine. Although Augustine retains the other archic variables of Genesis, he adopts the noumenal reality of Plato and Plotinus, and supports this shift by a surprising reading of the opening sentence of Genesis. Augustine argues that this sentence describes the initial creation by God of a timeless noumenal heaven and a timeless chaotic earth out of which the visible heavens and earth were formed in the seven days of creation:

> This, my God, is what I feel when I hear your Scripture saying: *In the Beginning God made heaven and earth; and the earth was invisible*

and without form, and darkness was upon the deep. And when Scripture makes no mention of the day on which you made these, I conclude that this is because what is meant by "heaven" is the *heaven of heavens*, that intellectual heaven, where it is the property of the intellect to know all things in one act, not *in part*, not *darkly*, not *through a glass*, but as a whole, *in manifestation, face to face*; not to know one thing at one time and one at another, but, as has been said, to know everything together without any vicissitude of time. And I assume that by "earth" is meant that *earth invisible and without form*, not subject to the vicissitude of time in which there occurs now "this" and now "that," because where there is no form, there is no "this" and no "that."[4]

Augustine thus has the same archic profile as Plato except for the creative principles, and the contrast is clear in their respective accounts of creation. For Augustine, the noumenal reality is itself the result of the creator, whereas for Plato in the *Timaeus* the noumenal reality pre-exists and is used as a pattern by the creator.

The creative principle in man is examined by Augustine in *On the Free Choice of the Will*. He argues that what is superior or equal to man will not compel him to sin, and what is inferior to him cannot, and consequently he sins only by his own will and free choice:

> Since, because of justice, whatever is equal or superior to the mind that possesses virtue and is in control does not make the mind a slave to lust; and since, because of its weakness, whatever is inferior to the mind cannot do this (as the things we have established prove)—therefore it follows that nothing can make the mind a companion of desire except its own will and free choice (*voluntas et liberum arbitrium*).[5]

Creative principles are also found in the Greek tradition, beginning with Thales. Thales held that all things are full of gods and that the magnet has soul because it moves iron. To say that all things are full of gods means that they have within them the power of activity of gods. The creative power present in all things is signified materially by water. Aristotle conjectures that Thales made water the principle because of its creative potentialities:

> Thales, the founder of this type of philosophy, says the principle is water (for which reason he declared that the earth rests on water), getting the notion perhaps from seeing that the nutriment of all things is moist, and that heat itself is generated from the moist and kept alive by it (and that from which they come to be is a principle of all things).

> He got his notion from this fact, and from the fact that the seeds of all things have a moist nature, and that water is the origin of the nature of moist things.[6]

The evidence for the earth's crust floating on water is found in its motion in earthquakes: "For he said that the world is held up by water and rides like a ship, and when it is said to 'quake' it is actually rocking because of the water's movement."[7] Thales' plan to unite the Ionian cities and prevent their conquest by Croesus by having a single deliberative chamber at Teos is a plan by which independent centers of activity can be coordinated in a common effort. The prediction of the eclipse with which Herodotus credits Thales may involve thinking of it as a recurrent encounter of independently moving deities.

The wisdom of Protagoras is also a creative principle, the power to effect changes from what appears bad to what appears good. Protagoras says in Plato's *Theaetetus,*

> By a wise man I mean precisely a man who can change any one of us, when what is bad appears and is to him, and make what is good appear and be to him. In this statement, again, don't set off in chase of words, but let me explain still more clearly what I mean. Remember how it was put earlier in the conversation. To the sick man his food appears sour and is so; to the healthy man it is and appears the opposite. Now there is no call to represent either of the two as wiser—that cannot be—nor is the sick man to be pronounced unwise because he thinks as he does, or the healthy man wise because he thinks differently. What is wanted is a change to the opposite condition, because the other state is better. And so too in education a change has to be effected from the worse condition to the better; only, whereas the physician produces a change by means of drugs, the Sophist does it by discourse.[8]

The sophist invents a speech which affects the minds of others and so changes the world. Isocrates praises the power of speech as the key to man's creative activity:

> For in the other powers which we possess, as I have already said on a former occasion, we are in no respect superior to other living creatures; nay, we are inferior to many in swiftness and in strength and in other resources; but, because there has been implanted in us the power to persuade each other and to make clear to each other whatever we desire, not only have we escaped the life of wild beasts, but we have come together and founded cities and made laws and invented arts; and,

generally speaking, there is no institution devised by man which the power of speech has not helped us to establish.[9]

History becomes the record of the creative activities of great individuals, as in Isocrates' account of the role of his art of speech in the development of Athens:

> First of all was Solon. For when he was placed at the head of the people, he gave them laws, set their affairs in order, and constituted the government of the city so wisely that even now Athens is well satisfied with the polity which was organized by him. Next, Cleisthenes, after he had been driven from Athens by the tyrants, succeeded by his eloquence in persuading the Amphictyons to lend him money from the treasury of Apollo, and thus restored the people to power, expelled the tyrants, and established that democracy to which the world of Hellas owes its greatest blessings. After him, Themistocles, placed at the head of our forces in the Persian War, counselled our ancestors to abandon the city (and who could have persuaded them to do this but a man of surpassing eloquence?), and so advanced their circumstances that at the price of being homeless for a few days they became for a long period of time the masters of the Hellenes. Finally, Pericles, because he was both a good leader of the people and an excellent orator, so adorned the city with temples, monuments, and other objects of beauty, that even to-day visitors who come to Athens think her worthy of ruling not only the Hellenes, but all the world.[10]

The fusion of the creative tradition stemming from Genesis with the creative tradition stemming from the Greek sophists can be seen in the Renaissance humanists. Pico della Mirandola, for example, tells us how Adam was addressed by his Creator:

> He therefore took man as a creature of indeterminate nature and, assigning him a place in the middle of the world, addressed him thus: "Neither a fixed abode nor a form that is thine alone nor any function peculiar to thyself have we given thee, Adam, to the end that according to thy longing and according to thy judgment thou mayest have and possess what abode, what form, and what functions thou thyself shalt desire. The nature of all other beings is limited and constrained within the bounds of laws prescribed by Us. Thou, constrained by no limits, in accordance with thine own free will, in whose hand We have placed thee, shalt ordain for thyself the limits of thy nature."[11]

The arbitrary beginnings of creative principles were attached to the necessary sequences of logistic by Calvin in the 16th century and by Hobbes, Locke, Newton, and others, in the 17th century. In the objective perspective of Locke, the idea of a God who created us and the idea of ourselves as rational beings provide a basis for a law of nature and for a demonstrative science of morals: "The idea of a supreme Being, infinite in power, goodness, and wisdom, whose workmanship we are, and on whom we depend; and the idea of ourselves, as understanding rational beings; being such as are clear in us, would, I suppose, if duly considered and pursued, afford such foundations of our duty and rules of action as might place morality amongst the sciences capable of demonstration."[12] In the personal perspective of Hobbes, however, the state of nature is a state of war, and the escape from it depends on reducing the wills of all to the single arbitrary will of an artificial person.

> The only way to erect such a Common Power, as may be able to defend them from the invasion of Forraigners, and the injuries of one another, and thereby to secure them in such sort, as that by their owne industrie, and by the fruites of the Earth, they may nourish themselves and live contentedly; is, to conferre all their power and strength upon one Man, or upon one Assembly of men, that may reduce all their Wills, by plurality of voices, unto one Will: which is as much as to say, to appoint one Man, or Assembly of men, to beare their Person; and every one to owne, and acknowledge himselfe to be Author of whatsoever he that so beareth their Person, shall Act, or cause to be Acted, in those things which concerne the Common Peace and Safetie; and therein to submit their Wills, every one to his Will, and their Judgements, to his Judgment.[13]

We may note here a similar combination of creative beginnings with necessary consequences in the so-called Legalist school in China and in the social science of Max Weber. In the Legalist doctrine as formulated by Han Fei Tsu, the creative initiative comes from the ministers, and the ruler uses rewards and punishments to insure that the actions of the ministers correspond to their words. The ministers in turn use rewards and punishments to insure that the actions of the people correspond to the laws that the ministers have promulgated. By these means the internal order and external security of the state can be established and maintained.[14]

Max Weber, with his objective perspective on an existential reality, sees creativity not in the will of God but in the charismatic individuals who claim to represent this will. The arbitrary creativity of charismatic individuals becomes routinized in rational and traditional authority, but it is itself a specifically revolutionary force:

Charismatic authority is thus specifically outside the realm of every-day routine and the profane sphere. In this respect, it is sharply opposed both to rational, and particularly bureaucratic, authority, and to tradi-tional authority, whether in its patriarchal, patrimonial, or any other form. Both rational and traditional authority are specifically forms of everyday routine control of action; while the charismatic type is the direct antithesis of this. Bureaucratic authority is specifically rational in the sense of being bound to intellectually analysable rules; while charismatic authority is specifically irrational in the sense of being for-eign to all rules. Traditional authority is bound to the precedents handed down from the past and to this extent is also oriented to rules. Within the sphere of its claims, charismatic authority repudiates the past, and is in this sense a specifically revolutionary force.[15]

Darwin, like Genesis, accounts for things by their genesis. He is con-cerned with the origin of biological species in general in *On the Origin of Species*, with the origin of the distinctive features of man, such as his moral and intellectual qualities and the differentiation of male and female, in *The Descent of Man and Selection in Relation to Sex*, and with the origin of the expression of emotions in *The Expression of the Emotions in Animals and Man*. He begins his account of the origin of species not with a creating God, but with two chapters on variation, and first with varia-tion under domestication, where it is greatest: "When we look to the individuals of the same variety or sub-variety of our older cultivated plants and animals, one of the first points which strikes us, is, that they gener-ally differ much more from each other, than do the individuals of any one species or variety in a state of nature." Such variation provides the novelty, which, preserved and accumulated through natural selection and inheritance, eventuates in new species. Species originate through the logistic addition and subtraction of variations.

Combinations of creative principles with a dialectical method, as in Genesis, have not been wanting in the 19th and 20th centuries. Marx came from a rabbinical family, but Marx secularized the creative dialectic of Genesis by applying it to a material reality. The primary creator thus becomes man in his capacity as a worker or producer. "For socialist man, the whole of what is called world history is nothing but the creation of man by human labour, and the emergence of nature for man; he, therefore, has the evident and irrefutable proof of his self-creation, of his own origins."[16] The chosen group that represents this creative power and by whom the world is to be reformed becomes the Communist Party. The stages by which a creative dialectic reforms the world are represented in Genesis by the sequence from Abraham through Jacob to Joseph, and in Marxism by the sequence from Marx through Lenin to Stalin. The first stage requires faith in the future reality of the promised land, a stage represented by Abraham and by the *Communist Manifesto*. The second stage requires the uncompromising perseverance and tenacity of Jacob or Lenin that refuse to settle for immediate satisfactions or anything less than control of the means of production. (Capitalistic exploitation is represented in Genesis by Laban.) The third stage requires the wisdom of Joseph to collectivise the land and reconcile the brothers. Stalin lacked the dialectical wisdom of his namesake, and dealt with conflicts by starvation and purges rather than by food and reconciliation, and the result, according to some critics, was a god that failed.

Heidegger approximates still more closely to the creativity of Genesis by returning to an essential reality. In Heidegger the God and man of Genesis become Being and Dasein. The names have changed, but they remain co-creators. The manifestation of God in time that we find in Genesis reappears in Heidegger as the temporality of Being, and man's freedom to obey or disobey reappears in Heidegger as Dasein's freedom to choose itself.

Whitehead also uses a creative dialectic to order an essential reality. He concludes one of his accounts of the various grades of actualities by saying that it is "nothing else than a modern rendering of the oldest of civilized reflections on the development of the Universe as seen from the perspective of life on this earth,"[17] by which he means it is a modern rendering of the account of creation in Genesis. Creativity, according to Whitehead, is an ultimate principle by which actual occasions introduce novelty into the universe:

> "Creativity" is the principle of *novelty*. An actual occasion is a novel entity diverse from any entity in the "many" which it unifies. Thus "creativity" introduces novelty into the content of the many, which are the universe disjunctively. The "creative advance" is the application of this ultimate principle of creativity to each novel situation which it originates.[18]

God is himself created and is the primordial creature, the unconditioned conceptual though unconscious valuation of the entire multiplicity of eternal objects. The eternal objects as unrealized possibilities thus become available to other actual occasions, and particularly to man, who is specialized for the conceptual entertainment of unrealized possibilities:

When we come to mankind, nature seems to have burst through another of its boundaries. The central activity of enjoyment and expression has assumed a reversal in the importance of its diverse functionings. The conceptual entertainment of unrealized possibility becomes a major factor in human mentality. In this way outrageous novelty is introduced, sometimes beatified, sometimes damned, and sometimes literally patented or protected by copyright. The definition of mankind is that in this genus of animals the central activity has been developed on the side of its relationship to novelty.[19]

Whitehead's *Process and Reality* is a work in the discipline of speculative philosophy rather than of revealed religion, and his perspective is disciplinary rather than revelatory, but his archic elements are otherwise the same as those of Genesis. Theologians have therefore been able to use Whitehead to develop a process theology that brings traditional religious conceptions into harmony with advances in the scientific disciplines. Theologians who prefer to retain a revelatory perspective and look down on the scientific disciplines can use Heidegger to bring Genesis up to date.

A creative dialectic with an existential reality is found in existentialism. Man is not God's creature, but is thrown into the world. The perspective is personal and the primary creator is man in his individual subjectivity choosing for all men. Man cannot be guided in his choice by God or human nature or passion or some omen in the world, but is condemned at every moment to invent man:

> Dostoyevsky said, "If God didn't exist, everything would be possible." That is the very starting point of existentialism. Indeed, everything is permissible if God does not exist, and as a result man is forlorn, because neither within him nor without does he find anything to cling to. He can't start making excuses for himself.
>
> If existence really does precede essence, there is no explaining things away by reference to a fixed and given human nature. In other words, there is no determinism, man is free, man is freedom. On the other hand, if God does not exist, we find no values or commands to turn to which legitimize our conduct. So, in the bright realm of values, we have no excuse behind us, nor justification before us. We are alone, with no excuses.
>
> That is the idea I shall try to convey when I say that man is condemned to be free. Condemned, because he did not create himself, yet, in other respects is free; because, once thrown into the world, he is responsible for everything he does. The existentialist does not believe in the power of passion. He will never agree that a sweeping passion is a ravaging

torrent which fatally leads a man to certain acts and is therefore an excuse. He thinks that man is responsible for his passion.

The existentialist does not think that man is going to help himself by finding in the world some omen by which to orient himself. Because he thinks that man will interpret the omen to suit himself. Therefore, he thinks that man, with no support and no aid, is condemned every moment to invent man.[20]

When creative principles are used with a problematic method, they effect a real transformation of a problematic situation into one that is settled and determinate. Inquiry through the resolution of problems thus transforms the world.

Dewey wrote a lecture on the influence of Darwinism on philosophy which emphasized the creative power of Darwin's work. According to Dewey, it introduced a mode of thinking that was bound to transform the logic of knowledge, and hence the treatment of morals, politics, and religion:

> That the publication of the "Origin of Species" marked an epoch in the development of the natural sciences is well known to the layman. That the combination of the very words origin and species embodied an intellectual revolt and introduced a new intellectual temper is easily overlooked by the expert. The conceptions that had reigned in the philosophy of nature and knowledge for two thousand years, the conceptions that had become the familiar furniture of the mind, rested on the assumption of the superiority of the fixed and final; they rested upon treating change and origin as signs of defect and unreality. In laying hands upon the sacred ark of absolute permanency, in treating the forms that had been regarded as types of fixity and perfection as originating and passing away, the "Origin of Species" introduced a mode of thinking that in the end was bound to transform the logic of knowledge, and hence the treatment of morals, politics, and religion.[21]

Dewey's own philosophy must in these terms be counted among those influenced by Darwinism, for he here and elsewhere inveighs against the conceptions which he says reigned for two thousand years, conceptions resting upon the assumption of the superiority of the fixed and final and upon treating change and origin as signs of defect and unreality. Dewey in his *Logic*, for example, attempts to do for present science and culture what Aristotle did for the science and culture of his time, and summarizes the difference between the ancient and modern conception of nature as follows: "The change in the conception of Nature is expressed in summary form in the idea that the universe is now conceived as open and in process while classical Greece thought of it as finite in the sense in which finite means finished, complete and perfect."[22] It should be noticed that differences of principle here become historical differences. An historical or genetic method is always found in some form when the principles are creative—in Genesis, for example, which is a history, in Augustine's *Confessions* and *City of God*, in the account of the state of nature in Hobbes and Locke, or in Locke's "historical, plain method" of investigating the human understanding, in Berkeley's genetic account of the origin of our ideas, in Darwin's account of the origin of species, in Marx's history of class struggles, in Heidegger's task of destroying the history of ontology, and in Whitehead's adventures of ideas.

My own personal history illustrates the contrast between creative principles and other kinds of principles. I was first attracted to philosophy by Dewey, found in him the true philosophy, and was encouraged in the pursuit of philosophy by Dewey himself. The present work accords with Dewey in its disciplinary perspective, essential signification, and problematic method, but it departs from Dewey in abandoning creative principles. This revolution in my thinking was occasioned by study with Richard McKeon. There is a great difference, as Dewey says, and as I experienced, between understanding things in relation to their historical origin and understanding them in relation to a principle of completeness or perfection. In making this change I was abandoning the principles that predominated in my family, in my neighborhood, in my schooling, in my nation, and in the whole tradition of the West. It was an escape from a provincialism so pervasive and so extensive that it seemed not to be a provincialism at all. And I expect that for many of my readers the chief difficulty of this book will be that it treats doctrines as relative to philosophic principles rather than philosophic principles as relative to historical situations.

Dewey treats the conception of the primacy of the changing over the unchanging as itself having an historical origin in Darwin's *Origin of Species*, whereas I have treated this conception as a possibility for thought from its very beginnings, and one which is found already in Genesis. Biological species in Genesis may be stable (although varied by Jacob's art), but this should not lead one to overlook the fact that they were created, and that the treatment of morals, politics, and religion in Genesis reveals a creative advance of a kind that Dewey sees as a result of Darwinism. And it is not only in Genesis that one finds, before Darwin, a conception of things open and in process. One might also think of the Sophists in ancient Greece, who were, after all, far more numerous than the Platonists and Aristotelians with their stable forms whom Dewey treats as representing Greek science. Nor should we overlook the Book of Lord Shang and the

Legalist school in China, already mentioned, which represent creative principles in that tradition.[23] Of course there is a reciprocal priority here: the appearance of creative principles in history can be treated as the consequence of creative beginnings, or the creative beginnings can be treated as consequences of unchanging principles. But at the present stage of intellectual history the development of the latter possibility reveals intelligible relations among doctrines that tend to be obscured when philosophic principles are treated as relative to their historical situation, as they are by Dewey.

In summary, then, creative principles appear early and often in the West. They are found in both the Hebrew and Hellenic traditions. They are exemplified on the one hand by Genesis, the orthodox Christianity of St. Augustine, and the Koran, and on the other by Thales and by the Greek Sophists such as Protagoras and Isocrates. The two traditions are brought together in the Renaissance humanists such as Pico della Mirandola. Creative principles originate logistic sequences in Calvin, Hobbes, Locke, the Chinese Legalists, and Max Weber; they originate agonistic struggles in Michelangelo; they originate dialectical syntheses in Marx, Heidegger, Whitehead, and Sartre; and they originate problematic resolutions in John Dewey.

2. Elemental Principles

It may be held that to account for functionings by arbitrary causes is not to account for them at all, but to abandon causality. An uncaused cause, it may be held, should not be conceived as something that is unaffected by its antecedents and therefore arbitrary in its action, but as something that has no antecedents because it has always existed. Things in general come into being from their antecedents, and these in turn from other antecedents, and so on without limit, but the reason why the whole series of things is what it is lies in that which persists through these changes and does not itself change. Changing things are the variable manifestations of a cause that always exists and does not change. They are what they are not because of a principle of novelty, but because of a principle of sameness. An unchanging principle that persists through all changes is a first principle; a principle that persists through a particular change but is itself brought into being by something else is a principle but not a first principle.

Such principles can be called conservational or inertial or simple or elemental principles. "Conservational" and "inertial" may suggest too narrow a meaning, while any kind of principle may be simple in the sense of being without parts.[24] I will therefore call this second kind of principles *elemental* principles. Elemental principles are familiar in the views that the more things change, the more they remain the same, or that the fundamental laws of physics govern all changes but do not themselves change.

An elemental principle appears in Western philosophy in Anaximenes' air. According to Anaximenes, all things are modifications of air. Theophrastus' account is as follows:

> Anaximenes son of Eurystratus, of Miletus, a companion of Anaximander, also says that the underlying nature is one and infinite like him, but not indefinite, as Anaximander said but definite, for he identifies it as air; and it differs in its substantial nature by rarity and density. Being made finer it becomes fire, being made thicker it becomes wind, then cloud, then (when thickened still more) water, then earth, then stones; and the rest come into being from these.[25]

The sameness of the substratum grounds the many samenesses of small and large: As our soul, being air, holds us together and controls us, so does wind or air enclose the whole world.[26] The sun is flat like a leaf,[27] the earth is supported like a lid,[28] the stars are like nails in the crystalline,[29] they move round the earth like a felt cap turning round our head;[30] clouds are produced from air by "felting,"[31] lightning is like the phosphorescence of the sea when it is cleft by oars,[32] and earthquakes are the result of drought or rain drying up and cracking the earth or crumbling it apart as we see in the case of mud on a small scale.[33] Heating and cooling in the cosmos occur by the same process as in our mouths: "The dictum is not an unreasonable one, that man releases both warmth and cold from his mouth: for the breath is chilled by being compressed and condensed with the lips, but when the mouth is loosened the breath escapes and becomes warm through its rarity."[34]

Air is thus the common substratum of all things and also the cause of their functioning, and similar modifications of air function in similar ways. The absolute Being of Parmenides is a different kind of elemental principle, noumenal rather than substrative, but similarly uncreated and imperishable:

> One way is left to be spoken of, that it *is*; and on this way are full many signs that what is is uncreated and imperishable, for it is entire, immovable and without end. It *was* not in the past, nor *shall* it be, since it *is* now, all at once, one, continuous; for what creation wilt thou seek for it? How and whence did it grow?[35]

Empedocles' agonistic materialism is governed by the eternal elemental antagonists Love and Strife, which generate all compound things by putting together or taking apart the four roots, fire, water, earth, and air. Love brings the elements together, producing finally the "rounded sphere rejoicing in his circular solitude,"[36] while Strife when his turn comes takes them apart again. "And these things never cease from continual shifting, at one time all coming together, through Love, into one, at another each borne apart from the others through Strife."[37]

In the culminating phase of Hellenic philosophy, Leucippus and Democritus materialized and pluralized the noumenal one of Parmenides so that it became the atoms of pure being. The atoms differ in rhythm, contact, and turning, and these differences in the elements are the causes of all other qualities, as Aristotle tells us in a passage from the *Metaphysics*:

> Leucippus and his associate Democritus say that the full and the empty are the elements, calling the one being and the other non-being—the full and solid being being, the empty non-being (whence they say being no more is than non-being, because the solid no more is than the empty); and they make these the material causes of things. And as those who make the underlying substance one generate all other things by its modifications, supposing the rare and the dense to be the sources of the modifications, in the same way these philosophers say the differences in the elements are the causes of all other qualities. These differences, they say, are three—shape and order and position. For they say the real is differentiated only by "rhythm" and "inter-contact" and "turning"; and of these rhythm is shape, inter-contact is order, and turning is position; for A differs from N in shape, AN from NA in order, Z from N in position. The question of movement—whence or how it is to belong to things—these thinkers, like the others, lazily neglected.[38]

The reference to those who generate all things by the modifications of one underlying substance, and suppose the rare and the dense to be the sources of the modifications, is to Anaximenes and his followers. Aristotle's criticism that Anaximenes and the atomists lazily neglected the question of motion is evidence of the difference of principle between Aristotle and the elementalists. For the latter, motion is the result of antecedent motion, and there is no principle or beginning of motion. As Aristotle says in another context,

> Those are wrong, and fail to state the causal necessity, who say that things have always happened so and that this explains their beginning.

So Democritus of Abdera says that there is no beginning of the infinite, that a cause is a beginning and what is everlasting is infinite; therefore to ask "why?" in a case like this is to look for a beginning of the infinite.[39]

Elemental principles are conservative or inertial principles in accordance with which things are the same throughout all time.

In the Hellenistic period the noumenal one of Parmenides reappears as the One of Plotinus, but joined to a dialectical method. For Plotinus, all things emanate from the One, which is itself without any definite characteristics:

> As The One begets all things, it cannot be any of them—neither thing, nor quality, nor quantity, nor intelligence, nor soul. Not in motion, nor at rest, not in space, nor in time, it is "the in itself uniform," or rather it is the "without-form" preceding form, movement, and rest, which are characteristics of Being and make Being multiple.[40]

One cannot be aware of the One by knowing, for this already implies a duality of knower and known, but only by becoming one with the One:

> The chief difficulty is this: awareness of The One comes to us neither by knowing nor by the pure thought that discovers the other intelligible things, but by a presence transcending knowledge. When the soul knows something, it loses its unity; it cannot remain simply one because knowledge implies discursive reason and discursive reason implies multiplicity. The soul then misses The One and falls into number and multiplicity.
>
> Therefore we must go beyond knowledge and hold to unity. We must renounce knowing and knowable, every object of thought, even Beauty, because Beauty, too, is posterior to The One and is derived from it as, from the sun, daylight. That is why Plato says of The One, "It can neither be spoken nor written about." If nevertheless we speak of it and write about it, we do so only to give direction to urge towards that vision beyond discourse, to point out the road to one desirous of seeing. Instruction goes only as far as showing the road and the direction. To obtain the vision is solely the work of him who desires to obtain it.[41]

A dialectic leading to unity with the One transcends knowledge and is thus mystical in its nature.

From Plotinus, elemental principles enter the Christian tradition through the Christian neo-Platonists such as Dionysius the Aeropagite, and were continued by John Scotus Eriugena, Nicholas of Cusa, and others. This elementalist tradition is a subordinate strain in Christianity opposed to the orthodox Augustinian creationism. Elemental dialectics tend to be dialectics of departure and return, for the principles being a perpetual sameness, there is nowhere for the dialectic to go but away and back again. We may note in this connection the elemental dialectics of departure and return that are found in the Indian and Chinese traditions. The Upanishads teach in countless ways the elemental principle that is the same in all things. Here is an example from the Chhāndôgya Upanishad:

> Uddālaka said, "My son! You think such a lot of yourself, but did you ask your teacher about that initiation, which makes a man hear what is not heard, think what is not thought, know what is not known?"
> "What is that initiation, Lord?" said Shwetaketu. Uddālaka said: "By knowing a lump of clay you know all things made of clay; they differ from one another as it were in language and in name, having no reality but their clay;
> "By knowing one nugget of gold you know all things made of gold; they differ from one another as it were in language and in name, having no reality but their gold;
> "By knowing one piece of base metal you know all things made of that metal; they differ from one another as it were in language and in name, having no reality but that metal.
> "For the like reason, after that initiation, you know everything."[42]

A later excerpt makes clear that all things originate from and return to this principle, like the rivers from and to the sea:

> "My son! Rivers, flowing east and west, rise from the sea, return to the sea, become the sea itself, forget their identities.
> "These creatures do not know that they have risen from that Being, or returned to that Being.
> "Whatever that may be, tiger, lion, wolf, boar, worm, moth, gnat, mosquito, they become aware of particular life when they are born into it or awake.
> "That Being is the seed; all else but His expression. He is truth. He is Self. Shwetaketu! You are That."[43]

The elemental principle from which all things originate and to which they return is personified in the Bhagavad Gita:

All beings, son of Kunti,
   Pass into My material nature
At the end of a world-eon; them again
   I send forth at the beginning of a (new)
   world-eon.

Taking as base My own material-nature
   I send forth again and again
This whole host of beings,
   Which is powerless, by the power of (My)
   material nature.[44]

This same dialectic of departure and return is found in the Chinese tradition in the *Tao-te ching*.

All things come into being,
And I see thereby their return.
All things flourish,
But each one returns to its root.[45]

The Tao, like the One, can itself have no definite essence:

We look at it and do not see it;
   Its name is The Invisible.
We listen to it and do not hear it;
   Its name is The Inaudible.
We touch it and do not find it;
   Its name is The Subtle (formless).
These three cannot be further inquired into,
And hence merge into one.
Going up high, it is not bright, and coming
   down low, it is not dark.
Infinite and boundless, it cannot be given
   any name;
It reverts to nothingness.
This is called shape without shape,
Form (*hsiang*) without object.
It is the Vague and Elusive.
Meet it and you will not see its head.
Follow it and you will not see its back.
Hold on to the Tao of old in order to master
   the things of the present.
From this one may know the primeval beginning.
This is called the bond of Tao.[46]

The most important source of elemental principles in the modern Western tradition is Newton, in spite of the fact that Newton himself uses creative rather than elemental principles. We see in Newton one way in which creative principles can subsume elemental principles, for the creator may so create things that their continued functioning can be understood in terms of their elements. It was not difficult for subsequent thinkers to detach the elements from their creator, or Newton's science from his theology, and make the elements themselves the principles. For Newton himself, however, passive or inertial principles are insufficient to explain the functioning of the world.

> The *Vis inertiae* is a passive Principle by which Bodies persist in their Motion or Rest, receive Motion in proportion to the Force impressing it, and resist as much as they are resisted. By this Principle alone there never could have been any Motion in the World. Some other Principle was necessary for putting Bodies into Motion; and now they are in Motion, some other Principle is necessary for conserving the Motion.[47]

And if matter is formed in particles so very hard as never to wear or break in pieces, it is because God in the beginning formed it that way:

> All these things being consider'd, it seems probable to me, that God in the Beginning form'd Matter in solid, massy, hard, impenetrable, movable Particles, of such Sizes and Figures, and with such other Properties, and in such Proportion to Space, as most conduced to the End for which he form'd them; and that these primitive Particles being Solids, are incomparably harder than any porous Bodies compounded of them; even so very hard, as never to wear or break in pieces; no ordinary Power being able to divide what God himself made one in the first Creation.[48]

In Newton, creation is prior to conservation, and if anything is conserved, it is because things were created so that there would be this conservation. Blind metaphysical necessity (" 'The stars,' she whispers, 'blindly run.' ") did not produce this system of the world: "This most beautiful system of the sun, planets, and comets, could only proceed from the counsel and dominion of an intelligent and powerful Being . . . . Blind metaphysical necessity, which is certainly the same always and everywhere, could produce no variety in things."[49] Laplace's nebular hypothesis, however, accounts for the order of the cosmos in a way that recalls the cosmogenic hypothesis of Leucippus and Democritus rather than the creation of Genesis. With this hypothesis, Laplace had no need for the hypothesis of God, and the order of the universe is determined throughout infinite time by the state of the universe at any one time and the laws governing the interactions of its particles.

Hume, like Laplace, is a follower of Newton who has no need of the hypothesis of a God. Hume seeks the principles by which ideas are connected in our mind, and finds that they are resemblance, contiguity, and cause or effect:

> Though it be too obvious to escape observation, that different ideas are connected together; I do not find that any philosopher has attempted to enumerate or class all the principles of association; a subject, however, that seems worthy of curiosity. To me, there appear to be only three principles of connexion among ideas, namely, *Resemblance,Contiguity* in time or place, and *Cause* or *Effect*.[50]

All our reasonings concerning matters of fact are founded on the relation of cause and effect. The foundation of all our reasonings and conclusions concerning cause and effect is experience. And the foundation of all conclusions from experience is the principle of custom or habit:

> This principle is Custom or Habit. For wherever the repetition of any particular act or operation produces a propensity to renew the same act or operation, without being impelled by any reasoning or process of the understanding, we always say, that this propensity is the effect of *Custom*. By employing that word, we pretend not to have given the ultimate reason of such a propensity. We only point out a principle of human nature, which is universally acknowledged and which is well known by its effects. Perhaps we can push our enquiries no further, or pretend to give the cause of this cause; but must rest contented with it as the ultimate principle, which we can assign, of all our conclusions from experience.[51]

This principle of custom or habit is a kind of inertia of the mind, by which it is led to expect that the future will resemble the past.

In his inquiry concerning the principles of morals Hume finds in human nature a principle of sympathy or humanity which connects our own happiness and misery with the happiness and misery of others. Like the principle of custom, it is for us an ultimate principle:

> It is needless to push our researches so far as to ask, why we have humanity or a fellow-feeling with others. It is sufficient, that this is experienced to be a principle in human nature. We must stop somewhere in our examination of causes; and there are, in every science, some general principles, beyond which we cannot hope to find any principle more general.[52]

The principle of humanity is a particular example of the relation of cause and effect, and is an elemental principle in the moral sphere. Just as the principle of custom determines the mind to connect past and future because of their similarity, so the principle of humanity determines the mind to connect its feelings with those of other individuals because of their similarity to ourselves.

Elemental principles are more in evidence in the sciences than in the philosophy of the West. We have already noted that Laplace's nebular hypothesis made astronomical order the consequence of the basic laws of physics rather than of a creating God. In chemistry, John Dalton used an atomic theory to treat chemical combination as the combination of elementary atoms attracting each other to form compound atoms. The definite weight ratios in which chemical elements combine to form compounds are for Dalton the result of their atoms combining in simple ratios to form compound atoms. Mendeleev uses the atomic weights to which Dalton's theory led as elemental principles by which to explain the other properties of the elements and their compounds. He emphasizes that at the time he is writing the only known numerical property of elements that remains invariant in all their compounds is the atomic weight:

> And yet, everyone of us understands that in spite of all the changes in the properties of simple bodies, in their free state, *something* remains constant, and when an element enters into compounds this something is material and determines the character of the compounds which contain the given element. In this respect, up to the present time only one numerical fact is known, namely, the atomic weight peculiar to the element.[53]

Just as the atomic weight of the elements, or Anaximenes' air, or the Tao, is one and the same through all changes, so what Helmholtz calls force or energy is conceived by him as one thing appearing in multiple forms:

Whilst the foregoing considerations chiefly seek to elucidate the logical value of the law of the conservation of force, its actual signification in the general conception of the processes of nature is expressed in the grand connection which it establishes between the entire processes of the universe, through all distances of place or time. The universe appears, according to this law, to be endowed with a store of energy which, through all the varied changes in natural processes, can neither be increased nor diminished, which is maintained therein in ever-varying phases, but, like matter itself, is from eternity to eternity of unchanging magnitude; *acting in space*, but not *divisible*, as matter is, with it. Every change in the world simply consists in a variation in the mode of appearance of this store of energy. Here we find one portion of it as the *vis viva* of moving bodies, there as regular oscillation in light and sound; or again, as heat, that is to say, the irregular motion of invisible particles; at another point the energy appears in the form of the weight of two masses gravitating towards each other, then as internal tension and pressure of elastic bodies, or as chemical attraction, electrical tension, or magnetic distribution. If it disappears in one form, it reappears as surely in another; and whenever it presents itself in a new phase we are certain that it does so at the expense of one of its other forms.[54]

Both Nietzsche's will to power and Freud's psychic energy are elemental principles, although perhaps Nietzsche owes more to Schopenhauer and thus to the Indian tradition, and Freud to Helmholtz and the Newtonian scientific tradition. The similarity of Nietzsche and Freud has often been remarked, and their archic profiles are the same except for their perspectives. Nietzsche is a poet presenting his interpretation of reality; Freud is an objective scientist presenting reality as it is. But for both the phenomena are the manifestation of the underlying conflict of elemental forces.

Nietzsche makes the experiment of positing all causality as the causality of will, and all will as the will to power:

The question is in the end whether we really recognize the will as *efficient*, whether we believe in the causality of the will: if we do—and at bottom our faith in this is nothing less than our faith in causality itself—then we have to make the experiment of positing the causality of the will hypothetically as the only one. "Will," of course, can affect only "will"—and not "matter" (not "nerves," for example). In short, one has to risk the hypothesis whether will does not affect will wherever "effects" are recognized—and whether all mechanical occurrences are not, insofar as a force is active in them, will force, effects of will.

Suppose, finally, we succeeded in explaining our entire instinctive life as the development and ramification of *one* basic form of the will—

namely, of the will to power, as *my* proposition has it; suppose all organic functions could be traced back to this will to power and one could also find in it the solution of the problem of procreation and nourishment—it is *one* problem—then one would have gained the right to determine *all* efficient force univocally as—*will to power*. The world viewed from inside, the world defined and determined according to its "intelligible character"—it would be "will to power" and nothing else.—[55]

The will for Nietzsche is in a sense creative. It creates the phenomena, as do also Brahma or Mendeleev's atomic weights. It is creative because it aims at the expansion of power.[56] It aims at the expansion of power, however, not from *liberum arbitrium*, free choice, but from necessity—it can do nothing else. The will to power is in this sense an elemental will and opposed to a free will. Freedom of the will is for Nietzsche an illusion invented by the priests to expand their power by making us responsible for our actions and hence liable to punishment.[57] Our own sense of acting freely is an illusion that enhances our own feeling of power.[58] The death of God is for Nietzsche not only the death of God's order in the world, but also the death of creativity. The idea that the world eternally creates new things is one of the shadows of God. The creative advance of Genesis or Whitehead is replaced by eternal recurrence: "the whole music box repeats eternally its tune which may never be called a melody."[59]

Freud carries over the concept of energy from physics into psychology, and postulates a psychic energy that is definite in quantity but that manifests itself in multiple forms. As for Nietzsche, the method is agonistic and the phenomena result from the conflicts of opposed forces or instincts. Freud initially worked with the conflict of ego-instincts, such as hunger, and object instincts, such as love, but revised this theory to make the fundamental conflict the conflict between the instincts of life, or Eros, and of death, or Thanatos. Eros is creative in the sense of producing new unities, but, like Nietzsche's will to power, it creates not from free choice but as a necessary consequence of what it is. Freud noted the similarity between his primal instincts and the fundamental principles of Empedocles:

> The two fundamental principles of Empedocles—*philia* and *neikos*—are, both in name and function, the same as our two primal instincts, *Eros* and *destructiveness*, the first of which endeavors to combine what exists into ever greater unities, while the second endeavors to dissolve those combinations and to destroy the structures to which they have given rise.[60]

This recognition of the sameness of principle between one of the Greeks and himself may be contrasted with Dewey's formulation of the fundamental difference of principle between the Greeks and himself. Elemental principles are always the same; creative principles are always new.

Turning finally to the arts, elemental antagonists like those of Empedocles and Freud are evident in the plays of Euripides. The *Hippolytus*, for example, presents one episode in the endless agon between the forces personified by Artemis and Aphrodite. The elemental power of Aphrodite manifests itself in Phaedra, and leads her inevitably, step by step, to reveal her love for Hippolytus to Hippolytus himself, and his reaction, as a worshipper of Artemis, leads to the destruction of both. Those who deny elemental powers do so at their peril, as Pentheus also finds in the *Bacchae*.

As a final example of elemental principles, consider the principle of perverseness in Poe's "The Imp of the Perverse":

> Induction, *a posteriori*, would have brought phrenology to admit, as an innate and primitive principle of human action, a paradoxical something, which we may call *perverseness*, for want of a more characteristic term. In the sense I intend, it is, in fact, a *mobile* without a motive, a motive not *motivirt*. Through its promptings we act without comprehensible object; or, if this shall be understood as a contradiction in terms, we may so far modify the proposition as to say, that through its promptings we act, for the reason that we should *not*. In theory, no reason can be more unreasonable; but, in fact, there is none more strong. With certain minds, under certain conditions, it becomes absolutely irresistible. I am not more certain that I breathe, than that the assurance of the wrong or error of any action is often the one unconquerable *force* which impels us, and alone impels us to its prosecution. Nor will this overwhelming tendency to do wrong for the wrong's sake, admit of analysis, or resolution into ulterior elements. It is a radical, a primitive impulse—elementary.[61]

The same principle of perverseness controls Dostoyevsky's underground man, but since the signification there is existential it appears not as a general principle but as something peculiar to him, and since the method is agonistic rather than analytic, its effects are seen not in the ordering of a whole but in the multiple inner contradictions with which the underground man is afflicted. The objective perspective and substrative signification of Freud make the perverseness understandable in terms of unconscious forces that oppose the motives of which we are aware.

Let these suffice as our examples of elemental principles: air in Anaximenes, Being in Parmenides, Love and Strife in Empedocles, the

One in Plotinus, Brahma in the Upanishads, Krishna in the Bhagavad
Gita, the Tao in Lao Tzu, custom and humanity in Hume, material points
and force laws in Laplace, elementary atoms in Dalton, atomic weight in
Mendeleev, energy in Helmholtz, the will to power in Nietzsche, the instincts
in Freud, Aphrodite and Artemis in Euripides, and perverseness in Poe.

3. Comprehensive Principles

It is possible to reject the arbitrary causation of creative principles not
only by going to the unchanging elements from which things arise, but
also by going to the unchanging principle that determines the form of the
whole. Functioning is then the result neither of an arbitrary creator nor of
the elements from which things arise, but of the design of the whole.
Whatever functions does so because it contributes to this design. The
design of the whole as a cause of functioning can be called a *comprehensive*
principle. A comprehensive principle that determines all things is a first
principle, and a comprehensive principle that determines a particular whole
but is itself determined as part of a larger whole is a principle but not a
first principle. Comprehensive principles are familiar in the view that ultimately everything works out for the best.

The first comprehensive principle to appear in the Western tradition
was the *apeiron*, or unlimited, of Anaximander. "And the source of coming-
to-be for existing things is that into which destruction, too, happens,
'according to necessity; for they pay penalty and retribution to each other
for their injustice according to the assessment of Time,' as he describes it
in these rather poetical terms."[62] Here a principle of justice or balance or
symmetry controls the sequence of becomings in time, the sequence of
the seasons, for example. The impossibility of understanding functioning
without understanding the whole is evident in Anaximander at many points:
The earth is at rest because the symmetry of the cosmos provides no
sufficient reason for its moving one way rather than another: "For it behoves
that which is established at the centre, and is equally related to the extremes,
not to be borne one whit more either up or down or to the sides; and it is
impossible for it to move simultaneously in opposite directions, so that it
stays fixed by necessity."[63] Similarly, the orbits of the stars are conceived
as complete material wholes, with breathing-holes where we see their light.
Anaximander's interest in the whole made him the first to draw a map of
the earth and sea, and he also constructed a celestial globe.[64] The cosmos
has its origin as an enclosed whole: "He says that that which is productive
from the eternal of hot and cold was separated off at the coming-to-be of
this world, and that a kind of sphere of flame from this was formed round

the air surrounding the earth, like bark round a tree."[65] Living creatures
have their origin in an analogous process: "the first living creatures were
born in moisture, enclosed in thorny barks.[66] The same way of thinking of
functioning as dependent on the whole leads him to suppose that man
must have been nurtured at the beginning by another animal: "In the
beginning man was born from creatures of a different kind; because other
creatures are soon self-supporting, but man alone needs prolonged nursing.
For this reason he would not have survived if this had been his original
form."[67]

Heraclitus' Logos is another comprehensive principle. His method is
agonistic, as we have already noted, the signification substrative ("Nature
loves to hide"[68]), and the perspective diaphanic ("Listening not to me but
to the Logos"[69]). The result is the revelation of a world in tension everywhere but everywhere governed by the hidden harmony of the Logos. The
comprehensive unity is evident in fragments such as "It is wise, listening
not to me but to the Logos, to agree that all things are one."[70] "The wise
is one, knowing the plan by which it steers all things through all."[71] "The
wise is one alone, unwilling and willing to be spoken of by the name of
Zeus."[72] The principle unites agonistic opposites in a paradoxical unity:
"They do not comprehend how a thing agrees at variance with itself; it is
an attunement turning back on itself, like that of the bow and the lyre."[73]
"The way up and down is one and the same."[74] "Cold warms up, warm
cools off, moist parches, dry dampens."[75] All things happen according to
this Logos, even the prevailing ignorance of it:

> Of the Logos which is as I describe it men always prove to be uncompre-
> hending, both before they have heard it and when once they have heard
> it. For although all things happen according to this Logos men are like
> people of no experience, even when they experience such words and
> deeds as I explain, when I distinguish each thing according to its constitu-
> tion and declare how it is.[76]

The comprehensive justice that orders the activity of things for
Anaximander and Heraclitus also appears in Herodotus and Aeschylus
and Plato, giving comprehensive principles a powerful representation in
Hellenic thought. The fullest philosophic development is in Plato. The
comprehensive nature of principles in Plato is clear enough, even though
they transcend our apprehension and we can only conjecture about them.
In the *Republic*, the idea of the good is said to be the cause not only of the
being known of the things that are known, but also of their being and

essence, just as the sun is not only the cause of the being seen of the things that are seen, but also of their generation, growth, and nourishment.[77] The virtue of wisdom relates this good to the state or individual, temperance insures its rule within the state or individual, courage prevents external interference, and justice is the functioning of the whole, each part doing its own work. The good determines a functioning that is at once justice and happiness.

In the *Timaeus*, the goodness of the creator is said to be the cause of the world of generation, and is responsible for its functioning as a living animal.

> Let me tell you then why the creator made this world of generation. He was good, and the good can never have any jealousy of anything. And being free from jealousy, he desired that all things should be as like himself as they could be. This is in the truest sense the origin of creation and of the world, as we shall do well in believing on the testimony of wise men. God desired that all things should be good and nothing bad, so far as this was attainable.[78]

Even if we are ignorant of the good, as we are, it can determine the activity of inquiry that proceeds toward it. Since it unifies all things, the partial unifications that we discover are, so to speak, glimpses of it. In the *Phaedo*, in the absence of a knowledge of the good, a second-best method seeks the highest and most inclusive hypothesis. Since a comprehensive principle orders all things, intimations of it can be found everywhere, and not only by reasoning. It may inspire poets and rhapsodes to function as poets and rhapsodes, and the fact that Ion functions only in relation to Homer, and falls asleep when other poets are discussed, indicates that his functioning is by inspiration rather than art. In the *Symposium* love is a messenger between ourselves and the divine, and through it our activity is determined by the divine. In the *Apology*, the authoritative voice of conventional religion, the Delphic oracle, causes Socrates to function in a way that might in turn put the state in motion. In the *Crito*, the laws of Athens speak with a divine voice that answers Crito's arguments for escape and causes Socrates to remain in prison. In general, each of the Platonic dialogues exhibits a different way in which the comprehensive principle of the good can be a cause of functioning.

A reinterpretation of the Christian tradition in terms of a Platonic rule of the good can be found in Leibniz. His *Discourse on Metaphysics* begins with an article, "Concerning the divine perfection and that God does everything in the most desirable way."[79] The second article argues against the dominant creationism of the Western tradition: "Against those who hold that there is in the works of God no goodness, or that the principles of goodness and beauty are arbitrary."[80] The contrast between the view that things are good because God made them and the view that God made them because they are good is the contrast between creative and comprehensive principles.

The third article is "Against those who think that God might have made things better than he has."[81] In the catch phrase associated with Leibniz, this is the best of all possible worlds. Leibniz summarizes his view in the *Monadology*:

> Now, as there is an infinity of possible universes in the ideas of God, and as only one of them can exist, there must be a sufficient reason for the choice of God which determines him to select one rather than another.
>
> And this reason can only be found in the *fitness*, or in the degrees of perfection, which these worlds contain, each possible world having a right to claim existence according to the measure of perfection which it possesses.
>
> And this is the cause for the existence of the Best; namely, that his wisdom makes it known to God, his goodness makes him chose it, and his power makes him produce it.[82]

If, like Voltaire in *Candide*, we do not perceive the goodness of things, it is because our view is not comprehensive enough—it is as if we were to judge a large painting from seeing only a small fragment of it.

The way in which a comprehensive principle determines the whole can be illustrated by the way the formula for a line determines all its points. Leibniz says, in arguing that it is not possible to conceive of events that are not regular,

> Let us suppose for example that some one jots down a quantity of points upon a sheet of paper helter skelter, as do those who exercise the ridiculous art of Geomancy; now I say that it is possible to find a geometrical line whose concept shall be uniform and constant, that is, in accordance with a certain formula, and which line at the same time shall pass through all of those points, and in the same order in which the hand jotted them down; also if a continuous line be traced, which is now straight, now circular, and now of any other description, it is possible to find a mental equivalent, a formula or an equation common to all the points of this line by virtue of which formula the changes in the direction of the line must occur.[83]

In a similar way, the concept of an individual substance includes all its properties: "We have said that the concept of an indiviual substance includes once for all everything which can ever happen to it and that in considering this concept one will be able to see everything which can truly be said concerning the individual, just as we are able to see in the nature of a circle all the properties which can be derived from it."[84] The essence of bodies does not consist in extension, however, and is not mathematical. Their essence is rather an internal principle of activity, a substantial form or entelechy:

> The name of *entelechies* might be given to all simple substances or created monads, for they have within themselves a certain perfection (*echousi to enteles*); there is a certain sufficiency (*autarcheia*) which makes them the sources of their internal activities, and so to speak, incorporeal automata.[85]

Leibniz is here using an Aristotelian vocabulary, but the activity of the monad is the consequence of the comprehensive principle that makes it what it is. Thus each of the infinite simple substances in the world has its own comprehensive principle that determines its activity, and all together are determined by the one comprehensive principle of the good.

The leading non-Western exemplification of comprehensive principles is found in the Confucian tradition. This tradition traces its origins to a time long before Confucius himself, to the legendary emperors Yao and Shun. The greatness of their achievements, according to the *Analects*, was the result of their placing themselves in accord with Heaven:

> The Master said, "Great indeed was Yao as a sovereign! How majestic was he! It is only Heaven that is grand, and only Yao corresponded to it. How vast was his virtue! The people could find no name for it.
> "How majestic was he in the works which he accomplished! How glorious in the elegant regulations which he instituted!"[86]

> Confucius said, "To have taken no action and yet have the empire well governed, Shun was the man! What did he do? All he did was to make himself reverent and correctly face south."[87]

The fate of succeeding emperors and dynasties depended on their maintaining through reverence and virtue the accord with Heaven. "The Mandate of Heaven is not easily [preserved]. Heaven is hard to depend on. Those who have lost the mandate did so because they could not practice and carry on the reverence and the brilliant virtue of their forefathers."[88] The Mandate of Heaven passed from the Hsia dynasty to the Shang or Yin dynasty, and from the Yin to the Chou dynasty. The Duke of Chou says:

> We should not fail to mirror ourselves in the lords of Hsia; we likewise should not fail to mirror ourselves in the lords of Yin. We do not presume to know and say that the lords of Hsia undertook Heaven's mandate so as to have it for so-and-so many years; we do not presume to know and say that it could not have been prolonged. It was that they did not reverently attend to their virtue, and so they prematurely renounced their mandate. We do not presume to know and say that the lords of Yin received Heaven's mandate for so-and-so many years; we do not know and say that it could not have been prolonged. It was that they did not reverently attend to their virtue and so they prematurely threw away their mandate.[89]

The *Book of Odes* confirms the lesson of the *Book of History*:

> Always strive to be in harmony with Heaven's Mandate.
> Seek for yourselves the many blessings.
> Before Yin lost its army,
> Its kings were able to be counterparts to the Lord on High.
> In Yin you should see as in a mirror
> That the great mandate is not easy [to keep].[90]

The fate of empires thus depends upon the comprehensive principle of a cosmic moral order. Confucius continues this tradition and gives more definite content to the reverence and virtue that bring the ruler into accord with Heaven. He tells us that at fifty he knew the Mandate of Heaven,[91] and when at fifty-four an attempt was made to assassinate him, he could say, "Heaven produced the virtue that is in me; what can Huan T'ui do to me?"[92] Similarly, when at the age of fifty-six he was again in personal danger, he said,

> Since the death of King Wen, is not the course of culture (*wen*) in my keeping? If it had been the will of Heaven to destroy this culture, it would not have been given to a mortal [like me]. But if it is the will of Heaven that this culture should not perish, what can the people of K'uang do to me?[93]

The culture which Confucius received from Heaven orders human relationships by principles that determine the relationship as a whole rather than by selfish or partisan interests. This can be clearly seen with respect to the key moral terms of humanity (*ren*) and justice (*yi*). Confucius says, "If you set your mind on humanity, you will be free from evil."[94] "A man of humanity, wishing to establish his own character, also establishes the character of others, and wishing to be prominent himself, also helps others to be prominent. To be able to judge others by what is near to ourselves may be called the method of realizing humanity."[95] In judging others by what is near to oneself one must put oneself in the place of the other. Confucius is reported as saying,

> There are four things in the Way of the superior man, none of which I have been able to do. To serve my father as I would expect my son to serve me: that I have not been able to do. To serve my ruler as I would expect my ministers to serve me: that I have not been able to do. To serve my elder brothers as I would expect my younger brothers to serve me: that I have not been able to do. To be the first to treat friends as I would expect them to treat me: that I have not been able to do.[96]

The standard for a relationship can be reached through humanity, and as a standard it is justice. "A superior man in dealing with the world is not for anything or against anything. He follows justice as the standard."[97] "The superior man regards justice as the substance of everything. He practises it according to the principles of propriety. He brings it forth in modesty. And he carries it to its conclusion with faithfulness. He is indeed a superior man!"[98] Propriety provides for the characteristic determination of detail by its relation to the whole: "When his mat was not straight [Confucius] did not sit on it."[99]

In the Neo-Confucianism of Chu Hsi, all things are understood as composites of form (*li*) and matter (*qi*). "Each particular thing possesses a form, and the many kinds of form coalesce into the unity of form."[100] The Great Principle (*Tai-Ji*) is the principle of form: "When all the forms of heaven and earth and the myriad things are put together, that is the Great Principle."[101] This principle of form evidently resembles the Platonic form of the good.[102]

Kepler is an example of a scientist who sought explanations in comprehensive principles determining the form of the whole. The three things at rest in the universe, the sun, the stars, and the intermediate space, correspond respectively to the Father, the Son, and the Holy Spirit. In his first work, the forerunner of a cosmographic dissertation, Kepler attempted to account for the number of planets in the intermediate space and their respective distances from the sun by means of the five regular solids, one solid fitting into each of the five spaces between the six planetary bodies. The agreement with the observed distances was not exact and the order of the solids required special justification. The three laws of planetary motion for which Kepler is best known represent for Kepler partial orderings along the way to the comprehensive harmony of the whole system. The law of areas, in accordance with which a line from the sun to the planet sweeps out equal areas in equal times, was supposed by Kepler to be a consequence of the sun's moving the planets around their orbits with a force acting in the plane of the orbit at right angles to the radius from the sun and varying inversely as the distance from the sun. The elliptical shape of the planetary orbits, with the sun at one focus, is a comprehensive principle by which all points on the orbit are determined, and, with the law of areas, the relative speeds of the planet at all points of its orbit are also determined. The relative velocities of the different planets are determined by the harmonic law, that the squares of the times required by the planets to complete their revolution around the sun are proportional to the cubes of their mean distance from the sun. It remains to account for the eccentricities of the orbits, and Kepler did this by seeking an harmonic ratio between the maximum angular velocity of a planet about the sun, when it is nearest the sun, and its minimum angular velocity, when it is farthest from the sun, and seeking further harmonic ratios between the fastest and slowest angular velocities of all the different planets. The music that they play together, the harmony of the world, is the true comprehensive principle of the system, and Kepler used it to correct the planetary distances determined approximately by the five regular solids. It should be noted that in this system of the world nothing is arbitrary, that a reason can in principle be given for everything, as Plato and Leibniz require. Newton's system of the world, on the other hand, left the initial conditions determining the number of planets, their distance from the sun, and the eccentricity and orientation of their orbits, outside of his science and dependent on the will of the creator. The science that Kepler was seeking was a much stronger one than Newton's. Laplace, as we have seen, eliminates the arbitrary will of God from Newton's system, and in one sense makes everything determinate, but from Kepler's point of view at the price of leaving everything without a reason.

Einstein returned to Kepler's search for the divine in an order of the world free of arbitrariness, and his scientific career parallels that of Kepler in its splendid partial successes on the way toward an end which proved elusive. In Einstein, comprehensiveness appears in the endeavor to attain the greatest possible logical unification (*Einheitlichkeit*) of the foundations of science, i.e., the greatest possible reduction of the independent concepts which form the axiomatic foundation of a theory. The special theory of relativity removes the incoherence between classical mechanics and the theory of electricity and magnetism by making the velocity of light the same in all frames of reference for which the law of inertia holds, even though they may be moving relatively to one another; the general theory of relativity removes the incoherence between mechanics and the theory of gravitation by accounting for the equivalence between the effects of a uniform gravitational field and a uniform acceleration of one's frame of reference; the field theory that Einstein sought in his later years would remove the incoherence between fields and material particles by exhibiting material particles as solutions of the field equations.

The existence of a comprehensive order which eludes our grasp has also been apprehended poetically. Walt Whitman writes, "While I cannot understand it or argue it out, I fully believe in a clue and purpose in Nature, entire and several."[103] Each individual thing is therefore perfect, as it should be: I believe a leaf of grass is no less than the journey-work of the stars."[104] Anything is but a part, however,[105] and the meaning of the whole emerges from all the parts taken together. Hence the many enumerations in his poems. We have already noted the personal perspective in Whitman, and out of all that he encounters Whitman weaves the song of himself. "To me the converging objects of the universe perpetually flow, All are written to me, and I must get what the writing means."[106] The principle is not present in the whole as a part, however, but emerges from the whole: "Do you see O my brothers and sisters? It is not chaos or death—it is form, union, plan—it is eternal life—it is Happiness."[107] Whitman's true songs are not in his songs, but rise above them:

> Thy very songs not in thy songs,
> No special strains to sing, none for itself,
> But from the whole resulting, rising at last and floating,
> A round full-orb'd eidólon.[108]

Because the ultimate principle always transcends what one already encompasses, one must always explore further:

O my brave soul!
O farther farther sail!
O daring joy, but safe! are they not all the seas of God?
O farther, farther, farther sail![109]

Tolstoy has a similar incomprehensible comprehensive principle, determining each part but by its nature eluding our grasp: "As the sun and
each atom of ether is a sphere complete in itself, and yet at the same time
only a part of a whole too immense for man to comprehend, so each
individual has within himself his own aims and yet has them to serve a
general purpose incomprehensible to man."[110] Tolstoy presents in *War
and Peace* a comprehensive series of events, a movement and counter-
movement that recalls Anaximander's statement that things pay penalty
and retribution to each other for their injustice according to the assessment of Time:

> In 1789 a ferment arises in Paris; it grows, spreads, and is expressed
> by a movement of peoples from west to east. Several times it moves
> eastward and collides with a countermovement from the east westward.
> In 1812 it reaches its extreme limit, Moscow, and then, with remarka-
> ble symmetry, a countermovement occurs from east to west, attracting
> to it, as the first movement had done, the nations of middle Europe.
> The countermovement reaches the starting point of the first move-
> ment in the west—Paris—and subsides.[111]

The movement and counter-movement are not explained by power or intellectual activity, but only as the activity of all the people who participate:
"The movement of nations is caused not by power, nor by intellectual
activity, nor even by a combination of the two as historians have supposed,
but by the activity of *all* the people who participate in the events."[112]
These people all follow their own purposes, but in so doing they serve
more general purposes of which they are not aware. It is necessary, says
Tolstoy in concluding his work, "to renounce a freedom that does not
exist, and to recognize a dependence of which we are not conscious."[113]
All of Tolstoy's archic elements can be seen in this conclusion: his work
is a revelation of a substrative necessity ordered to a transcendent end.

All these authors, then, have endeavored to apprehend the comprehensive principle that governs all things but always remains beyond our
knowledge: Anaximander, Heraclitus, Herodotus, Aeschylus, Plato, Leibniz,
Confucius, Chu Hsi, Kepler, Einstein, Whitman, and Tolstoy.

4. Reflexive Principles

If one denies that functioning is caused either by an arbitrary creator or by the functioning thing itself either in its elements or in its design, does any alternative remain? All of the causes of functioning so far considered account for functioning as a result of something other than the functioning itself. The remaining possibility is that it is functioning that causes functioning. This view alone makes functioning a principle and a cause, and a cause of itself. Functionings that cause functionings can be called *reflexive* principles. If a reflexive principle is an absolutely self-sufficient or independent functioning, then it is a first principle. If it depends for its functioning on other functionings, then it is a principle but not a first principle. Reflexive principles are familiar in the views that make activities ends in themselves—knowledge for its own sake, virtue its own reward, and art for art's sake.

Reflexive principles differ from creative principles because they do not determine consequences arbitrarily, but in accordance with what they themselves already are. They differ from elemental principles because they are functionings or activities rather than that out of which these functionings or activities emerge. They differ from comprehensive principles because things are complete when they function rather than function when they are complete. A creative first principle creates all things but is not itself created; an elemental first principle gives rise to all things out of itself but nothing gives rise to it; a comprehensive first principle orders all things but is not itself ordered; a reflexive first principle is a functioning or activity that causes all other functionings and activities but is not itself caused by anything else.

It is remarkable that all four kinds of principle appear in the great initial phase of Hellenic thought in Ionia in the 6th century B.C. Thales' water is a creative cause of activity, Anaximander's *apeiron* or unlimited is a comprehensive cause of activity, Anaximenes' air is an elemental cause of activity, and, finally, Xenophanes' mind is a reflexive cause of activity. Mind is a reflexive cause of activity when its own activity or functioning, thought, is self-determining and the cause of the activity or functioning of other things. The activity of the mind of Xenophanes' god is an effortless intellectual activity by which all things are moved: "Always he remains in the same place, moving not at all; nor is it fitting for him to go to different places at different times, but without toil he shakes all things by the thought of his mind."[114] The activity of material things is reflexively self-determining when it is cyclic, and Xenophanes notes the cycle by which water is drawn up from the sea and returns to it again, and also a cyclic process by which the earth rises from the sea and sinks into it again:

> Xenophanes thinks that a mixture of the earth with the sea is going
> on, and that in time the earth is dissolved by the moist. He says that he
> has demonstrations of the following kind: shells are found inland, and
> in the mountains, and in the quarries in Syracuse he says that an impres-
> sion of a fish and of seaweed has been found, while an impression of a
> bay-leaf was found in Paros in the depth of the rock, and in Malta flat
> shapes of all marine objects. These, he says, were produced when every-
> thing was long ago covered with mud, and the impression was dried in
> the mud. All mankind is destroyed whenever the earth is carried down
> into the sea and becomes mud; then there is another beginning of
> coming-to-be, and this foundation happens for all the worlds.[115]

The human mind is also a reflexive principle, controlling itself and its
body. The autonomy of mind in controlling its thoughts and its body
provides a principle for determining how much to drink:

> There is nothing wrong in drinking as much as a man can hold with-
> out having to be taken home by a servant, unless of course he is very
> old. The man to be praised is he who, after drinking, can still express
> thoughts that are noble and well-arranged. But let him not repeat those
> old hackneyed tales of Titans or Giants or Centaurs, nor those of vio-
> lent civil broils; there is nothing to be gained from all that.[116]

There are other ways besides drunkenness in which the mind can abandon
its autonomy, as when the Greeks of Xenophanes' native Colophon imi-
tated the Lydians: "having learned useless kinds of luxury from the Lydians,
as long as they were free from the tyrant's yoke they used to stroll into the
marketplace, perhaps a thousand of them, boastful, overdressed in purple
garments, anointed with rare perfumes, making a show of their hairdresser's
art."[117]

Anaxagoras is known for his doctrine of the rule of self-ruling mind.
Mind rules all things that have soul, both the greater, the cosmos, and the
lesser, living things within the cosmos:

> All other things have a portion of everything, but Mind is infinite and
> self-ruled (autokrates), and is mixed with nothing but is all alone by
> itself. For if it was not by itself, but was mixed with anything else, it
> would have a share of all things if it were mixed with any; for in
> everything there is a portion of everything, as I said earlier; and the

things that were mingled with it would hinder it so that it could control nothing in the same way as it does now being alone by itself. For it is the finest of all things and the purest, it has all knowledge about everything and the greatest power; and mind controls (*kratei*) all things, both the greater and the smaller, that have life.[118]

The primacy of the activity of thinking reaches its fullest development in the Hellenic period in the philosophy of Aristotle. All of Aristotle's sciences represent the activity of thought, and the functioning of each is governed by reflexive principles. The principle of first philosophy is thought thinking itself. Because thought thinks itself, its activity or functioning is self-caused. If the content of thought were other than the activity of thinking itself, then the principle would lie outside the activity and in that content—in, say, the creation of things, or their elements, or their order—and the principle would not be reflexive. The whole of first philosophy is thought thinking itself. The opening sentence, "All men by nature desire to know," indicates the way in which this principle moves us toward itself, and the initial definition is the science's definition of itself, of wisdom. Wisdom throughout is investigating what it itself is. At the beginning the wisdom is human wisdom, but at the end we see that the principle that has been determining our wisdom from the beginning is the divine principle of thought thinking itself. Metaphysics is in this sense an itinerary of the mind to god, but one that depends on the progressive recognition through reflection of the principle of divine activity that was present in metaphysical thought from the beginning.

The principles of physics, or natural science, are natures, and natures are internal principles of motion or rest. These are reflexive in the sense that the principle initiating the motion actualizes itself through the motion, like a doctor doctoring himself:

For those things are natural which, by a continuous movement originated from an internal principle, arrive at some completion: the same completion is not reached from every principle; nor any chance completion, but always the tendency in each is towards the same end, if there is no impediment. . . . It is absurd to suppose that purpose is not present because we do not observe the agent deliberating. Art does not deliberate. If the shipbuilding art were in the wood, it would produce the same results by nature. If, therefore, purpose is present in art, it is present also in nature. The best illustration is a doctor doctoring himself: nature is like that.[119]

This is a linear process with a beginning and an end, but such linear processes can be repeated and persist only if they are incorporated in some cyclic process. Imperishable things are moved by the prime mover in a cyclical motion without beginning or end. This eternal cyclic motion in turn determines eternal cycles of becoming. The elements are transformed into one another, and there are multiple meteorological cycles of the kind we have seen in Xenophanes. Living things not only move to realize their own ends, but their individual life cycles depend on the cycle of reproduction by which the species is preserved, and this in turn depends upon other biological cycles and upon the cycles of the elements and of the environment, and these ultimately upon the cosmic cycles and the prime mover.

In living things that are rational various kinds of self-determination through reason, corresponding to the various disciplinary interests, become possible. The theoretical sciences, such as first philosophy and physics, realize a theoretical interest, and the practical sciences a practical interest. The principle of ethics is happiness, which is activity in accordance with virtue. The whole of the *Ethics* is the thought through which happiness actualizes itself, although of course it is not actualized until the thought becomes effective in determining our actions. And it is real happiness, not simply the thought of happiness, that actualizes itself through ethics, for one knows the goodness of the good only through experiencing it, and so for it to become effective in one's action one must in a sense already have experienced it; that is, one must have been brought up in good habits. For the actualization of happiness is a reflexive process by which our character determines our apprehension of what is good, this influences how we act, and our actions in turn affect our character.

In the *Poetics*, the principle is the art form, and in particular the definition of tragedy. This is actualized through the work of the poet, but the end here is not in the making but in the thing made, and the work is made as a self-actualizing whole. Each art form has its own power, and in the case of tragedy it is the power to achieve through pity and fear the catharsis of such emotions. Aristotle first treats the plot as a self-determining whole, and then the emotions proper to the art form as qualifying the plot. Feeling or emotion is here an end-in-itself, and is a reflexive principle in the sense that it selects and orders the means by which it is realized. The opening chords of a Verdi opera, analogous to the opening sentences of the *Metaphysics*, are determined by the emotions that are to be actualized in the opera.

In the *Rhetoric*, the principle is the power of observing in any given case the available means of persuasion. Just as the tragic effect actualizes itself in the tragedy, so persuasion actualizes itself in the speech. The speech is a process by which the hearer, beginning from his own convictions as to what is advantageous, noble, or just, guided by a speaker whom he believes will lead him where he wants to go, as well as by his own feelings and character, uses his own mind to reach his own decision. The mind in the rhetorical speech does not think itself, as in metaphysics, but creates itself from what it already is and in accordance with the forms of creativity.

In the Hellenistic period, reflexive principles were continued in the sciences of the Stoics. In logic, the criterion of truth was the apprehensive presentation, or *kataleptic phantasia*, and this was the criterion of itself as well as of other things:

> It is not absurd to consider a thing as its own criterion. For the straight line is capable of testing both itself and other lines, and the balance measures the equality of other things and of itself as well, and light reveals not only other objects but itself also. Thus the criterion can be established as a criterion of itself and of other things too.[120]

The Stoic reality was material, so in physics the ruling mind containing the reasons of all things was identified with fire, and the universe itself was subject to periodic conflagrations: "The whole world, at certain fated periods, is dissolved by fire, and then formed again into a world. Now the primary fire is like a kind of seed, containing the reasons of all things and the causes of everything, past, present, and future."[121] There is similarly in the individual soul a highest and ruling part, the hegemonic part. The method is dialectical, and so in ethics the ruling part of the soul assimilates itself to the rationality of the universe:

> The end may be defined as life in accordance with nature, or, in other words, in accordance with our own human nature as well as that of the universe, a life in which we refrain from every action forbidden by the law common to all things, i.e., the right reason which pervades all things, and is identical with this Zeus, lord and ruler of all that is. And this very thing constitutes the virtue of the happy man and the smooth current of life, when all actions promote the harmony of the spirit dwelling in the individual man with the will of him who orders the universe.[122]

The texts of Aristotle were largely unknown to the Christian tradition until their translation into Latin in the 12th and 13th centuries. We have already noted that the dominant Christian orthodoxy followed St. Augustine in using creative principles, but that the subordinate neo-Platonic strain deriving from Plotinus and represented by Dionysius the Aeropagite, John Scotus Eriugena, and others, interpreted Christianity in terms of elemental principles, while the possibility of an interpretation in terms of comprehensive principles is represented by Leibniz. The remaining alternative, an interpretation in terms of reflexive principles, was carried through by St. Thomas Aquinas. From Aristotle he derived the doctrine that "nothing can be reduced from potentiality to actuality, except by something in a state of actuality."[123] This is equivalent to our statement that it is functioning that causes functioning. By treating existence itself as an act, St. Thomas made all existence depend upon a God whose nature is his act of existing, and thus the creation described in Genesis becomes the work of a reflexive principle.

> Everything, then, which is such that its act of existing is other than its nature must needs have its act of existing from something else. And since every being which exists through another is reduced, as to its first cause, to one existing in virtue of itself, there must be some being which is the cause of the existing of all things because it itself is the act of existing alone.[124]

This re-interpretation by St. Thomas was of decisive importance for later thought. Descartes studied in the Jesuit college at La Flèche, and sought to establish a firm and permanent structure in the sciences by beginning from a personal rather than a divine reflexivity: "I think, therefore I am." Thought thinking itself here recognizes existence as implicated in its activity. Descartes in the *Meditations* establishes the foundations of the sciences in the knowledge of three reflexively self-determining substances. The first is the thinking self, recognizing its existence in the Second Meditation, determining its own cognitive content throughout the *Meditations*, and explicitly aware of itself as so doing in the Fourth Meditation. The second substance is God, encountered by the self as existing in the Third Meditation, and known in His own reflexive self-determination in the Fifth. The third kind of substance is extended, treated as reflexively determining its own properties at the beginning of the Fifth Meditation, and as encountered by us in its existence in the Sixth Meditation.

Spinoza adopts the reflexive principles of Descartes, but, as we saw earlier, shifts from a personal to an objective perspective, and therefore finds reflexive beginnings for existence, knowledge, and action. The first definition of Spinoza's *Ethics* states the reflexive principle from which all existence proceeds: "By cause of itself I understand that whose essence involves existence, or that whose nature cannot be conceived unless existing."[125] This cause of itself is identified with substance as that which is in itself and is conceived through itself, and God as substance consisting of infinite attributes is the only substance and the only *causa sui*. Thus whatever is, is in God, and nothing can either be or be conceived without God.[126] Knowledge as well as being begins from reflexive principles, for it begins from adequate ideas that determine their own consequences, like the ideas of the thinking self or of god or of extended things in Descartes. "By adequate idea I understand an idea which, in so far as it is considered in itself, without reference to the object, has all the properties or internal signs of a true idea."[127] The adequate idea is, like the Stoic apprehensive presentation, its own criterion of truth:

> For no one who has a true idea is ignorant that a true idea involves the highest certitude; to have a true idea signifying just this—to know a thing perfectly or as well as possible. No one, in fact, can doubt this unless he supposes an idea to be something dumb, like a picture on a tablet instead of being a mode of thought, that is to say, intelligence itself. Moreover, I ask who can know that he understands a thing unless he first of all understands that thing? That is to say, who can know that he is certain of anything unless he is first of all certain of that thing? Then, again, what can be clearer or more certain than a true idea as the standard of truth? Just as light reveals both itself and the darkness, so truth is the standard of itself and of the false.[128]

Not only being and knowledge, but also action, begins from reflexive principles. For we desire to further our own being, and we further our own being so far as we are self-determining or free. And we are self-determining or free so far as our action follows from ideas that are adequate in us, for these as we have said are self-determining. "Our mind acts at times and at times suffers: in so far as it has adequate ideas, it necessarily acts; and in so far as it has inadequate ideas, it necessarily suffers."[129] Further, we necessarily rejoice insofar as we act, for action furthers our own being. And since God is the cause of the adequate ideas which cause our action and rejoicing, these are accompanied by an intellectual love of God, which is, however, the very love with which God loves himself.[130] The *Ethics* as a whole thus traces out a line of causation that passes through the individual and returns to God, a line of causation which constitutes our blessedness and salvation, and is one of the infinite ways in which God is a cause of himself.

Kant continues the tradition of reflexive principles, but in a disciplinary perspective, and the functioning of each of his three critiques depends upon a reflexive principle. The highest principle in the sphere of knowledge is the original synthetic unity of apperception by which different intuitions are united in one consciousness. Through this principle the knowing mind determines itself, for the categories of the understanding correspond to the conditions of such unification. This principle is analogous to thought thinking itself in Aristotle. In the practical sphere, the moral law formulates the condition for the self-determination by reason of action. This is analogous to the self-determination of happiness in Aristotle. And the principle of purposiveness in the *Critique of Judgment* is a principle by which objects are judged as purposive for us or for themselves, corresponding to the self-determining principles of art and nature in Aristotle.

Hegel, finally, retains the reflexive principles of Kant but shifts to a diaphanic perspective that unites the separate sciences in absolute knowledge. The epigraph to Hegel's *Phenomenology of Spirit* consists of two quotations from Aristotle's *Metaphysics*. The first identifies the process toward a principle that is common to both works: "It is our task to start from what is more knowable to oneself and make what is knowable by nature knowable to oneself."[131] The second identifies the principle towards which both works proceed: "Its thinking is a thinking on thinking."[132] The reflexive self-actualization of mind characterizes both works. The Preface to the *Phenomenology* presents this self-actualization as follows:

> What has just been said can also be expressed by saying that Reason is *purposive activity*. The exaltation of a supposed Nature over a misconceived thinking, and especially the rejection of external teleology, has brought the form of purpose in general into discredit. Still, in the sense in which Aristotle, too, defines Nature as purposive activity, purpose is what is immediate and *at rest*, the unmoved which is also *self-moving*, and as such is Subject. Its power to move, taken abstractly, is *being-for-self* or pure negativity. The result is the same as the beginning, only because the *beginning* is the *purpose*; in other words, the actual is the same as its Notion only because the immediate, as purpose, contains the self or pure actuality within itself.[133]

We may add a note on John Stuart Mill, who exhibits the influence of reflexive principles on the British empirical tradition. Mill's archic profile is the same as Hume's, except that he substitutes reflexive principles for Hume's elemental principles. He represents in this respect a synthesis of Hume and Kant. Knowledge of cause and effect does not depend for Mill on the elemental principle of habit, but on the reflexive principle of the uniformity of nature, by which all past uniformities are brought to bear on our knowledge of the future. Similarly, Mill substitutes for Hume's elemental principle of sympathy the reflexive principle of utility, by which our past experience of goods and bads is brought to bear on future action.

The philosophers who have used reflexive principles constitute a formidable tradition: Xenophanes, Anaxagoras, Aristotle, the Stoics, Aquinas, Descartes, Spinoza, Kant, Hegel, and Mill, and we may also add Husserl with his transcendental ego. This so-called rationalist tradition originated in the Hellenic period, was represented by the Stoics in the Hellenistic period, was used by St. Thomas in the Medieval period to challenge the prevailing orthodoxy of creative principles stemming from Genesis, and in the modern period became the dominant tradition on the Continent.

Let us now turn to one or two examples of reflexive principles in science and literature.

The development of the science of electricity and magnetism in the 19th century took place in the context of a contrast between elemental and reflexive principles. This was a reincarnation of the ancient contrast between the particle physics of Democritus and the field physics of Aristotle. Aristotle explained both inertial and gravitational motion as a consequence of the action of the field upon bodies, but Newton treated both as consequences of powers belonging to bodies taken in isolation. Inertia for Newton is an innate force belonging to all bodies and proportional to their quantity of matter, and gravity is a power of impressing a force on other bodies that also belongs to all bodies and is also proportional to their quantity of matter. The Newtonian model was followed in the early development of the science of electricity by Coulomb, Weber, and others, but Faraday develops an alternative possibility at every point. He never conceives forces as belonging to isolated bodies but always thinks of them as closed systems of action. Thus Faraday does not think of magnetic poles as centers of force, and prefers not to use the word "pole" at all, but treats polarity as a difference of direction along the closed lines of force that constitute a magnetic field. Similarly, electric charges are not isolated centers of force, but are always connected to equal and opposite charges by electrical lines of force. Electric currents for Faraday are never open in the sense of having a beginning and end, but are always closed upon themselves like the lines of magnetic force. Even a charge moved from one point to another in empty space is for Faraday a part of a closed current.[134] Instead of atomic weights belonging to the atoms of different elements taken in isolation, Faraday uses electrochemical equivalents, which are the relative weights of the different elements that would be liberated in electrolysis by the same quantity of electricity. The series of electrochemical equivalents is thus analogous to a closed line of force. The different kinds of force may also be transformable into one another in accordance with definite equivalents in a closed system. Faraday himself discovered the action of magnetism in inducing electric currents, the definite chemical action of electricity, and the action of magnetism on light. He sought in vain for an experimental connection between electricity and gravity. Faraday's interlocking cycles of force are the closest approximation in modern physics to the interlocking cycles of Aristotle's physics, but it is remarkable that Faraday seems to have been influenced by no previous user of reflexive principles. Influences are perhaps easier to discern in the adoption of principles than in the adoption of the other archic variables, yet, as the example of Faraday indicates, the archic elements are always essential possibilities for thought, quite apart from any question of influences.

Maxwell gave mathematical form to Faraday's principles of electricity and magnetism. The electric field arises from electric charges and from changes in the magnetic field, and the magnetic field arises from the motion of electric charges and from changes in the electric field. The term in Maxwell's equations giving the contribution to the magnetic field of changes in the electric field corresponds to Faraday's view that all currents are closed. The reciprocal determination of changes in the electric and magnetic fields by each other gives rise to the possibility of a self-sustaining process of electromagnetic radiation. Light, as understood in terms of Maxwell's equations, is a self-determining activity.

Chaucer's *Canterbury Tales* provides a literary example of reflexive principles. The telling of the tales is an end in itself, the self-enjoyment by the pilgrims of their own actuality. And each of the pilgrims actualizes himself through the story he tells for the entertainment of the others.

Perhaps I may be permitted here a more detailed account of one of the *Canterbury Tales*, the Manciple's Tale, since it has never, so far as I know, been understood or interpreted correctly, and yet, once the reflexivity of the tale is recognized, its many puzzles and difficulties are easily resolved. The Manciple's tale is a retelling of the old story of how the crow lost its white plumage and beautiful voice by informing Apollo of his wife's infidelity. The Manciple's version, however, appears artistically inferior to the prototype in Ovid and to the other versions. It portrays Phoebus as a model of perfection who, upon hearing the crow's report, first rashly murders his wife, and then, reversing himself, irrationally ignores the evidence the crow has presented, accuses the crow of falsehood, and punishes it by depriving it of feathers, song, and speech, and slinging it out the door. So there is first of all the problem of why the Manciple has modified the tale by making the punishment of the crow patently unjust, as well as by giving it a domestic setting, omitting any reference to an unborn child, and dwelling on the terrible details of the punishment, which are in fact repeated twice over, since Phoebus first says what he is going to do, and then does it. The behavior of the Manciple himself in the Prologue to his tale is also puzzling, for it seems to lack adequate motivation. He first excoriates the Cook unmercifully for his drunkenness, and then, after a word of caution from the Host, he goes to the other extreme of pandering to the Cook's vice by offering him a drink of the excellent wine he carries in his gourd.

Further, the Manciple accompanies his tale with a series of glosses of his own to the effect that people are animals enslaved to their lusts, and these glosses give rise to further difficulties. For, first, there seems to be no reason why the Manciple should take such a dim view of human nature. Further, the Manciple repeats the pattern of the Prologue several times by saying something and then immediately taking it back or denying what he has said. In explaining why Phoebus' wife prefers her worthless paramour to her divine husband, he cites the predominance of natural appetites in the bird, the cat, and the she-wolf, and then immediately denies their obvious application, saying they apply only to men, not to women:

> Alle thise enasamples speke I by thise men
> That been untrewe, and nothyng by wommen.[135]

He also seems unable to cite a text without claiming to be "noght textueel." Further, the Manciple's glosses are inconsistent with his tale, for in the tale the crow is fostered in a cage, and part of his punishment is to be slung out the door, and yet the Manciple tells us in his gloss that any bird fostered in a cage would prefer to live in a forest that is rude and cold.

Finally, and most egregious of all, the Manciple concludes his tale by telling us that he learned it from his mother, and proceeds to go on for forty-five lines tediously repeating his mother's morals about holding one's tongue, as if he had no sense of the applicability of what he was saying to himself. And yet Chaucer has told us in the General Prologue that the author of this demented performance was one of the shrewdest men in England:

> Now is nat that of God a ful fair grace
> That swich a lewed mannes wit shal pace
> The wisdom of an heep of lerned men?[136]

There were more than thirty lawyers in the Manciple's temple, a dozen of them worthy to manage the estate of any lord in England,

And yet this Manciple sette hir aller cappe.[137]

What are we to make of this puzzling Manciple, who conceals his knowledge and wit behind a facade of ignorance and stupidity, gives way to apparently unmotivated accusations and retractions, tells a defective and immoral tale, makes people into animals, continually unsays what he has said, and finally says too much about not saying too much? All the puzzles of the Manciple can be resolved if we suppose that in telling us the story of the crow the Manciple has told us the story of himself, that he himself is the truth-telling crow. He is then the witness to his mother's infidelity, and threatened by her, through the tale of the crow modified to suit her own purposes, with terrible punishment should he tell his father. The Manciple remains dominated by the need to expose for all to see the vices of others, and by the fear of what will happen to him if he does so. His jaundiced view of human nature, as well as his choice of profession, also have their origin in that early lesson learned at his mother's bedside: in a world of animals it is best to be the one who controls the food and drink. The telling of the tale, it should be added, is the Manciple's own action; he is not asked to do so by the Host, who in fact asked the Cook. And at the end of the tale there are for once no apologies and no taking back of what has been said: he has fulfilled his destiny: by telling the story of the truth-telling crow, the Manciple has actualized himself as the truth-telling crow.

No detailed analysis is required to show the presence of reflexive principles in the writings of James Joyce; they are suggested even by the titles of his works. Perhaps both he and Descartes were influenced in their adoption of reflexive principles by their Jesuit education, which connected them with the tradition of Aquinas and Aristotle. In the *Portrait of the Artist as a Young Man*, art is the cause of itself in the sense that the art of the artist produces its own genesis. Nothing can be reduced from potentiality to actuality except by something in a state of actuality. In *Ulysses* art is the cause of itself in the sense that the art of the *Odyssey* produces its own re-enactment in a Dublin day. In *Finnegans Wake* art is the cause of itself in the sense that the end of the work joins the beginning to produce a wholemole millwheeling vicociclometer.

Let these suffice as our examples of authors who have used reflexive principles: Xenophanes, Anaxagoras, Aristotle, the Stoics, Saint Thomas,

Descartes, Spinoza, Kant, Hegel, Faraday and Maxwell, Chaucer, and James Joyce.

Our four kinds of principles, then, are creative, elemental, comprehensive, and reflexive. If they are grouped in pairs, the following features emerge: (1) Creative and elemental principles cause functioning by virtue of their potentiality, an indeterminate potentiality in the one case and a determinate potentiality in the other. Comprehensive and reflexive principles, on the other hand, cause functioning by virtue of their actuality, the actuality of the totality of things in the one case and of functioning in the other. (2) Creative and comprehensive principles transcend what is given, going beyond it either because the functioning they cause is without limit or because the functioning of all things transcends any given thing. Elemental and reflexive principles, on the other hand, are immanent in what is given, either as that from which the functioning emerges or as the functioning itself. (3) Creative and reflexive principles are different for different things, and are either indeterminate or determinate in the kind of functioning they can cause. Elemental and comprehensive principles, on the other hand, are ultimately the same for all things, either because all things are the same in their being or because all things are differentiated parts of a single whole.

It remains to consider whether the different kinds of principle are reciprocally prior to one another.

Creative principles include all other principles as their own creations, as coming into existence in time. Even though other principles may claim to be eternal, they are principles for us only as they appear in history. The predominant way of understanding principles in the West is as coming into being in particular historical situations, as then perhaps continuing through a series of "influences," and thus becoming ingredient in the progress of history toward a future that becomes determinate only as actualized in time.

Elemental principles include all other principles as emerging out of themselves. "Supporter of beings, and not resting in beings, Is My Self, that causes beings to be."[138] In the Indian tradition, the dates and authorships and influences that are so important to Western scholarship cease to be essential; for the Mimamsa school, for example, the Veda is valid precisely because it has no author: "If the Veda be eternal its denotation cannot but be eternal; and if it be non-eternal, then it can have no validity."[139]

Comprehensive principles include all other principles within themselves, for otherwise they would not be comprehensive. The Confucian tradition continually reviews the old so as to find the new,[140] and Leibniz found most of the sects right in a good part of what they propose, if not in what they deny.[141] Leibniz says,

> Our age has already saved from contempt the corpuscles of Democritus, the ideas of Plato, and the tranquillity of the Stoics which arises from the best possible connection of things; now we shall reduce the Peripatetic tradition of forms or entelechies, which has rightly seemed enigmatic and scarcely understood by its authors themselves, to intelligible concepts. Thus we believe that this philosophy, accepted for so many centuries, must not be discarded but be explained in a way that makes it consistent within itself (where this is possible) and clarifies and amplifies it with new truths.[142]

Reflexive principles include all others insofar as they function, for the functioning of any principle can always be treated as an end for which the principle is required, and the principle as actualizing itself in the functioning. The whole to which the principle belongs is then a self-actualizing whole. Hegel, for example, treats all philosophies as self-actualizing components of the self-actualization of spirit. And we have similarly treated all the kinds of principles as principles by which texts actualize themselves.

We have now reached the result that the values of each of the four archic variables are reciprocally prior to one another. This means that every archic profile specifies a potentially adequate philosophy if any archic profile does so, a philosophy able to include within itself architectonically all the other philosophies and their results. An architectonic art is one that orders subordinate arts to the attainment of an end; architectonic, according to Kant, is the art of system.[143] The discovery of the principles of pluralism is thus the discovery of an architectonic of architectonics, in which each philosophy subordinates all the others to the end of its own self-actualization, and yet all are components of a single architectonic of self-actualization.

This result deserves to be emphasized. It means that the diverse philosophic traditions of the world, and all the diverse philosophies that each of them contains, have become, in fact and not merely in idea, components of a single philosophic science. This science, far from subordinating these multiple traditions and philosophies to a single point of view, rather enhances each of them by making it architectonic with respect to the entire worldwide or universal tradition. We have here a community analogous to Kant's kingdom of ends, a universal republic of philosophers in which every philosopher is at once member and sovereign.

In conclusion, the present architectonics of meaning may be related to its predecessors in ontic and epistemic epochs. Aristotle's *Metaphysics* is an architectonics of being. Being is self-determining in substances, and substances are self-determining through their principles and causes. The *Metaphysics* seeks the principles and causes through which all substances are self-determining, each in its own way. Kant's *Critique of Pure Reason* is an architectonics of knowing. Knowing is self-determining in sciences, and sciences are self-determining through their a priori elements. The *Critique* seeks the a priori elements through which all sciences are self-determining, each in its own way. The present work is an architectonics of meaning. Meaning is self-determining in texts, and texts are self-determining through their archic elements. This work seeks the archic elements through which all texts are self-determining, each in its own way.

VI. Archic Analysis

1. The Archic Matrix

Archic Variables

Pure Modes	PERSPECTIVE	REALITY	METHOD	PRINCIPLE
SOPHISTIC	Personal	Existential	Agonistic	Creative
DEMOCRITEAN	Objective	Substrative	Logistic	Elemental
PLATONIC	Diaphanic	Noumenal	Dialectic	Comprehensive
ARISTOTELIAN	Disciplinary	Essential	Problematic	Reflexive

The archic variables and their possible values are recapitulated in the above table. It is a matrix of possible starting points for the constitution of meaning, and will be called the *archic matrix*. Each element of the matrix, that is, each of the possible values for an archic variable, is what we have called an *archic element*.

It will have been noticed that certain values for different archic variables seem to belong together, or to be suited to one another, or to have an affinity for one another. Such elements will be called *affinitive*, and they have been placed in the same column of the matrix. A set of values for the archic variables, one for each variable, constitutes an *archic profile*, in David Dilworth's apt phrase, and such a profile defines the *archic mode* of a text or author. An archic mode constituted from a set of affinitive elements is a *pure* mode; the others are *mixed* modes. Thus in the matrix each column corresponds to a pure mode. The pure modes have been named for the philosophers who first exemplify them: the Sophists, Democritus, Plato, and Aristotle.

The elements of the sophistic mode are at once human and liberating. Our perspective is whatever perspective we have, our reality whatever is real for us, our method whatever method works for us, and our principle our own freedom. We are liberated from all external or a priori restrictions. We are free to affirm or deny anything whatever. There is here a quite characteristic kind of liberation or enlightenment that can never be specified, even by specifying that it can never be specified. The sceptic must beware of asserting dogmatically that nothing can be known, and the Buddhist liberating himself from attachments must beware of an attachment to nothingness. Nagarjuna's fourfold negation applies to any property that we might attempt to attach to the sophist or to sophistic—elusive, for example. The sophist is neither elusive, nor not elusive, nor both elusive and not elusive, nor neither elusive nor non-elusive. Language in particular provides unlimited opportunities for the creativity of the sophist.

Shakespeare has the sophistic profile except for his objective perspective. The pure sophist is everywhere at the center of his work, but in his plays Shakespeare himself is nowhere to be seen. His creativity takes the form of a creative but objective mirroring of the human world in all its agonistic flux. Our sense that he includes all philosophies without himself having a philosophy, that all categories can be found in him but that he is above all categories, is our sense of the liberation characteristic of the sophistic mode:

> Others abide our question. Thou art free.
> We ask and ask—Thou smilest and art still,
> Out-topping knowledge.[1]

The use of sophistic elements in combination with non-sophistic ones introduces openness in particular respects. Descartes, for example, leaves the truth of his philosophy to be established by each individual for himself; Einstein leaves unrestricted the concepts we may invent to order our sensations; Milton argues for the unrestricted play of all doctrines, even those of Satan; Genesis leaves open the future moral development of mankind, and Darwin's theory leaves open the question of what biological species will emerge in the course of evolution.

The sophistic tradition, great and important as it is, has not been well recognized as such either by those who continue it or by others. The principal reason for this is the diversity and elusiveness of the sophistic approach itself. Also, the good sophist is always new and different and without precedent in the earlier tradition; it is the nature of this tradition to be open and creative. Further, few of the writings of the early sophists, and particularly of Protagoras, have survived, so the tradition has had to bear the heavy burden of the unanswered arguments against it in the writings of Plato and Aristotle, which *have* survived, and later sophists have been reluctant to call themselves by that name. Already in the time of Protagoras, if we are to believe the Platonic dialogue that bears his name, the name of sophist had acquired a pejorative connotation, thus leading sophists to abandon the name and obscure their tradition. I do not suppose that very many sophists, either before or after Protagoras, have, in order to avoid opprobrium, consciously concealed their identity behind some more reputable profession; they have simply been unaware of their tradition. The archic matrix, however, restores the sophistic mode to its essential position co-ordinate with the other pure modes, and we can now follow the excellent example of Protagoras, and reclaim the name of sophist for a great and honorable, though unrecognized, tradition.[2]

The Democritean mode counters at each point the subjectivity and indeterminacy of the sophistic mode with an inhuman determinateness. Instead of the subjectivity of personal perspectives we have objective perspectives that mirror the world as it is. Instead of the human reality of appearances we have the inhuman reality of what underlies the appearances. Instead of methods by which we order the world we have inhuman logical or physical necessity. Instead of principles which make the world depend upon us and our creative actions, we have inhuman principles that are always and everywhere the same. The elements of the Democritean mode rose into prominence with the beginnings of modern science in the 17th century, above all in the great achievement of Newton, and the subsequent revolutions in science have been departures in one respect or another from this mode.

The elements of the Platonic mode reject the arbitrary freedom of sophistic, but instead of the inhuman valuelessness of the Democritean mode they move at each point toward an ideal or perfect case in which all values are realized. Any perspective bears witness to a higher perspective; appearances intimate a higher order of things; rhetorical and logistic methods are subsumed by dialectic; and the ultimate principle always lies beyond any principle that one has. Platonic elements became associated with Christian doctrine, and it is from its affiliations with Christianity and other religions that the Platonic tradition is most familiar to us. Those who speak glibly of "Western metaphysics" or "onto-theology" usually have some form of Platonism in mind.

The elements of the Aristotelian mode preserve the cognitive content of all the other modes in a determinate pluralism that avoids the arbitrariness of sophistic, the reductions of atomistic, and the transcendence of Platonism. These elements determine multiple modes of actualization, and above all the actualization of knowing. Disciplinary perspectives determine the multiple ways in which the knower is related to things; essential realities determine the multiple things that are knowable; problematic methods determine the multiple forms that knowledge takes; and reflexive principles determine multiple actualizations and above all the actualization of knowing. If the sophists are everywhere and nowhere, the Democriteans most in evidence in classical mechanics, and the Platonists in religion, the Aristotelian tradition is perhaps most evident in universities with their full range of autonomous disciplines, theoretical, practical, and poetic.

The four pure modes were all developed in the great culminating phase of Hellenic philosophy, from the sophists to Aristotle. The sophistic mode came first, and the other three developed out of it and in reaction to it. I have followed this historical sequence in developing the archic matrix here. In the subsequent history, the endeavor to unite the different modes, and in particular those represented by the philosophies of Plato and Aristotle, as well as the endeavor to advance beyond what had already been done, led to the development of mixed modes.

It may be questioned whether the pure modes are in some way superior to the mixed modes. The pure modes have a coherence, simplicity, and elegance that distinguish them from the mixed modes and give them an archetypal role, but, on the other hand, they can easily degenerate into thinness and triviality. The synthesis of heterogeneous elements in the mixed modes presents difficulties at the sutures, but, on the other hand, the unity of discordant elements can give a philosophy unusual interest and power. Think for example of Leibniz as a logistic Platonist: the method requires that the monads be independent of one another, or windowless, while the principle requires them to be organically related, reflecting the whole of which they are a part, and both together lead to a system of pre-established harmony by which each monad from its own nature reflects all the others. Or consider Hume as an existential Democritean, binding together the existential world by a necessity for which it supplies no reason. Or consider Kant as a noumenal Aristotelian: there is scientific knowledge of experienced things, as for Aristotle, and yet these experienced things are only phenomenal, and a noumenal reality lies beyond all that is scientifically known. Or think of Berkeley as a diaphanic sophist, seeing in the flux of appearances the discourse of God.

The archic variables are formally independent, and there is no formal reason to prefer the pure to the mixed modes, or indeed any modes to any other. The pure modes are as different from one another as it is possible to be, and each is in its own terms superior to the others, and yet, because of the reciprocal priority of their elements, there is no absolute sense in which one is superior to the others. There is, we may say, a formal parity of all archic modes, whether pure or mixed.

The formal parity of archic modes does not, of course, imply that all philosophies are equal. There are countless ways in which one philosophy can be better than another. Everything depends on the way the starting-points are developed and worked out. Any philosophy, no matter how deficient, is capable of improvement in accordance with the potentialities of its mode. This is one reason why philosophers who encounter difficulties and objections to their philosophy seldom abandon it for another, but remain convinced that it is fundamentally sound and that difficulties can be overcome and objections answered. And of course the endeavor to defend a philosophy often does lead to its improvement.

The question whether the pure modes are superior to the mixed modes is not the only question that might be raised about the archic matrix. Above all, there is the question of why there is such a matrix at all. It may order intellectual history and provide a key to the interpretation of any text, but why it is able to do so remains a total mystery. Why are there four columns and four rows, and why these particular columns and rows? And what mode are we in when we talk about the matrix itself?

Inquiry into questions in which the matrix itself, apart from the materials it orders, becomes the subject of inquiry runs the danger of degenerating into sterile formalism. The validity of the matrix depends on its ability to order intellectual history, not upon its formal derivation from some higher principle. Nevertheless, we must do what we can to elucidate the mystery of why there should be such a matrix. I think this problem can best be treated by referring to the philosophy of Aristotle, even though this will make the discussion somewhat technical.

Why, then, are there four archic variables, or four columns in the matrix, and why these four? In seeking these variables, we were seeking the same sort of thing that Aristotle sought as *aitiai*, that is, as "responsibles," causes, reasons, determinants, factors. There are, according to Aristotle, four kinds of causes: the matter or substratum, the beginning of motion or change, the essence or form, and that for the sake of which or the end. Let us first consider whether the archic variables are indeed instances of Aristotle's causes. If they are, then questions about the derivation of the variables will become questions about the derivation of the Aristotelian causes.

The archic variables, as causes of texts in general, do not correspond to any particular set of causes in Aristotle. There are three uses of the causes in Aristotle, however, that resemble in one way or another the project attempted here, and the comparison with them will clarify the relation of the archic variables to the causes. The present project resembles the *Metaphysics* in its concern with what is primary and universal, but its subject matter is texts rather than the things that are. Allowing for this difference, however, the analogy can be seen. The first major segment of the *Metaphysics*, Books I-III, is concerned with the origin of metaphysics in the human mind. This corresponds to our concern with the origin of a text in the mind of its author. The second major segment of the *Metaphysics*, Books IV-V, is concerned with the conditions of signification and with the meanings of metaphysical terms. This corresponds to our concern with the signification of the terms of a text. The third major segment of the *Metaphysics*, Books VI-X, is concerned with the forms of being in its various senses, being as known, as substance, as actuality and potentiality, as one and many. This corresponds to our concern with the general forms or methods by which texts and their reality are ordered. The final segment of the *Metaphysics*, Books XI-XIV, is concerned with the principles of all things, and primarily with the prime mover that causes the whole to function. The analogue of this in the case of a text is the principle that causes the text to function.

Aristotle's *Organon*, unlike the *Metaphysics*, could be said to be concerned with texts, although with a specific kind of texts, namely, those that present logical or seemingly logical arguments. Although our concern is with texts in general, and not just with logical or even with verbal texts, a comparison with the *Organon* will be useful in showing how the causes apply to one important kind of text. Signification is found already in the individual terms (and is carried forward into the larger verbal units) and corresponds to the signification of things by terms as treated in the *Categories*. Perspective appears in the combination of terms in a proposition, for this implies the mind of the author, and this corresponds to the combination of terms by the mind treated in *On Interpretation*. Method appears when three terms are related in an argument, and this corrresponds to the treatment of the syllogism in the *Prior Analytics*. Principles appear when terms, propositions, and arguments are organized with respect to a function, and this corresponds to the concern of the remaining works of the *Organon* with the kinds of principles, scientific, dialectical, and sophistic, that cause arguments to function.

Aristotle's *Poetics*, although limited to imitative poetry, has the advantage of not being limited to logical or even verbal texts, and further, in the first use of the causes in the *Poetics* they function as variables, as they do in their use here. It will therefore be instructive to compare the archic variables with this set of causes also. Signification as a variable corresponds to the various possible means of imitation: figure and color, or rhythm, language, and harmony, in their various possible combinations. Method as a variable corresponds to the various possible objects of imitation: the actions of those like ourselves or better or worse. Perspective as a variable corresponds to the various possible manners of imitation: narrative, mixed, or dramatic. Principle as a variable corresponds to the various possible pleasures that can organize a work of art, the catharsis of pity and fear in the case of tragedy. An art form defined as a particular combination of means, object, manner, and end is analogous to what we have called an archic mode, and a particular instance of an art form, the play *Oedipus* as an instance of tragedy, for example, corresponds to a philosophy as an instance of an archic mode.

These analogies justify us in supposing that the archic variables can indeed be viewed as instances of the causes when these are sought in texts in general. But why should there also be four rows in the matrix, that is, four pure modes? The four elements in each column are not the elements of any whole and do not correspond in a direct way to the causes. Nevertheless, the nature and number of the four pure modes leads one to suspect that here too the causes are at work, although in a different and an indirect way.

The problem is whether the causes that determine the complementary aspects of a single whole such as a particular doctrine also determine a set of different and independent wholes or doctrines. And once the question is stated in this way, the answer is not difficult to find. For the causes do not each cause a part of the whole; rather, each is a cause of the whole and can subordinate the other causes to itself. In fact, the causes are the archetypal set of reciprocally prior starting-points for the determination of a functioning whole.

In all of Aristotle's treatises there is manifest a tendency for each of the causes to become archical or architectonic and to take over the whole. But because they are being used within a single metaphysical or archical frame, the incompatibility of the approaches determined by the different causes is easily seen to be procedural and not substantive: the different causes are after all causes of the same thing. But when they are freed from the restraint of a single metaphysics or archic mode, the different causes no longer generate complementary parts of a single doctrine, but different doctrines that appear to be substantively incompatible. The incompatibility, however, is still procedural, but it is not the incompatibility of two procedures within a single science, but the incompatibility of two sciences each of which implicates a different metaphysics or archic mode. It is now no longer a case of the same thing being investigated by different methods within a single discipline, but rather of disciplines that are different because implicating procedural differences at the metaphysical or archic level, and what is common to different metaphysics is not any one subject, but the totality of all subjects. That is, the procedural difference no longer lies simply in the way a particular subject is approached, but in the way all subjects are approached.

In Aristotle's *Politics*, for example, there are four methods corresponding to different senses of the word "best" and dealing with problems in which the art is progressively more limited or restricted by given conditions. (This sequence corresponds to the order of books as determined by the internal references.) In considering what state is best absolutely, one can assume what one likes, although nothing that is impossible. For what is best in general, one must assume conditions that generally prevail, but one is unrestricted as to the kind of constitution one proposes. For what is best on hypothesis, one begins from a given kind of constitution and is unrestricted as to the means used to preserve it. And for what is best under the circumstances, one begins from a set of actual conditions and seeks to reform the constitution in a way appropriate to them. So conceived, it is evident that the four methods can be parts of a single politics, but McKeon has also argued that each can become an independent mode of political analysis: ideal, as in Plato; constitutional, as in Spinoza; revolutionary, as in Machiavelli; and circumstantial, as in Aristotle.[3]

The same sort of shift from the causes as determining different approaches within a science to the causes as determining different forms of the science itself can be seen in other subjects. In Aristotle's *Ethics*, for example, the consideration of character, thought, the irrational, and the good of activity all form parts of a single doctrine, but one can also use these causes to distinguish four possible kinds of ethics: a voluntaristic ethics such as that of Nietzsche, a formal or deontological ethics such as that of Kant, a material or hedonistic ethics such as that of Epicurus, and a functional ethics such as that of Aristotle.[4]

But the tendency of the causes to become architectonic is nowhere more apparent than in the *Metaphysics*, for there is here not even a single definition of the science, but rather three different ones. The science is first defined in relation to man as the intellectual virtue of wisdom, the science of first principles and causes, then in relation to being as the science of being *qua* being, and then in relation to that which is first in being as theology, the science of that which exists separately and is immovable. (Within the third of these sciences, Aristotle considers the different forms of being before turning to the proper subjects of theology.) Now just as in the case of politics and ethics, each of the causes treated in the *Metaphysics* can become primary and subordinate the others, and thus they can generate four different metaphysical doctrines. And in fact this is what has happened in our development of the archic matrix: the four pure modes correspond to the possibility of each of the causes becoming architectonic.

The first part of the *Metaphysics* is concerned with man as the generator of metaphysics, and for the sophists it is man that is the measure of all things, of the being of the things that are and the not-being of the things that are not. Man appears in the archic matrix as the author with his personal perspective, and when this determines the other variables the result is the sophistic mode. The real is what is real for us, the method is the way we order the real, and the cause of functioning is ourselves. The world of the sophist is determined by himself: he creates his world.

The second part of the *Metaphysics* is concerned with being *qua* being, common to all things, and for the atomists, it is the common substratum of being and not-being that explains all things. This common substratum appears in the archic matrix as the substrative reality, and when this determines the other variables the result is the Democritean mode. The author is a part of the material cosmos into which the cosmos is reflected in an objective perspective, the order of the real is determined by its material parts, and the principle is the ultimate unchanging matter that underlies all things. The world of the Democritean is determined by its ultimate substratum, the atoms and the void.

The third part of the *Metaphysics* is concerned with the forms of being, and for Plato it is formal connectedness that explains all things. Formal connectedness appears in the archic matrix as the connectedness of dialectic, and when this determines the other variables the result is the Platonic mode. The author reveals it more or less in his diaphanic perspective, the real is just the intelligible reality of the objects of thought, and the principle is the form that determines all other forms, the form of the good. The world of the Platonist is determined by its ultimate form, the form of the good.

The fourth part of the *Metaphysics* is concerned with the pure actuality of thought thinking itself which governs all things. This is primary in Aristotle's own metaphysics. It appears in the archic matrix as a reflexive principle, and when the activity of knowing determines the other variables the result is the Aristotelian mode. The disciplinary perspective is that of a knower, knowable essences are what is real, and they are ordered as knowledge. The world of the Aristotelian is determined by its ultimate activity or functioning, the activity of knowing.

In a word, the Sophist begins from man, the Democritean from matter, the Platonist from form, and the Aristotelian from functioning.

The causes or reponsibles are thus reponsible for both axes of the archic matrix, but in different ways. As responsibles within a single whole they give rise to the different archic variables within a single text, that is, to the different columns of the matrix, and as assuming priority over one another they give rise to the different pure modes, that is, to the different rows of the matrix. The matrix itself is organic in the sense that it can be generated from any of its elements. One can begin from any element and show that it implicates the other elements of its pure mode, and then generate the other pure modes by shifting the primacy of elements within the first one. The matrix schematizes the organic structure of knowing in its multiple modes.

We can now return to the problem from which we began, why is there an archic matrix at all? It is clear from what has been said that it arises because each of the causes can be taken as prior to the others, that is, because they are reciprocally prior to one another. This identifies the arbitrary or conventional element that we suspected from the very beginning must be present in all thought.

The causes can be reciprocally prior to one another because they are different ways of knowing one thing. If we ask why there are different ways of knowing one thing, we are asking for a cause of the causes. If the set of causes is complete, this cause will turn out to be one of the four we have already identified, and, because of their reciprocal priority, the plurality will reappear. The basic fact here is just that the one world can be known in multiple ways, and the causes, and the archic matrix, identify these ways. The whole of every text is the work of an author, is about a reality, is an ordering of parts in a whole, and is for the sake of some function, and we can approach the whole text through any of these as a starting point. The archic matrix and particular texts are not two different things that mysteriously correspond; they are the same thing in universal and in particular form. The mystery that the archic matrix should order intellectual history is just the mystery that any subject should be knowable through universals.

The formulation of universals in any subject gives rise to a science, and the formulation of the archic matrix gives rise to a scientific form that philosophy is assuming today, and which I will call *archic analysis*. The archic profile of this discipline has already been specified in the earlier chapters with respect to each variable taken in isolation, and the results can be brought together here. The discipline interprets a semantic rather than an ontic or epistemic subject matter, and being and knowing are included as they are expressed in texts. (1) The perspective is disciplinary, for personal views and objective mirrorings and approximations to the divine are all included as ways in which the mind constitutes its point of view on the world. (2) The signification is essential, for unique meanings and hidden meanings and higher meanings are all included as essential possibilities of meaning. (3) The method is analytic, for competition and axiomatic derivation and higher syntheses are all included as methods by which form and matter are unified. (4) The principle is reflexive, for creativity and conservation and comprehensiveness are all included as requisite to the functioning of texts, and thus this functioning is a cause of itself.

2. Interpretation of Texts and of the World

The archic matrix orders the diverse approaches possible in philosophy and in the special arts and sciences, and by so doing makes possible the discovery of a more thoroughgoing scientific order in their respective subject matters. Let us consider literary theory, or poetics, as an example. It is remarkable that many great literary works, like great philosophic works, are virtually one of a kind. Think for example of Dante's *Divine Comedy*, or Chaucer's *Canterbury Tales*, or Cervantes' *Don Quixote*, or Walt Whitman's *Song of Myself*, or Kafka's *The Trial*, or Joyce's *Finnegans Wake*. Traditional literary genres, such as lyric, epic, and dramatic, or tragic and comic, etc., are not adequate to determine the essential features of such works. If, on the other hand, they are considered simply in their uniqueness, no science of them is possible. The archic matrix makes it possible to define the specific literary or poetic projects of these and other works, and to understand the work as the realization of this project., These literary projects thus replace traditional art forms as principles for understanding literary works. Each project is in itself a general one, although it may have only one exemplification. The understanding of a literary work as the realization of a specific project may not be required for the enjoyment of the work, but it is a knowledge of why the work is enjoyable. And this knowledge is in fact the very same knowledge in accordance with which the work might have been produced. It is thus poetic or productive knowledge in the strict sense, the knowledge by which the work could be produced. Criticism occupies a rather small place within this poetic knowledge, comparable to the place occupied in Aristotle's *Poetics* by the consideration of problems and their solutions in Chapter 25. When a criticism of a work is placed in the context of the work's own poetic project, it can often be answered without difficulty, or, if it cannot be answered, then it is a fault of the work. In general, the archic matrix provides the basis for a new poetics analogous to Aristotle's poetics, but more adequate to the diversity of literary forms that have appeared since Aristotle wrote.

The archic matrix orders not only expressions of thought about the world in poetic or scientific texts, but also interpretations of texts by one another. There is this difference, however, between the world and a text, that the world is not itself an interpretation and has no archic mode, but a text is an interpretation and does have an archic mode. Consequently in the interpretation of a text two archic profiles are involved, the archic profile of the text being interpreted and the archic profile of the interpreter. Abstractly considered, there are 4^4 or 256 possible profiles, and 256^2 or 65,536 possible combinations of profiles in the simplest case of interpretation. Now it might be thought that special interest would attach to that subclass of these possibilities in which text and interpreter have the same profile. Interpretation in such a case we might call *homo-archic interpretation*, as distinguished from the more usual case of *hetero-archic interpretation*. Here at last, it might be thought, we have a clear specification of what it means to "interpret a text in its own terms," and a criterion for the correctness of an interpretive framework.

And yet the requirement that interpretation be in the same mode as the text being interpreted approaches the limiting case where interpretation ceases to be interpretation at all. If someone were to copy a text word for word and claim to have produced a correct interpretation of the text, we would say that he had copied the text rather than interpreted it. And if he were to paraphrase or restate the text, we would still not call it an interpretation, but rather a paraphrase or a restatement. Just as translation implies that a text is not only re-presented, but re-presented in another language, so interpretation seems to imply some difference in the point of view of text and interpreter. Commentaries that do no more than repeat what the text has already said are of limited value.

Yet homo-archic interpretations are of special value in two sorts of situations. The first is one in which one wants to stay as close as possible to the given text within the constraints imposed by one's project, as for example if one is illustrating a text or translating it from one language to another.

The second sort of situation occurs when the same archic profile occurs in radically different circumstances. Jane Austen speaks with a comic voice, as we have already noted, the individual characters and incidents in her novels have a universal significance, the plots are resolutive, and each novel is organized by the discovery of a virtue. Her archic profile is thus the same as Aristotle's, and the comparison of her treatment of character and Aristotle's treatment of character in the *Ethics* may be expected to be of special interest. *Sense and Sensibility* is concerned with the precondition for ethics, the disposition to follow reason rather than the passions, and is organized by the ethical mean. *Pride and Prejudice* is organized by pride, *Northanger Abbey* by truthfulness, *Mansfield Park* by justice, *Emma* by practical wisdom, and *Persuasion* by courage. In each of these novels, the primary couple exhibits complementary and usually imperfect forms of the virtue, while other couples or characters exhibit the absence of this virtue or the corresponding vices. Ethical problems for the characters and for the reader are resolved through the discovery of the virtue: Is it not best to trust one's feelings rather than reason? Isn't pride a fault? Isn't truth dull compared to imaginative invention? Isn't it best to have a detached attitude with respect to morality, and to be able, like an actor, to act morally or not, as one choses? Isn't it best to mind one's own business and not meddle with other people's affairs? Isn't it best to give up a hopeless love? The difference in the circumstances of Aristotle and Jane Austen combined with their essential similarities makes their works unsurpassed commentaries on one another.

But the power of an interpretive mode is shown by its ability to interpret all sorts of texts, and not just those that are homo-archic with itself. And, on the side of the interpreted work, interpretation from a standpoint different from that of the work itself can give us new insights into the work and enhance our appreciation of it. But how can the interpretation of the work in alien terms be anything but distorting? The answer to this question is by now evident. Because the archic modes are reciprocally prior to one another, and thus only procedurally and not substantively incompatible, they can all give us the same truth. We do not distort a measured quantity by converting it to other units, provided the conversion is correctly carried out. A text although written in a particular mode does not have meaning only in that mode; it has a meaning in any mode, a meaning that is brought out by interpretations formulated in the interpreting mode. In hetero-archic interpretation the archic matrix can make clear what is going on and why the interpretation comes out as it does. Think for example of any interpretation—of Freud's interpretation of Sophocles' *Oedipus*, or Heidegger's interpretation of the Pre-Socratics, or Derrida's interpretation of Rousseau or Plato. In all of these a determinate and understandable process is going on, and its determinateness becomes clear when the interpretation is understood in relation to the respective archic modes of the interpreted and the interpreter. And the full power of an archic mode becomes clear when we see how it can interpret the range and variety of both the world and the other texts that have interpreted the world. Each of the great philosophers has shown us a way in which this can be done, and thus the power of their respective archic modes.

3. Historical Interaction of Archic Modes

The use of the archic modes always occurs in concrete historical circumstances, and a recognition of the formal parity of modes should not lead us to neglect or minimize the different ways in which they bear upon concrete situations. What is easy in one mode is often difficult in another, and there is seldom a straightforward translation from one mode to another. Because of the great differences in the way the world appears in different modes, important new discoveries and achievements in every field are usually associated with a shift of archic mode. A great pioneer in any subject usually has an experiential grasp of his domain that permits him to show the superiority of his own formulation to the alternative formulations or revisions that are proposed during his own lifetime. Thus the discoveries may seem indissolubly linked to the mode in which they were made, and it is only after they become familiar from long experience that ways are found of translating them into other modes. Newton, for example, pointed out that Huygens was unable to account for the phenomena of polarization by his wave theory of light, and that the motion of the comets presented an insuperable difficulty to the Cartesian theory of vortices. But later generations of scientists, trained and experienced in the new orthodoxy, were able to propose alternative formulations that did not sacrifice the successes of the original theory. When Young and Fresnel revived the wave theory of light in the early 19th century, there were no optical phenomena explained by Newton that they could not also explain. And when Einstein restored physical properties to space in a way reminiscent of Descartes, his equations yielded Newton's law of gravitation as a first approximation. Similarly, Freud was able to point out empirical inadequacies in the revisions of psychoanalysis that appeared in his own lifetime, such as those of Adler and Jung. "From the History of an Infantile Neurosis" presents a difficulty for those who denied the significance of infantile factors in the genesis of neurosis not unlike the difficulty of the comets for the Cartesians. But today we see those trained and experienced in the psychoanalytic orthodoxy endeavoring to substitute other archic frameworks for Freud's Helmholtzian energetics without sacrificing Freud's achievements.[5] This interplay of different archic modes in the development of the special sciences is a vast field of inquiry which I can only touch on here.

The larger traditions of a culture or civilization are also susceptible of analysis in archic terms. Any intellectually vital culture or tradition will exhibit a plurality of archic modes, and yet the dominant character of a tradition or culture can often be specified in archic terms. If a culture or tradition has a basic text or set of texts, then the archic elements, and particularly the principles, of these basic texts will tend to prevail in that culture or tradition. The most basic text of the Western tradition is Genesis; the three great religions of the West have all sprung from it, and all have retained the creative principle that characterizes it. The belief in creative novelty at a fundamental level is almost a hallmark of the Western tradition— consider, for example, philosophers as diverse as Augustine, Pico, Hobbes, Locke, Berkeley, Kierkegaard, Marx, Bergson, James, Heidegger, Dewey, Whitehead, and Sartre. Progress and advancement are keynotes of the Western tradition.

In the Indian tradition, on the other hand, with its basic texts in the Vedas and Upanishads, elemental principles have played a dominant role. Fatalism and an acceptance of what it is not in one's power to change are more evident here than in the West. The Buddhist tradition, although departing from the Hindu in other respects, has tended to retain the ele- mental principle of the Buddha-nature.

The most basic text of the Chinese tradition is the Confucian *Analects*, and the Confucian tradition has always been guided by the harmonizing power of comprehensive principles. The fundamental sense of harmony that is said to pervade the Chinese tradition has its source here.

Sometimes also pairs of texts with different archic profiles will define a polarity running through an entire tradition. Plato and Aristotle define such a polarity within the Western tradition, and Confucius and Lao Tzu within the Chinese tradition.[6] The way in which such a polarity is con- ceived will depend upon the principles of the tradition. The saying, "Everyone is born either a Platonist or an Aristotelian," makes the polarity conse- quent upon an arbitrary creation. The saying, "A Confucian in office, a Taoist in retirement," makes the polarity into complementary aspects of a comprehensive whole.

Speaking roughly, then, one can say of the three great philosophic tradi- tions that creative principles have been dominant in the West, elemental principles in India, and comprehensive principles in China. In no cultural tradition have reflexive principles been dominant. As we have seen, however, reflexive principles bring the different philosophies of the different tradi- tions together as complementary components of a single science, and thus provide a basis for the new universal tradition that is now emerging. The archic matrix makes clear the sense in which different traditions that appear to be incompatible need not be really so, but are determinately related to each other as participants in a common enterprise that respects rather than jeopardizes the integrity of its component traditions. It is doubtful to what extent the national antagonisms that today threaten to express them-

selves in catastrophic destruction derive from philosophic differences, but
to the extent that they do, there is now if ever a need for a doctrine such
as the present one that shows the ultimate compatibility of diverse
philosophies.

4. The Progress of Awareness

The archic elements were developed as essential features of individual
texts rather than of authors or traditions, and yet authors in general have
the same archic profile in all their works, and even whole traditions can
be characterized by their archic elements. It might seem that there is no
reason why one author should not write texts in different archic modes,
but this seldom occurs. And in fact a change in even a single archic
variable can constitute a fundamental revolution in an individual mind. It
is paradoxical that what is merely arbitrary or conventional should be a
matter of fundamental importance to an individual or tradition.

We must distinguish here between the archic element taken by itself
and the archic element taken as functioning to form a mind or tradition.
It is not as if the mind or tradition first existed as what it is and then
selected its archic elements; rather it is the archic elements that make the
mind or tradition what it is. The selection of archic elements taken in
isolation may be a matter of indifference, but when they have been used
to constitute a mind or tradition, the integrity of that mind or tradition is
inseparable from the archic elements by which it is constituted. There is
an analogy here to the choice of units of measure. When units of measure
are taken in isolation the choice among them may be a matter of indifference,
but when they have become embodied in a technology, the foot-pound-
second system in the United States technology, for example, the system is
not easily changed.

We can conceive the individual mind, then, as having two components,
an archic component and what I will call a factual component. The archic
elements form the factual materials into a functioning whole, and the
stability of the archic elements is a consequence of this unity. A change in
an archic element entails a re-organization of the mind in one of its aspects.
The protean sophist, who can assume any archic profile, is not attached to
that profile in the same way as the genuine holder of the profile is; this is
the reason why the sophist is viewed with suspicion. The sophist, however,
has his own archic elements like everyone else: they are those that liberate
him from attachments.

Archic elements, or philosophic principles, function in the minds of
most people more or less implicitly, and are not clearly thought out and

brought into awareness. Encounters with others who have different archic profiles or who have thought them out more clearly may stimulate the development of awareness and lead toward the clarity and explicitness that we find in the great philosophers. In general, when two individual minds encounter one another, they will differ in both their archic and factual components. Each of course must interpret the other in its own terms. Since the archic elements pervade the whole, disagreements on particular issues will in general involve an archic component. Since the factual component, the materials which the archic elements organize, can be made more or less the same for both parties, disagreements will tend to focus on the archic elements. So long as the true nature of the archic components remains unrecognized, it is natural for the parties involved to try to reach agreement on the archic elements and to interpret factual inadequacies as evidence of the inadequacy of the archic elements themselves. This endeavor to reach agreement on philosophic principles culminates in the works of the great philosophers. The philosophers of antiquity brought all of the archic elements into awareness, and the philosophers of the modern period, reflecting self-consciously on these elements, have endeavored to account for all of them within their own philosophies. But agreement even on the mode of taking into account all other principles has proved elusive, and it was this fact from which the present work began. This work attempts to further the developing self-consciousness of the modern period with respect to philosophic principles by making explicit their nature and reciprocal priority.

Once this reciprocal priority is recognized, the situation is radically altered. The endeavor to reach agreement on philosophic principles, although valuable in bringing to light the nature of these principles, cannot ultimately succeed, and if it did succeed would stultify rather than advance thought, and in any case is pointless, in view of the parity of archic modes. To those who have understood the arguments of this book, it will seem that anyone who today undertakes to refute the principles of a great philosopher, or to expose his fundamental errors or oversights, can have little understanding of the nature of philosophy or of what he is attempting. Yet if there are such benighted souls, we must be grateful to them for their Sisyphean labors, for the harder they work at their impossible task, the more clearly do archic differences and their reciprocal priorities emerge. In the end, those who are most tenacious in their efforts to refute pluralism provide the best evidence for it. In saying this I do not mean to deny the validity of an objectivist profile that attempts to eliminate pluralism by bringing thought into accord with reality as it is in itself. It is rather that such an approach today, if it is to be effective, must proceed in a different way than formerly, and explain objectively the reciprocal priority of the objective and other approaches.

With the abandonment of the attempt to secure agreement on philosophic principles, the nature of discussion and debate on particular issues is also radically altered. It becomes important to discriminate archic differences, which are undecidable, from factual differences, which are decidable. This of course is not easy, for what the facts are depends on the principles by which they are known. But by making this discrimination, one can avoid futile controversies on undecidable questions and direct one's efforts toward decidable ones.

I have in this book sought to bring into awareness the multiple modes in which we become aware of the world. The result is therefore an awareness of the intrinsic diversity present in awareness itself. And this diversity must qualify even the awareness of this diversity. Agreement is therefore not to be expected on the results of this book. The archic matrix emerges within a particular archic mode, and thinkers in other modes cannot be expected to agree either on the existence of such a matrix or on its particular elements. Were everyone to agree on the archic matrix, it would *ipso facto* be refuted.

To those in the sophistic tradition, the approach followed here must appear restrictive at every point. The perspective is my perspective, or an Aristotelian perspective, or a Western perspective, but in any case an idiocentric perspective, and it should be recognized that other perspectives are also possible. The approach depends on particular interpretations of texts, but an acquaintance with either traditional or contemporary scholarship shows that other interpretations are also possible. The method imposes the same Procrustean categories on everyone, and thus distorts or truncates their views; everyone should be allowed to speak for himself. The approach attempts to classify all possible philosophies, but the history of thought is not bound by static categories, and we should today attempt to find new ways of dealing with the newly discovered openness of thought rather than try to close it off with categories from the past.

To those in the Democritean tradition, on the other hand, the approach must appear indeterminate at every point. It resembles the approach of the discredited system-builders of the past rather than the scientific approach of the mainstream of philosophy today. It plays a jejune dialectical game with philosophies and never deals with the essential questions of their truth and adequacy. Its terms are so imprecise and its arguments so inconsequential that nothing is proved, to which the pluralistic conclusion bears witness. It treats our thought as a measure of the world, rather than the world as a measure of our thought.

To the Platonic tradition, finally, the approach must appear limited and partial at every point. It is limited by its attempt to make philosophies the subject of a science, for the task of philosophy is precisely to transcend the limitations of science. It is limited by its uncritical acceptance of other doctrines at face value, and even by the language in which it is stated, for meaning transcends linguistic formulation. It is limited by merely classifying doctrines instead of bringing them into dialogue with each other through which new insights could emerge. It is limited by its adherence to a single set of categories as if they were complete and final, for no set of categories is ever complete and final.

All such criticisms serve to confirm the matrix and establish its validity.

The matrix can, however, be confirmed by assimilation as well as by rejection. The principle of translatability requires that the discoveries presented here can be assimilated by the other modes, each in its own way. In fact, rejection and assimilation are by no means mutually exclusive, but proceed simultaneously. The sophistic mode has always been pluralistic, and far more so than the essentialist mode. Therefore the approach presented here can be seen as liberating, and its distinctions, treated as provisional and heuristic, can open up new possibilities of discovery and interpretation. The Democritean mode tends to be non-pluralistic, and this is one reason for the present division of philosophers in this country into so-called analysts and pluralists, the pluralists including everyone who is not an analyst. But the matrix can lead to greater precision in understanding the doctrines of others, even if only as a means to their eventual refutation. Platonic philosophies, finally, require other philosophies to assimilate, and the views presented here provide new possibilities for incorporation and transcendence.

This assimilation in multiple modes is one phase of the progress of philosophy, or the progress of awareness. The progress of awareness, so long as the continuity of thought is maintained, is irreversible. A higher level of awareness, once attained, is not voluntarily abandoned for a lower one.

All human progress is fundamentally progress in awareness. The end of the special theoretical sciences is simply to increase our awareness of the various special domains of natural science and mathematics. Progress is here marked by an increase in awareness which is sought and valued as such. In the practical sciences, our awareness of ourselves and our situation and of ends worth seeking is what makes it possible to attain these ends, and above all others the end of awareness itself. Technological advance is the result of the awareness of the means through which new technological ends can be attained, and the fine arts represent the possibility of bringing into awareness emotional experiences of a depth and order and completeness seldom found in the experiences of ordinary life. But if awareness is the progressive factor in all these domains, then progress in the awareness of awareness, or philosophic progress, would seem to be the most fundamental of all.

The advance in the awareness of awareness presented here is certainly not a final one. To suppose this would be to ignore the whole history of thought. In Aristotle the divine thought is a thinking on thinking that orders the world as an object of love. In our progression toward the divine, motivated by this love, we are far from realizing the perfection that would complete this progress. In Hegel, thought becomes aware of itself as realized in world history. But even understanding the whole of world history as the self-realization of spirit does not complete that history. The insight presented here into the archic determinants of our thought, an insight appropriate to a semantic epoch, is one further step in the progressive realization of thought by itself.

Notes

The worldwide or universal tradition that is the subject of this book involves the printing of the same work in many different languages and editions. It is desirable to have methods of citing passages in these works that are independent of the particular language and edition. Such methods have already been developed for classical works, and it is to be hoped that translators and editors of modern classics will include in their editions numbers indicating the paragraphing or pagination of the original. (A. V. Miller, for example, indicates the original paragraphing in his translation of Hegel's *Phenomenology*, and Norman Kemp Smith indicates the original pagination in his translation of Kant's *Critique of Pure Reason*.) In citing widely-published works in what follows, I have endeavored to include, where possible, forms of reference that apply to most editions.

Chapter I. Archic Variables

1. See Walter Watson, "Principles for Dealing with Disorder," *Journal of Chinese Philosophy*, VIII (1981), 349-70.

2. Francis Bacon, *Novum Organum*, Bk. I, aph. 1, trans. in *The Works of Francis Bacon*, ed. James Spedding, Robert Leslie Ellis, and Douglas Denton Heath, 14 vols. (London, 1857-74), IV, 47.

3. David Hume, *A Treatise of Human Nature*, ed. L. A. Selby-Bigge (Oxford: Clarendon Press, 1888), Introduction, par. 6, p. xx.

4. *Immanuel Kant's Critique of Pure Reason*, trans. Norman Kemp Smith (New York: Macmillan Co., 1929), Preface to Second Edition, B xvi, p. 22. (Page numbers of the first edition [Riga, 1781] are preceded by the letter A, of the second edition [Riga, 1787] by the letter B.)

5. G. E. Moore, "An Autobiography," in *The Philosophy of G. E. Moore*, ed. Paul Arthur Schilpp, The Library of Living Philosophers, Vol. IV (Evanston: Northwestern University, 1942), p. 14.

6. Rudolf Carnap, *The Logical Syntax of Language* (London: Routledge and Kegan Paul, 1937), sec. 86, pp. 332-33.

7. Bacon, *Novum Organum*, Bk. I, aph. 76, trans. in *Works*, IV, 75-76.

8. See Richard McKeon, *Freedom and History* (New York: Noonday Press, 1952),

pp. 11-12, and "A Philosopher Meditates on Discovery," in *Moments of Personal Discovery*, ed. R. M. MacIver (New York: Institute for Religious and Social Studies, 1952), pp. 120-23.

Chapter II. Perspective

1. Wayne C. Booth, *The Rhetoric of Fiction* (Chicago: University of Chicago Press, 1967), p. 20.

2. Hermann Diels and Walther Kranz, eds., *Die Fragmente der Vorsokratiker*, 7th ed. (Berlin: Weidmannsche Verlagsbuchhandlung, 1954) (cited hereafter as DK), 21 B 22. In citations of this work, the first number is the number assigned by Diels-Kranz to the philosopher, the letter A indicates testimony about the philosopher or his doctrines and the letter B quotations from his writings, and the final number is the number assigned by Diels-Kranz to the testimony or quotation.

3. DK 21 B 7.

4. DK 21 B 38.

5. DK 21 B 14+16+15.

6. DK 21 B 23.

7. DK 21 B 18.

8. DK 21 B 34.

9. Plato *Theaetetus* 152b.

10. Aristotle *Metaphysics* iv. 5. 1009a6.

11. Sextus Empiricus *Outlines of Pyrrhonism* i. 216, trans. R. G. Bury in *Sextus Empiricus*, Vol. I, Loeb Classical Library (London: William Heinemann, 1933), p. 131.

12. Michel de Montaigne, *Essais*, 1st ed. (Bordeaux, 1580), Au Lecteur.

13. Søren Kierkegaard, *Either/Or*, Part II, trans. Walter Lowrie, rev. Howard A. Johnson (Garden City, N.Y.: Doubleday and Co., 1959), p. 356.

14. Søren Kierkegaard, *The Point of View for My Work as an Author: A Report to History, and Related Writings*, trans. Walter Lowrie (New York: Harper and Brothers, 1962), p. 143.

15. *Ibid.*, pp. 50-51.

16. *Ibid.*, p. 148.

17. *Ibid.*, p. 117.

18. *Ibid.*, p. 122.

19. Friedrich Nietzsche, *The Gay Science*, trans. Walter Kaufmann (New York: Vintage Books, 1974), art. 249, p. 215.

20. *Ibid.*, art. 374, p. 336.

21. Friedrich Nietzsche, *Beyond Good and Evil*, trans. Walter Kaufmann (New York: Vintage Books, 1966), art. 6, p. 13.

22. William James, "*On a Certain Blindness in Human Beings*," last par., in *Talks to Teachers on Psychology; and to Students on Some of Life's Ideals* (New York: Henry Holt and Co., 1901), p. 264.

23. Maurice Merleau-Ponty, *Phenomenology of Perception*, trans. Colin Smith (London: Routledge and Kegan Paul, 1962), Preface, par. 2, p. viii.

24. P. W. Bridgman, *The Way Things Are* (New York: Viking Press, 1961), p. 6.

25. *Ibid.*, pp. 3-4.

26. Walt Whitman, "A Backward Glance O'er Travel'd Roads" (1888), par. 38, in *Leaves of Grass*, ed. Harold W. Blodgett and Sully Bradley, Comprehensive Reader's

Edition (New York: New York University Press, 1965), pp. 573-74.

27. Fyodor Dostoyevsky, *Notes from Underground*, trans. Andrew R. MacAndrew (New York: New American Library, 1961), p. 90.

28. DK 67 A 30.

29. DK 68 B 189.

30. Bacon, *Novum Organum*, Bk. I, aph. 124, trans. in *Works*, IV, 110.

31. David Hume, "My Own Life," par. 11, in *Essays Moral, Political, and Literary*, ed. T. H. Green and T. H. Grose, 2 vols. (London, 1875), I, 4.

32. David Hume, *Enquiry concerning the Principles of Morals*, sec. 9, pt. 2, par. 1, in *Enquiries concerning the Human Understanding and concerning the Principles of Morals*, ed. L. A. Selby-Bigge, 2d ed. (Oxford: Clarendon Press, 1902), p. 278.

33. Charles Darwin, *On the Origin of Species* (London, 1859; facsimile reprint, Cambridge: Harvard University Press, 1946), chap. iii, par. 3, p. 62.

34. Sigmund Freud, *New Introductory Lectures on Psychoanalysis*, lect. xxxv, par. 25, trans. James Strachey in *The Standard Edition of the Complete Psychological Works of Sigmund Freud*, ed. James Strachey, 24 vols. (London: Hogarth Press, 1953-74), XXII, 170.

35. *Ibid.*, par. 31, p. 174. See also *The Interpretation of Dreams*, chap. vii, sec. F, par. 1, in *Standard Edition*, V, 610.

36. Max Weber, "The Meaning of 'Ethical Neutrality' in Sociology and Economics," in *Max Weber on the Methodology of the Social Sciences*, trans. and ed. Edward A. Shils and Henry A. Finch (Glencoe, Ill.: Free Press, 1949), p. 11.

37. Freud, *New Introductory Lectures*, lect. xxxv, par. 3, in *Standard Edition*, XXII, 158.

38. Hume, *Treatise*, Introduction, par. 7, pp. xx-xxi.

39. William Shakespeare, Sonnet 30.

40. Shakespeare, Sonnet 144.

41. Shakespeare, Sonnet 147.

42. Shakespeare, Sonnet 137.

43. DK 28 B 1-2, trans. in G. S. Kirk and J. E. Raven, *The Presocratic Philosophers* (Cambridge: University Pres, 1969), pp. 267, 269.

44. See Walter Watson, "The Voices of the God," *New Essays on Socrates*, ed. Eugene Kelly (Lanham, Maryland: University Press of America, 1984), pp. 173-79.

45. St. Augustine *De civitate Dei* viii. 7.

46. St. Augustine *De magistro* 14, trans. George G. Leckie in *Concerning the Teacher and On the Immortality of the Soul* (New York: Appleton-Century-Crofts, 1938), p. 55.

47. Gottfried Wilhelm Leibniz, "Discourse on Metaphysics," art. 28, trans. George Montgomery, rev. Albert R. Chandler, in *Leibniz Selections*, ed. Philip P. Wiener (New York: Charles Scribner's Sons, 1951), p. 329.

48. *Ibid.*, p. 330.

49. Gottfried Wilhelm Leibniz, "Monadology," art. 83, trans. Philip P. Wiener in *Leibniz Selections*, p. 550.

50. G. W. F. Hegel, *Phenomenology of Spirit*, trans. A. V. Miller (Oxford: Oxford University Press, 1977), Preface, par. 28, p. 16.

51. Henri Bergson, *An Introduction to Metaphysics*, trans. T. E. Hulme (New York: Liberal Arts Press, 1949), p. 48.

52. Leo Tolstoy, *The Christian Teaching*, Preface, trans. Aylmer Maude in Leo

Tolstoy, *Selected Essays* (New York: Modern Library, 1946), p. 6.

53. Leo Tolstoy, *What is Religion?*, sec. 17, trans. Aylmer Maude in *Selected Essays*, p. 94.

54. Bhagavad Gītā xviii:77, trans. Franklin Edgerton (New York: Harper and Row, 1946), p. 91.

55. Lao Tzu, *Tao-te ching* 7, in *A Source Book in Chinese Philosophy*, comp. and trans. Wing-tsit Chan (Princeton: Princeton University Press, 1963), pp. 142-43.

56. Chu Hsi, *Chu Tzu ch'uan-shu* 42:27a-b, trans. Chan, *Source Book*, p. 621.

57. Aristotle *Ethics* i. 2. 1094a26.

58. Aristotle *Metaphysics* i. 2. 982b4.

59. Aristotle *Physics* ii. 2. 1949a9-11, trans. R. P. Hardie and R. K. Gaye in *The Works of Aristotle*, ed. W. D. Ross, 12 vols. (Oxford: Oxford University Press, 1908-52), Vol. II.

60. St. Thomas Aquinas, *Summa Theologica*, Pt. I, Q. 1, art. 4, trans. in A. C. Pegis, *Introduction to Saint Thomas Aquinas* (New York: Modern Library, 1948), p. 9.

61. St. Thomas Aquinas, *Commentary on the Nichomachean Ethics*, Preface, trans. in *History of the Organization of the Sciences*, Selected Readings, Part I, for the Course in Observation, Interpretation, Integration, 1st ed. (Chicago: University of Chicago Bookstore, 1943), II-B2, p. 62.

62. Kant, *Critique of Pure Reason*, B xiii, p. 20.

63. Immanuel Kant, *Critique of Judgment*, trans. J. H. Bernard (New York: Hafner Publishing Co., 1951), Introduction, sec. 9, pp. 33-34.

64. John Dewey, *Art as Experience* (New York: Minton, Balch, and Co., 1934), chap. iii, par. 49, p. 55.

65. Friedrich Nietzsche, *The Genealogy of Morals*, Third Essay, art. 5, trans. Francis Golffing in *The Birth of Tragedy and The Genealogy of Morals* (Garden City, N.Y.: Doubleday & Co., 1956), p. 237. David Dilworth pointed out this passage.

66. Aristotle *On Sophistical Refutations* 9. 170a22.

67. John Locke, *An Essay concerning Human Understanding*, Bk. IV, chap. xxi, sec. 1, in *The Philosophical Works of John Locke*, ed. J. A. St. John, 2 vols. (London, 1908), II, 336-37.

68. St. Augustine *De civitate Dei* viii. 4.

69. *The Logic of Hegel*, trans. from *The Encyclopaedia of the Philosophical Sciences* by William Wallace, 2d. ed. (Oxford: Oxford University Press, 1892), Introduction, sec. 18, pp. 28-29.

70. Aristotle *Topics* i. 14. 105b19-26, trans. W. A. Pickard-Cambridge in *Works*, Vol. I.

Chapter III. Reality

1. Sextus Empiricus *Outlines of Pyrrhonism* i. 217-19, trans. Bury, pp. 131-33.

2. Aristotle *Metaphysics* iv. 5. 1010a6-14, trans. W. D. Ross in *Works*, Vol. VIII.

3. Aristotle *On Sophistical Refutations* 34. 183b37-184a7, trans. W. A. Pickard-Cambridge in *Works*, Vol. I.

4. Aristotle *Politics* i. 13. 1260a25-29.

5. Plato *Meno* 71e-72a, trans. W. K. C. Guthrie in *The Collected Dialogues of Plato*, ed. Edith Hamilton and Huntington Cairns (Princeton: Princeton University Press, 1963), p. 355.

6. Plato *Lesser Hippias* 368b-d, trans. Benjamin Jowett in *Collected Dialogues*, p. 206.

7. Plato *Greater Hippias* 287e, trans. Benjamin Jowett in *Collected Dialogues*, p. 1540.

8. Hume, *Treatise*, Bk. I, Pt. I, sec. 7, par. 1, p. 17.

9. David Hume, *Enquiry concerning Human Understanding*, sec. 2, par. 9, in *Enquiries*, ed. Selby-Bigge, p. 22.

10. Ernst Mach, *The Science of Mechanics*, trans. Thomas J. McCormack (La Salle, Ill.: Open Court Publishing Co., 1942), chap. iv, pt. 4, sec. 2, pp. 579-80.

11. *Ibid.*, p. 580.

12. Albert Einstein, "Physics and Reality," sec. 1, pars. 5-6, trans. Sonja Bargmann in *Ideas and Opinions* (New York: Crown Publishers, 1954), p. 291.

13. Max Weber, " 'Objectivity' in Social Science and Social Policy," in *Max Weber on the Methodology of the Social Sciences*, p. 84.

14. *Ibid.*, p. 111.

15. *Ibid.*, p. 93.

16. Ludwig Wittgenstein, *Philosophical Investigations*, trans. G. E. M. Anscombe (Oxford: Basil Blackwell, 1953), Pt. I, arts. 66-67, pp. 31-32.

17. Milindapañha 40, trans. in Henry Clarke Warren, *Buddhism in Translations* (Cambridge: Harvard University Press, 1896; New York: Atheneum, 1974), p. 149.

18. *Ibid.*, 25-27, pp. 129-33.

19. Nāgārjuna, *Mādhyamika-śāstra*, chap. xxv, st. 19, trans. Th. Stcherbatsky in *A Source Book in Indian Philosophy*, ed. Sarvepalli Radhakrishnan and Charles A. Moore (Princeton: Princeton University Press, 1957), p. 344.

20. William Shakespeare, *Hamlet*, Act III, scene 2.

21. Arthur Eddington, *The Nature of the Physical World* (New York: Macmillan Co., 1928), Introduction, pp. ix-xi.

22. DK 88 B 9.

23. Plato *Theaetetus* 156a.

24. DK 88 B 11.

25. DK 88 B 9.

26. Isaac Newton, *Mathematical Principles of Natural Philosophy*, trans. Andrew Motte, rev. Florian Cajori (Berkeley: University of California Press, 1947), Scholium to Definitions, pp. 6-7.

27. *Ibid.*, p. 8.

28. *Ibid.*, p. 12.

29. *Ibid.*, Preface, p. xvii.

30. Niccolò Machiavelli, *Discourses on the First Ten Books of Titus Livius*, Bk. I, Introduction, trans. Christian E. Detmold in *The Prince* and *The Discourses* (New York: Modern Library, 1940), p. 105.

31. *Ibid.*, chap. xxxix, p. 216.

32. Karl Marx and Frederick Engels, *Manifesto of the Communist Party*, trans. Samuel Moore, rev. Samuel Moore and Frederick Engels (London, 1888; Chicago: Charles H. Kerr and Co., 1946), Pt. II, pars. 58-59, p. 40.

33. Karl Marx, *A Contribution to the Critique of Political Economy*, trans. N. I. Stone (Chicago: Charles H. Kerr and Co., 1904), Preface, par. 4, p. 12.

34. Nietzsche, *Gay Science*, art. 354, pp. 298-99.

35. *Ibid.*, pp. 299-300.

36. Nietzsche, *Beyond Good and Evil*, art. 3, p. 11.

37. Sigmund Freud, *The Interpretation of Dreams*, chap. iv, par. 4, trans. James

Strachey in *Standard Edition*, IV, 135.

38. Leo Tolstoy, "The Death of Ivan Ilych," sec. 11, trans. Aylmer Maude in *The Death of Ivan Ilych and Other Stories* (New York: New American Library, 1960), p. 152.

39. Lao Tzu, *Tao-te ching* 41, trans. Chan, *Source Book*, p. 160.

40. Plato *Republic* vi. 508c.

41. Kant, *Critique of Pure Reason*, A 249, pp. 265-66.

42. DK 28 B 2.

43. Aristotle *Metaphysics* i. 6. 987a32-b10, trans. Ross in *Works*, Vol. VIII.

44. Plotinus *Enneads* i. 6, trans. Elmer O'Brien in *The Essential Plotinus* (New York: New American Library, 1964), p. 40.

45. St. Augustine *De civitate Dei* vii. 6, trans. R. McKeon in *Organizations of the Sciences* (see chap. ii, n. 61), Pt. I, III, p. 16.

46. The Koran, trans. J. M. Rodwell, Everyman's Library (London: J. M. Dent and Sons, 1909), ii:1, p. 338.

47. *Ibid.*, vii:45, p. 297.

48. Aristotle *Metaphysics* i. 6. 987b1-4, trans. Ross in *Works*, Vol. VIII.

49. Aristotle *On Sophistical Refutations* 1. 164a23-b28, trans. E. S. Foster, Loeb Classical Library (Cambridge: Harvard University Press, 1955), pp. 11-13.

50. Aristotle *Metaphysics* vi. 3. 1005b18-20, trans. Ross in *Works*, Vol. VIII.

51. *Ibid.*, 1006a18-23.

52. Aristotle *Ethics* i. 3. 1094b11-27, trans. W. D. Ross in *Works*, Vol. IX.

53. William Harvey, *Anatomical Studies on the Motion of the Heart and Blood*, trans. Chauncey D. Leake (Springfield, Ill.: Charles C. Thomas, 1969), chap. ii, p. 28.

54. *Hegel's Philosophy of Right*, trans. T. M. Knox (Oxford: Clarendon Press, 1942), Preface, p. 10, and *Logic of Hegel* (see chap. ii, n. 68), Introduction, sec. 6, p. 10.

55. Hegel, *Phenomenology*, chap. viii, par. 808, p. 493.

56. *Hegel's Science of Logic*, trans. W. H. Johnson and L. G. Struthers, 2 vols. (London: George Allen and Unwin, 1929), Introduction, par. 21; Vol. I, p. 60.

57. Edmund Husserl, *Ideas*, trans. W. R. Boyce Gibson (New York: Macmillan Co., 1931; New York: Collier Books, 1962), Pt. I, chap. i, sec. 2, p. 47.

58. Edmund Husserl, *The Crisis of European Sciences and Transcendental Phenomenology*, trans. David Carr (Evanston: Northwestern University Press, 1970), Pt. III, sec. 36, p. 139.

59. *Ibid.*

60. Martin Heidegger, *Being and Time*, trans. John Macquarrie and Edward Robinson (London: SCM Press, 1962), sec. 7A, p. 51.

61. Alfred North Whitehead, *Process and Reality* (New York: Macmillan Co., 1929), chap. i, sec. 1, p. 4.

62. Newton, *Principia*, Bk. III, Prop. VII, p. 414.

Chapter IV. Method

1. Diogenes Laertius ix. 52 (DK 80 A 1); Plato *Protagoras* 335a, but see *Theaetetus* 167e; Gorgias *Encomium of Helen* 13 (DK 82 B 11).

2. DK 87 B 49.

3. DK 82 B 8.

4. Diogenes Laertius ix. 51 (DK 80 A 1).

5. *Ibid.*, 53.

6. *Ibid.*, 55.

7. Antiphon *Tetralogies*, trans. J. S. Morrison in *The Older Sophists*, ed. Rosamund Kent Sprague (Columbia: University of South Carolina Press, 1972), pp. 136-63.

8. Sextus Empiricus *Outlines of Pyrrhonism* i. 8, trans. Bury, p. 7.

9. DK 22 B 10, trans. Kirk and Raven, p. 191.

10. DK 22 B 53, trans. Kirk and Raven, p. 195.

11. DK 22 A 22, trans. Kirk and Raven, p. 196.

12. DK 22 B 111, trans. Kirk and Raven, p. 189.

13. Ovid *Ars amatoria* iii. 1-6, trans. anonymously in *The Art of Love and Other Love Books of Ovid* (New York: Grosset and Dunlap, 1959), p. 169.

14. Andreas Capellanus *De amore* iii. 2, trans. John Jay Parry, *The Art of Courtly Love* (New York: Frederick Ungar, 1959), p. 187.

15. John Milton, *Areopagitica*, par. 7, in *Complete Prose Works of John Milton*, Vol. II (New Haven: Yale University Press, 1959), pp. 514-15.

16. Machiavelli, *Discourses*, Bk. I, chap. iv, trans. Christian E. Detmold in *The Prince and The Discourses*, p. 119.

17. *The Spirit of the Laws by Baron de Montesquieu*, trans. Thomas Nugent (New York: Hafner Publishing Co., 1949), Bk. XI, sec. 6, pp. 151-52.

18. *The Federalist* No. 51, par. 1, in *The Papers of James Madison*, Vol. X (Chicago: University of Chicago Press, 1977), p. 476.

19. Sigmund Freud, *Civilization and Its Discontents*, end of sec. 6, trans. James Strachey in *Standard Edition*, XXI, 122.

20. DK 67 B 2.

21. DK 68 A 66.

22. René Descartes, *Rules for the Direction of the Understanding*, Rule IV, trans. in *From Descartes to Kant*, ed. T. V. Smith and Marjorie Grene (Chicago: University of Chicago Press, 1933), p. 64.

23. *Ibid.*, Rule V, p. 68.

24. Thomas Hobbes, *Leviathan* (London, 1651; Oxford: Clarendon Press, 1909), Pt. I, chap. v, p. 18.

25. Benedict de Spinoza, *Ethics*, trans. J. Gutmann (New York: Hafner Publishing Co., 1949), Pt. I, Prop. 29, p. 65.

26. Gottfried Wilhelm Leibniz, "Preface to the General Science" and "The Art of Discovery," trans. Philip P. Wiener in *Leibniz Selections*, pp. 15, 51.

27. Gottfried Wilhelm Leibniz, "On Freedom," in *Philosophical Papers and Letters*, trans. Leroy E. Loemker, 2 vols. (Chicago: University of Chicago Press, 1956), I, 406-407.

28. Newton, *Principia*, Preface, pp. xvii-xviii.

29. Hume, *Enquiry concerning Human Understanding*, sec. 12, pt. 2, par. 7, p. 160.

30. Darwin, *Origin of Species*, chap. ii, pp. 74-75.

31. Max Weber, *The Protestant Ethic and the Spirit of Capitalism*, trans. Talcott Parsons (New York: Charles Scribner's Sons, 1958), p. 180.

32. *Ibid.*, p. 181.

33. Plato *Republic* vii. 537c, trans. Allan Bloom, *The Republic of Plato* (New York: Basic Books, 1968), p. 216; see also 531d, p. 211.

34. Alfred North Whitehead, *Adventures of Ideas* (New York: Macmillan Co., 1933), chap. vii, sec. 2, p. 134; sec. 3, pp. 137-38.

35. Edwin Markham, "Outwitted," in *The Shoes of Happiness and Other Poems* (Garden City, N.Y.: Doubleday, Page and Co., 1916), p. 1.

36. Norman O. Brown, *Life Against Death* (New York: Vintage Books, 1959), p. 83.

37. Karl Marx, *Capital*, Vol. I, trans. Eden and Cedar Paul, Everyman's Library (London: J. M. Dent and Sons, 1930), Preface to Second Edition, p. lix.

38. Jean-Paul Sartre, *Search for a Method*, trans. Hazel E. Barnes (New York: Vintage Books, 1968), Part III, pp. 151-52. Originally published as *Questions de méthode* (Paris, 1960).

39. *Ibid.*, Conclusion, p. 175.

40. *Ibid.*, p. 181.

41. Aristotle *On the Soul* i. 1. 402b16-403a2, trans. J. A. Smith in *Works*, Vol. III.

42. Aristotle *Prior Analytics* i. 1. 24b18-20.

43. Kant, *Critique of Pure Reason*, A 832, B 860, p. 653.

44. Immanuel Kant, *Critique of Practical Reason*, Preface, par. 11, trans. Thomas Kingsmill Abbot in *Kant's Critique of Practical Reason and Other Works on the Theory of Ethics*. 6th ed. (London: Longmans, Green, and Co., 1909), pp. 95-96. This passage was pointed out by David Dilworth.

45. Kant, *Critique of Pure Reason*, A 51, B 75, p. 93.

46. *Ibid.*, A 423-24, B 451-52, p. 395.

47. William Whewell, *The Philosophy of the Inductive Sciences Founded upon Their History*, 2d ed., 2 vols. (London, 1847), Bk. XI, chap. i; Vol. II, p. 3.

48. William Whewell, *Novum Organum Renovatum*, 3d ed. (London, 1858), Preface, p. iii.

49. John Dewey, *Logic: The Theory of Inquiry* (New York: Henry Holt and Co., 1938), chap. vi, par. 12, pp. 104-105.

50. *Ibid.*, par. 27, p. 111.

51. John Dewey, *Experience and Education* (New York: Kappa Delta Pi Publications, 1938; New York: Collier Books, 1963), Preface, p. 5.

52. Dmitri Mendeleev, "The Correlation between the Properties of the Elements and Their Atomic Weights," *Journal of the Russian Chemical Society*, I (1869), 60-77, par. 6, trans. Barry J. Rubin.

53. *Ibid.*, par. 12.

54. Edgar Allen Poe, "The Murders in the Rue Morgue," par. 1, in *The Complete Works of Edgar Allen Poe*, ed. James A. Harrison, 17 vols. (New York, 1902; New York: AMS Press, 1965), IV, 146-47.

55. *Ibid.*, par. 2, pp. 148-49.

Chapter V. Principle

1. For the interpretation of Genesis I am indebted to Leonard Gardner's "Heaven and Earth: A Study of the Book of Genesis."

2. Koran vi:39, trans. Rodwell, p. 320.

3. *Ibid.*, ii:284, p. 370.

4. St. Augustine *Confessiones* xii. 13, trans. Rex Warner, *The Confessions of St. Augustine* (New York: New American Library, 1963), p. 293.

5. St. Augustine *De libero arbitrio voluntatis* i. 11, trans. Anna S. Benjamin and

L. H. Hackstaff, *On Free Choice of the Will*, Library of Liberal Arts (Indianapolis: Bobbs-Merrill, 1964), p. 22.

6. Aristotle *Metaphysics* i. 3. 983b20-27, trans. Ross in *Works*, Vol. VIII.

7. DK 11 A 15, trans. Kirk and Raven, p. 92.

8. Plato *Theaetetus* 166d-167a, trans. F. M. Cornford in *Collected Dialogues*, pp. 872-73.

9. Isocrates *Antidosis* 253-54, trans. George Norlin in *Isocrates*, Vol. II, Loeb Classical Library (London: William Heinemann, 1929), p. 327.

10. *Ibid.*, 232-34, p. 315.

11. Giovanni Pico della Mirandola, "Oration on the Dignity of Man," trans. Elizabeth L. Forbes in *The Renaissance Philosophy of Man*, ed. Ernst Cassirer, Oskar Kristeller, and John Herman Randall, Jr. (Chicago: University of Chicago Press, 1948), pp. 224-25.

12. Locke, *Essay*, Bk. IV, chap. iii, sec. 18, in *Philosophical Works*, II, 154.

13. Hobbes, *Leviathan*, Pt. II, chap. xvii, p. 87.

14. See Watson, "Principles for Dealing with Disorder" (see chap. i, n. 1), pp. 356-57.

15. Max Weber, *The Theory of Social and Economic Organization*, trans. A. M. Henderson and Talcott Parsons (New York: Free Press, 1964), chap. iii, sec. 10, pp. 361-62. Originally published as *Wirtschaft und Gesellschaft*, Part I (Tübingen, 1921).

16. Karl Marx, "Economic and Philosophic Manuscripts of 1844," Third Manuscript, Private Property and Communism, MS p. XI, trans. T. B. Bottomore in *Karl Marx: Early Writings* (New York: McGraw-Hill Book Co., 1963), p. 166.

17. Alfred North Whitehead, *Modes of Thought* (New York: Macmillan Co., 1938), lect. ii, sec. 5, pp. 55-56.

18. Whitehead, *Process and Reality*, chap. ii, sec. 2, pp. 31-32.

19. Whitehead, *Modes of Thought*, lect. ii, sec. 2, p. 36.

20. Jean-Paul Sartre, *Existentialism*, trans. Bernard Frechtman (New York: Philosophical Library, 1947), pp. 27-28. Originally published as *L'existentialism est un humanisme* (Paris, 1946).

21. John Dewey, "The Influence of Darwinism on Philosophy," Pt. I, par. 1, in *The Influence of Darwin on Philosophy and Other Essays in Contemporary Thought* (New York: Henry Holt and Co., 1910), pp. 1-2.

22. Dewey, *Logic*, chap. v, par. 34, p. 93.

23. Watson, "Principles for Dealing with Disorder," pp. 354-59.

24. Thus for Berkeley "a Spirit is one simple, undivided, active being" (*A Treatise concerning the Principles of Human Knowledge*, Pt. I, par. 27); for Leibniz the monad is a simple substance and "God alone is the ultimate unity or the original simple substance" ("Monadology," art. 47, in *Leibniz Selections*, p. 542); and St. Thomas Aquinas says that "everyone admits the simplicity of the First Cause" (*On Being and Essence*, trans. Armand Augustine Maurer [Toronto: Pontifical Institute of Medieval Studies, 1949], chap. iv, p. 43.

25. DK 13 A 5, trans. Kirk and Raven, p. 14.

26. DK 13 B 2, trans. Kirk and Raven, p. 158.

27. DK 13 A 15, B 2a, trans. Kirk and Raven, p. 154.

28. DK 13 A 20, trans. Kirk and Raven, p. 153.

29. DK 13 A 14, trans. Kirk and Raven, p. 154.

30. DK 13 A 7, trans. Kirk and Raven, p. 154.

31. DK 13 A 7, trans. Kirk and Raven, pp. 144-45.

32. DK 13 A 17, trans. Kirk and Raven, p. 157.

33. DK 13 A 21, trans. Kirk and Raven, p. 158.

34. DK 13 B 1, trans. Kirk and Raven, p. 148.

35. DK 28 B 8, trans. Kirk and Raven, p. 273.

36. DK 31 B 27, 28, trans. Kirk and Raven, p. 326.

37. DK 31 B 17, trans. Kirk and Raven, p. 324.

38. Aristotle *Metaphysics* i. 4. 985b4-19, trans. Ross in *Works*, Vol. VIII.

39. Aristotle *On the Generation of Animals* ii. 6. 742b17.

40. Plotinus *Enneads* vi. 9, trans. O'Brien, p. 77.

41. *Ibid.*, p. 78.

42. Chhāndogya-Upanishad, Bk. VI, sec. 2, in *The Ten Principal Upanishads*, trans. Shree Purohit and W. B. Yeats (London: Faber and Faber, 1937), pp. 85-86.

43. *Ibid.*, sec. 11, p. 92.

44. Bhagavad Gītā ix:7-8, trans. Edgerton, p. 46.

45. Lao Tzu, *Tao-te ching* 16, trans. Chan, *Source Book*, p. 147.

46. *Ibid.*, 14, p. 146.

47. Isaac Newton, *Opticks*, 4th ed. (London, 1710; New York: Dover Publications, 1952), Bk. III, Pt. I, Q 31, p. 397.

48. *Ibid.*, p. 400.

49. Newton, *Principia*, General Scholium, pars. 3, 4, pp. 544, 546.

50. Hume, *Enquiry concerning Human Understanding*, sec. iii, par. 2, p. 24.

51. *Ibid.*, sec. 5, pt. 1, par. 5, p. 43.

52. Hume, *Enquiry concerning the Principles of Morals*, sec. 5, pt. 2, par. 2, note, pp. 219-20.

53. Mendeleev, "The Correlation between the Properties of the Elements and Their Atomic Weights" (see chap. iv, n. 52), par. 7, trans. Rubin.

54. Hermann Helmholtz, "The Aim and Progress of Physical Science," trans. W. Flight in *Popular Lectures on Scientific Subjects*, ed. E. Atkinson (New York, 1873), pp. 379-80.

55. Nietzsche, *Beyond Good and Evil*, art. 36, p. 48.

56. Nietzsche, *Gay Science*, art. 348, p. 291.

57. Friedrich Nietzsche, *Twilight of the Idols*, The Four Great Errors, sec. 7, in *The Portable Nietzsche*, sel. and trans. Walter Kaufmann (New York: Viking Press, 1954), pp. 499-500.

58. Nietzsche, *Beyond Good and Evil*, art. 19, p. 25.

59. Nietzsche, *Gay Science*, art. 109, p. 168.

60. Sigmund Freud, "Analysis Terminable and Interminable," sec. 6, trans. James Strachey in *Standard Edition*, XXIII, 246.

61. Edgar Allen Poe, "The Imp of the Perverse," par. 3, in *Complete Works*, VI, 146-47.

62. DK 12 A 9, trans. Kirk and Raven, p. 117.

63. DK 12 A 26, trans. Kirk and Raven, p. 134.

64. DK 12 A 1, trans. Kirk and Raven, p. 99.

65. DK 12 A 10, trans. Kirk and Raven, p. 131.

66. DK 12 A 30, trans. Kirk and Raven, p. 141.

67. DK 12 A 10, trans. Kirk and Raven, p. 141.

68. DK 22 B 123, trans. in Charles H. Kahn, *The Art and Thought of Heraclitus* (Cambridge: Cambridge University Press, 1979), p. 33.

69. DK 22 B 50, trans. Kirk and Raven, p. 188.

70. *Ibid.*

71. DK 22 B 41, trans. Kahn, p. 55.

72. DK 22 B 32, trans. Kahn, p. 83.

73. DK 22 B 51, trans. Kahn, p. 65.

74. DK 22 B 60, trans. Kahn, p. 75.

75. DK 22 B 126, trans. Kahn, p. 53.

76. DK 22 B 1, trans. Kirk and Raven, p. 187.

77. Plato *Republic* vi. 509b.

78. Plato *Timaeus* 29d-30a, trans. Benjamin Jowett in *Collected Dialogues*, p. 1162.

79. Leibniz, "Discourse on Metaphysics," art. 1, in *Leibniz Selections*, p. 290.

80. *Ibid.*, art. 2, p. 291.

81. *Ibid.*, art. 3, p. 292.

82. Leibniz, "Monadology," arts. 53-55, in *Leibniz Selections*, pp. 543-44.

83. Leibniz, "Discourse on Metaphysics," art. 6, in *Leibniz Selections*, p. 297.

84. *Ibid.*, art. 13, pp. 305-306.

85. Leibniz, "Monadology," art. 18, in *Leibniz Selections*, p. 536.

86. Confucius *Analects* 8:19, trans. James Legge in *Confucian Analects, The Great Learning and The Doctrine of the Mean* (Oxford: Clarendon Press, 1893; New York: Dover Publications, 1971), p. 214.

87. Confucius *Analects* 15:4, trans. Chan, *Source Book*, p. 43.

88. *Shu ching* (Book of history), "Prince Shih," trans. Chan, *Source Book*, p. 7.

89. *Ibid.*, "Shao kao," trans. in *Sources of Chinese Tradition*, Vol. I, ed. W. Theodore de Bary, Wing-tsit Chan, and Burton Watson (New York: Columbia University Press, 1964), p. 11.

90. *Shih ching* (Book of odes), no. 235, "King Wen," trans. Chan, *Source Book*, p. 7.

91. Confucius *Analects* 2:4, trans. Chan, *Source Book*, p. 22.

92. *Ibid.*, 7:22, p. 32.

93. *Ibid.*, 9:5, p. 35.

94. *Ibid.*, 4:4, p. 25.

95. *Ibid.*, 6:28, p. 31.

96. *Doctrine of the Mean* 13, trans. Chan, *Source Book*, p. 101.

97. Confucius *Analects* 4:10, trans. Chan, *Source Book*, p. 26.

98. *Ibid.*, 15:17, p. 43.

99. *Ibid.*, 10:9, p. 36.

100. Chu Hsi, *Chu Tzu yu-lui*, Bk. 94, quoted by Carsun Chang, *The Development of Neo-Confucian Thought* (New York: Bookman Associates, 1957), p. 282.

101. Chu Hsi, *Chu Tzu ch'uan-shu* 49:14b-15a, trans. Chan, *Source Book*, p. 641.

102. See Walter Watson, "Chu Hsi, Plato, and Aristotle," *Journal of Chinese Philosophy*, V (1978), 149-74.

103. Walt Whitman, "A Backward Glance O'er Travel'd Roads," par. 34, in *Leaves of Grass* (see chap. ii, n. 26), p. 573.

104. Walt Whitman, "Song of Myself," 31, in *Leaves of Grass*, p. 59.

105. *Ibid.*, 45, p. 82.

106. *Ibid.*, 20, p. 47.

107. *Ibid.*, 50, p. 88.

108. Walt Whitman, "Eidolons," lines 81-84, in *Leaves of Grass*, p. 8.

109. Walt Whitman, "Passage to India," 9, in *Leaves of Grass*, p. 421.

110. Leo Tolstoy, *War and Peace*, trans. Louise and Aylmer Maude (New York: Simon and Schuster, 1942), First Epilogue, sec. 1, p. 1264.

111. *Ibid.*, Second Epilogue, p. 1314.

112. *Ibid.*, p. 1335.

113. *Ibid.*, last sentence, p. 1351.

114. DK 21 B 26'25, trans. Kirk and Raven, p. 169.

115. DK 21 A 33, trans. Kirk and Raven, p. 177.

116. DK 21 B 1, trans. in Philip Wheelwright, *The Presocratics* (New York: Odyssey Press, 1966), p. 35.

117. DK 21 B 3, trans. Wheelwright, p. 36.

118. DK 59 B 12, trans. Kirk and Raven, p. 372.

119. Aristotle *Physics* ii. 199b15-31, trans. Hardie and Gaye in *Works*, Vol. II.

120. *Stoicorum veterum fragmenta*, ed. J. von Arnim, 4 vols. (Leipzig, 1905-24) (cited hereafter as SVF), II, 118, trans. in Jason L. Saunders, *Greek and Roman Philosophy after Aristotle* (New York: Free Press, 1966), p. 72.

121. SVF I, 98, trans. Saunders, p. 92.

122. SVF III, 4, trans. Saunders, p. 112.

123. St. Thomas Aquinas, *Summa Theologica*, Pt. I, Q. 2, art. 3, trans. Pegis, *Introduction*, p. 25.

124. St. Thomas Aquinas, *On Being and Essence*, chap. iv, p. 47.

125. Spinoza, *Ethics*, Pt. I, Def. 1, trans. Gutmann, p. 41.

126. *Ibid.*, Prop. 15, p. 52.

127. *Ibid.*, Pt. II, Def. 4, p. 79.

128. *Ibid.*, Prop. 43, Note, p. 114.

129. *Ibid.*, Pt. III, Prop. 1, p. 129.

130. *Ibid.*, Pt. V, Prop. 36, p. 274.

131. Aristotle *Metaphysics* vii. 3. 1029b7-8.

132. *Ibid.*, xii. 9. 1074b34.

133. Hegel, *Phenomenology*, Preface, par. 22, p. 12.

134. Michael Faraday, *Experimental Researches in Electricity*, 3 vols. (London, 1839-55; New York: Dover Publications, 1965), Nos. 1642-45; Vol. I, pp. 523-24.

135. Geoffrey Chaucer, *The Canterbury Tales*, The Manciple's Tale, lines 187-88, in *The Poetical Works of Chaucer*, ed. F. N. Robinson (Boston: Houghton Mifflin Co., 1933), p. 269.

136. *Ibid.*, General Prologue, lines 573-75, Robinson, p. 25.

137. *Ibid.*, line 586.

138. Bhagavad Gita ix:5, trans. Edgerton, p. 46.

139. Kumārila Bhaṭṭa, *Ślokavārtika*, trans. Ganganatha Jha in *Source Book in Indian Philosophy*, p. 505.

140. Confucius *Analects* 2:11, trans. Chan, *Source Book*, p. 23; Chu Hsi and Lü Tsu-ch'ien, *Reflections on Things at Hand: The Neo-Confucian Anthology*, trans. Wing-tsit Chan (New York: Columbia University Press, 1967).

141. Gottfried Wilhelm Leibniz, Letter to Nicolas Remond, 10 Jan. 1714, trans. Loemker, II, 1064.

142. Gottfried Wilhelm Leibniz, *Specimen Dynamicum*, Pt. I, par. 3, trans. Loemker, II, 713.

143. Kant, *Critique of Pure Reason* A 832, B 860, p. 653.

Chapter VI. Archic Analysis

1. Matthew Arnold, "Shakespeare," in *The Poetical Works of Matthew Arnold*, ed. C. B. Tinker and H. F. Lowry (London: Oxford University Press, 1950), p. 2.

2. Plato *Protagoras* 316d-317b.

3. Richard McKeon, "Discussion and Resolution in Political Conflicts," *Ethics*, LIV (1944), 235.

4. See Walter Watson, *Nature and Action* (Ann Arbor, Mich.: University Microfilms, 1958).

5. See Walter Watson, "The Existentializing of Psychoanalysis," *Cross Currents*, XXX (1980-81), 461-63.

6. See Watson, "Chu Hsi, Plato, and Aristotle" (see chap. v, n. 102).

Bibliography of Works Cited

Andreas Capellanus. *The Art of Courtly Love*. Translated by John Jay Parry. New York: Frederick Ungar, 1959.

Aristotle. *Aristotle's Prior and Posterior Analytics*. Edited by W. D. Ross. Oxford: Clarendon Press, 1949.

_____ . *On Sophistical Refutations*. With an English translation by E. S. Forster. (Loeb Classical Library). Cambridge: Harvard University Press, 1955.

_____ . *De generatione animalium*. Edited by H. J. Drossart Lulofs. Oxford: Clarendon Press, 1965.

_____ . *Metaphysica*. Edited by W. Jaeger. Oxford: Clarendon Press, 1957.

_____ . *Ethica Nicomachea*. Edited by I. Bywater. Oxford: Clarendon Press, 1894.

_____ . *Politica*. Edited by W. D. Ross. Oxford: Clarendon Press, 1957.

_____ . *The Works of Aristotle Translated into English*. Edited by W. D. Ross. 12 vols. Oxford: Oxford University Press, 1908-52.

Arnold, Matthew. *The Poetical Works of Matthew Arnold*. Edited by C. B. Tinker and H. F. Lowry. London: Oxford University Press, 1950.

Augustine, Saint. *On Free Choice of the Will*. Translated by Anna S. Benjamin and L. H. Hackstaff. (Library of Liberal Arts.) Indianapolis: Bobbs-Merrill, 1964.

_____ . *Concerning the Teacher* and *On the Immortality of the Soul*. Translated by George G. Leckie. New York: Appleton-Century Crofts, 1938.

_____ . *Confessions*. Translated by Rex Warner. New York: New America Library, 1963.

_____ . *The City of God*. Translated by Marcus Dods. New York: Modern Library, 1950.

Austen, Jane. *Sense and Sensibility*. Edited by James Kinsley and Claire Lamont. Oxford: Oxford University Press, 1980.

———. *Pride and Prejudice.* Edited by James Kinsley and Frank W. Bradbrook. Oxford: Oxford University Press, 1980.

———. *Mansfield Park.* Edited by James Kinsley and John Lucas. Oxford: Oxford University Press, 1980.

———. *Emma.* Edited by James Kinsley and David Lodge. Oxford: Oxford University Press, 1980.

———. *Persuasion.* Edited by John Davie. Oxford: Oxford University Press, 1980.

———. *Northanger Abbey, Lady Susan, The Watsons,* and *Sanditon.* Edited by John Davie. Oxford: Oxford University Press, 1980.

Bacon, Francis. *The Works of Francis Bacon.* Edited by James Spedding, Robert Leslie Ellis, and Douglas Denton Heath. 14 vols. London, 1857-74.

Bergson, Henri. *An Introduction to Metaphysics.* Translated by T. E. Hulme. New York: Liberal Arts Press, 1949.

———. *Creative Evolution.* Translated by Arthur Mitchell. New York: Modern Library, 1944.

Berkeley, George. *The Works of George Berkeley.* Edited by Alexander Campbell Fraser. 4 vols. Oxford: Clarendon Press, 1901.

The Bhagavad Gītā. Translated by Franklin Edgerton. New York: Harper and Row, 1946.

Booth, Wayne C. *The Rhetoric of Fiction.* Chicago: University of Chicago Press, 1967.

Bridgman, P. W. *The Way Things Are.* New York: Viking Press, 1961.

Brown, Norman O. *Life Against Death.* New York: Vintage Books, 1959.

Carnap, Rudolf. *The Logical Syntax of Language.* London: Routledge and Kegan Paul, 1937.

Cervantes, Miguel de. *Don Quixote.* Ozell's revision of the translation of Peter Motteus. New York: Modern Library, 1930.

Chan, Wing-tsit. *A Source Book in Chinese Philosophy.* Princeton: Princeton University Press, 1963.

Chang, Carsun. *The Development of Neo-Confucian Thought.* New York: Bookman Associates, 1957.

Chaucer, Geoffrey. *The Poetical Works of Chaucer.* Edited by F. N. Robinson. Boston: Houghton Mifflin Co., 1933.

Chu Hsi and Lu Tsu-Ch'ien. *Reflections on Things at Hand.* Translated by Wing-tsit Chan. New York: Columbia University Press, 1967.

Confucius. *Confucian Analects, The Great Learning* and *The Doctrine of the Mean.* Translated by James Legge. New York: Dover Publications, 1971.

Dante. *The Divine Comedy*. Translated by Laurence Binyon in *The Portable Dante*. New York: Viking Press, 1947.

Darwin, Charles. *On the Origin of Species*. A Facsimile of the First Edition. Cambridge: Harvard University Press, 1946.

———. *The Descent of Man and Selection in Relation to Sex*. In *The Origin of Species* and *The Descent of Man*. New York: Modern Library, n.d.

———. *The Expresion of the Emotions in Man and Animals*. Chicago: University of Chicago Press, 1965.

de Bary, Wm. Theodore, Chan, Wing-tsit, and Watson, Burton, eds. *Sources of Chinese Tradition*. 2 vols. New York: Columbia University Press, 1964.

Derrida, Jacques. *Of Grammatology*. Translated by Gayatri Chakravorty Spivak. Baltimore: Johns Hopkins University Press, 1976.

———. *Dissemination*. Translated by Barbara Johnson. Chicago: University of Chicago Press, 1981.

Descartes, René. *The Philosophical Works of Descartes*. Translated by Elizabeth S. Haldane and G. R. T. Ross. 2 vols. Cambridge: University Press, 1911.

Dewey, John. *The Influence of Darwinism on Philosophy and Other Essays in Contemporary Thought*. New York: Henry Holt and Co., 1910.

———. *Human Nature and Conduct: An Introduction to Social Psychology*. New York: Modern Library, 1930.

———. *Experience and Nature*. New York: W. W. Norton and Co., 1925.

———. *The Public and Its Problems: An Essay in Political Inquiry*. Chicago: Gateway Books, 1946.

———. *Art as Experience*. New York: Minton, Balch and Co., 1934.

———. *Experience and Education*. New York: Collier Books, 1963.

———. *Logic: The Theory of Inquiry*. New York: Henry Holt and Co., 1938.

Diels, Hermann, and Kranz, Walther, eds. *Die Fragmente der Vorsokratiker*. 3 vols. 7th ed. Berlin: Weidmannsche Verlagsbuchhandlung, 1954.

Diogenes Laertius. *Lives of Eminent Philosophers*. Translated by R. D. Hicks. 2 vols. (Loeb Classical Library.) Cambridge: Harvard University Press, 1966.

Dostoyevsky, Fyodor. *Notes from Underground*. Translated by Andrew R. MacAndrew. New York: New American Library, 1961.

Duyvendak, J. J. L. *The Book of Lord Shang*. Chicago: University of Chicago Press, 1963.

Eddington, Sir Arthur. *The Nature of the Physical World*. New York: Macmillan Co., 1928.

Einstein, Albert. *Ideas and Opinions*. New York: Crown Publishers, 1954.

Euripides. *Hippolytus*. Translated by David Grene. In *Euripides I*. Chicago: University of Chicago Press, 1955.

———. *The Bacchae*. Translated by William Arrowsmith. In *Euripides V*. Chicago: University of Chicago Press, 1959.

Faraday, Michael. *Experimental Researches in Electricity*. 3 vols. New York: Dover Publications, 1965.

Faulkner, William. *The Sound and the Fury* and *As I Lay Dying*. New York: Modern Library, 1946.

Freud, Sigmund. *The Standard Edition of the Complete Psychological Works of Sigmund Freud*. Edited by James Strachey. 24 vols. London: Hogarth Press, 1953-74.

Galileo Galilei. *Dialogues concerning Two New Sciences*. Translated by Henry Crew and Alfonso de Salvio. Evanston: Northwestern University, 1946.

———. *Dialogue on the Great World Systems*. Salusbury translation revised by Giorgio de Santillana. Chicago: University of Chicago Press, 1953.

Gardner, Leonard. "Heaven and Earth: A Study of the Book of Genesis."

Genesis. In *The Holy Bible*. King James Version, 1611. New York: American Bible Society, n.d.

Hardy, Thomas. *Tess of the d'Urbervilles*. London: Macmillan, 1974.

———. *Jude the Obscure*. London: Macmillan, 1975.

Harvey, William. *Anatomical Studies on the Motion of the Heart and Blood. Translated by Chauncey D. Leake. Springfield, Ill.: Charles C. Thomas, 1969.*

Hegel, Georg Wilhelm Friedrich. *Phenomenology of Spirit*. Translated by A. V. Miller. Oxford: Oxford University Press, 1977.

———. *Hegel's Science of Logic*. Translated by W. H. Johnson and L. G. Struthers. 2 vols. London: George Allen and Unwin, 1929.

———. *Encyclopadie der philosophischen Wissenschaften im Grundrisse*. 2d ed. Edited by Georg Lasson. Leipzig: Verlag von Felix Meiner, 1905.

———. *The Logic of Hegel*. Translated from the *Encyclopaedia of the Philosophical Sciences* by William Wallace. 2d ed. Oxford: Oxford University Press, 1892.

———. *Hegel's Philosophy of Right*. Translated by T. M. Knox. Oxford: Clarendon Press, 1942.

Heidegger, Martin. *Being and Time*. Translated by John Macquarrie and Edward Robinson. London: SCM Press, 1962.

Helmholtz, Hermann. *Popular Lectures on Scientific Subjects.* Edited by E. Atkinson. New York, 1873.

History of the Organization of the Sciences. Selected Readings, Part I, for the Course in Observation, Interpretation, Integration. 2 vols. 1st ed. Chicago: University of Chicago Bookstore, 1943.

Hobbes, Thomas. *Hobbes's Leviathan.* Reprinted from the edition of 1651. Oxford: Clarendon Press, 1909.

Hume, David. *A Treatise of Human Nature.* Edited by L. A. Selby-Bigge. Oxford: Clarendon Press, 1888.

———. *Enquiries concerning the Human Understanding and concerning the Principles of Morals.* Edited by L. A. Selby-Bigge. 2d ed. Oxford: Clarendon Press, 1902.

———. *The History of England from the Invasion of Julius Caesar to The Abdication of James the Second, 1688.* 3 vols. Philadelphia: Porter and Coates, n.d.

———. *Essays Moral, Political, and Literary.* Edited by T. H. Green and T. H. Grose. 2 vols. London, 1875.

Husserl, Edmund. *Ideas.* Translated by W. R. Boyce Gibson. New York: Collier Books, 1962.

———. *The Crisis of European Sciences and Transcendental Phenomenology.* Translated by David Carr. Evanston: Northwestern University Press, 1970.

Isidore of Seville, Saint. *Etymologiarum.* Edited by W. M. Lindsay. Oxford: Clarendon Press, 1957.

Isocrates. *Isocrates.* Vols. I and II translated by George Norlin; Vol. III translated by Larue van Hook. (Loeb Classical Library.) London: William Heinemann, 1928-45.

James, Henry. *Novels and Tales.* 23 vols. New York: Charles Scribner's Sons, 1907-9.

James, William. *Talks to Teachers on Psychology: and to Students on Some of Life's Ideals.* New York: Henry Holt and Co., 1901.

———. *The Varieties of Religious Experience.* New York: Modern Library, n.d.

Joyce, James. *A Portrait of the Artist as a Young Man.* New York: Viking Press, 1964.

———. *Ulysses.* New York: Modern Library, 1934.

———. *Finnegans Wake.* New York: Viking Press, 1945.

Kafka, Franz. *The Trial.* Translated by Willa and Edwin Muir. New York: A. A. Knopf, 1957.

Kahn, Charles H. *The Art and Thought of Heraclitus.* Cambridge: Cambridge University Press, 1979.

Kant, Immanuel. *Immanuel Kant's Critique of Pure Reason*. Translated by Norman Kemp Smith. New York: Humanities Press, 1950.

_____ . *Metaphysical Foundations of Natural Science*. Translated by James Ellington. (Library of Liberal Arts.) Indianapolis: Bobbs-Merrill Co., 1970.

_____ . *Kant's Critique of Practical Reason and Other Works on the Theory of Ethics*. Translated by Thomas Kingsmill Abbott. 6th ed. London: Longmans, Green, and Co., 1909.

_____ . *Critique of Judgment*. Translated by J. H. Bernard. New York: Hafner Publishing Co., 1951.

Kepler, Johannes. *Mysterium cosmographicum*. Translation by A. M. Duncan. New York: Abaris, 1981.

_____ . *Harmonice mundi*. Edited by Max Caspar. Vol. VI of *Gesammelte Werke*, edited by Walther von Duck and Max Caspar. Munich: C. H. Beck, 1937-.

Kierkegaard, Søren. *Either/Or*. Vol. I translated by David F. Swenson and Lillian Marvin Swenson. Vol. II translated by Walter Lowrie. Garden City, New York: Doubleday and Co., 1959.

_____ . *Kierkegaard's Concluding Unscientific Postscript*. Translated by David F. Swenson and Walter Lowrie. Princeton: Princeton University Press, 1944.

_____ . *Edifying Discourses*. Translated by David F. Swenson and Lillian Marvin Swenson. 4 vols. Minneapolis: Augsburg Publishing House, 1943-46.

_____ . *The Point of View for My Work as an Author: A Report to History, and Related Writings*. Translated by Walter Lowrie. New York: Harper and Brothers, 1962.

Kirk, G. S., and Raven, J. E. *The Presocratic Philosophers*. Cambridge: University Press, 1969.

The Koran. Translated by J. M. Rodwell. (Everyman's Library.) London: J. M. Dent and Sons, 1909.

Leibniz, Gottfried Wilhelm. *Leibniz Selections*. Edited by Philip P. Wiener. New York: Charles Scribner's Sons, 1951.

_____ . *Philosophical Papers and Letters*. Translated by Leroy E. Loemker. 2 vols. Chicago: University of Chicago Press, 1956.

The Lincoln-Douglas Debates of 1858. Edited by Robert W. Johannsen. New York: Oxford University Press, 1965.

Locke, John. *The Philosophical Works of John Locke*. Edited by J. A. St. John. 2 vols. (Bohn's Standard Library.) London: George Bell and Sons, 1908.

Mach, Ernst. *The Science of Mechanics*. Translated by Thomas J. Mc-Cormack. La Salle, Ill.: Open Court Publishing Co., 1942.

Machiavelli, Niccolò. *The Prince* and *The Discourses*. New York: Modern Library, 1940.

McKeon, Richard. "Discussion and Resolution in Political Conflicts." *Ethics*, LIV (1944), 235-62.

———. *Freedom and History*. New York: Noonday Press, 1952.

———. "A Philosopher Meditates on Discovery." In *Moments of Personal Discovery*, edited by R. M. MacIver. New York: Institute for Religious and Social Studies, 1952.

Madison, James. *The Papers of James Madison*. Edited by William T. Hutchinson and William M. E. Rachal. Chicago: University of Chicago Press, 1962.

Malthus, Thomas. *An Essay on Population*. (Everyman's Library.) London: J. M. Dent and Sons, 1914.

Markham, Edwin. *The Shoes of Happiness and Other Poems*. Garden City, New York: Doubleday, Page and Co., 1916.

Marx, Karl. *Early Writings*. Translated and Edited by T. B. Bottomore. New York: McGraw-Hill Book Co., 1963.

———. *A Contribution to the Critique of Political Economy*. Translated by N. I. Stone. Chicago: Charles H. Kerr and Co., 1904.

———. *Capital: Volume I Der Productionsprozess des Kapitals*. Translated from the 4th German edition by Eden and Cedar Paul. (Everyman's Library.) London: J. M. Dent and Sons, 1930.

Marx, Karl, and Engels, Frederick. *Manifesto of the Communist Party*. Translated by Samuel Moore, revised by Samuel Moore and Frederick Engels. Chicago: Charles H. Kerr and Co., 1946.

Melville, Herman. *Moby Dick*. Edited by Harrison Hayford and Hershel Parker. New York: W. W. Norton, 1976.

Mendeleev, Dmitri. "The Correlation between the Properties of the Elements and their Atomic Weights." *Journal of the Russian Chemical Society*, I (1969), 60-77. Translated by Barry J. Rubin.

Merleau-Ponty, Maurice. *Phenomenology of Perception*. Translated by Colin Smith. London: Routledge and Kegan Paul, 1962.

Mill, John Stuart. *A System of Logic*. London: Longmans, Green and Co., 1949.

———. *Utilitarianism*. In *The Philosophy of John Stuart Mill*. Edited by Marshall Cohen. New York: Modern Library, 1961.

Milton, John. *Complete Prose Works of John Milton*. Edited by Don M. Wolfe. New Haven: Yale University Press, 1953.

————. *Complete Poetry and Selected Prose of John Milton*. New York: Modern Library, n.d.

Montaigne, Michel de. *Essais*. 1st ed. Bordeaux, 1580.

Montesquieu. *The Spirit of the Laws by Baron de Montesquieu*. Translated by Thomas Nugent. New York: Hafner Publishing Co., 1949.

Moore, G. E. "An Autobiography." In *The Philosophy of G. E. Moore*, edited by Paul Arthur Schilpp. (The Library of Living Philosophers, Vol. IV.) Evanston: Northwestern University, 1942.

Newton, Sir Isaac. *Mathematical Principles of Natural Philosophy*. Translated by Andrew Motte, revised by Florian Cajori. Berkeley: University of California Press, 1947.

————. *Opticks*. 4th ed. New York: Dover Publications, 1952.

Nietzsche, Friedrich. *The Gay Science*. Translated by Walter Kaufmann. New York: Vintage Books, 1974.

————. *Beyond Good and Evil*. Translated by Walter Kaufmann. New York: Vintage Books, 1966.

————. *The Genealogy of Morals*. Translated by Francis Golffing. Garden City, N.Y.: Doubleday & Co., 1956.

————. *Twilight of the Idols*. Translated by Walter Kaufmann in *The Portable Nietzsche*. New York: Viking Press, 1954.

————. *Ecce Homo*. Translated by Walter Kaufmann in *Basic Writings of Nietzsche*. New York: Random House, 1968.

Ovid. *The Art of Love and Other Love Books of Ovid*. New York: Grosset and Dunlap, 1959.

Peirce, Charles Sanders. *Collected Papers of Charles Sanders Peirce*. Edited by Charles Hartshorne and Paul Weiss. 6 vols. Cambridge: Harvard University Press, 1931-35.

Pico della Mirandola, Giovanni. "Oration on the Dignity of Man." Translated by Elizabeth L. Forbes in *The Renaissance Philosophy of Man*, edited by Ernst Cassirer, Oskar Kristeller, and John Herman Randall, Jr. Chicago: University of Chicago Press, 1948.

Plato, *Platonis Opera*. Edited by John Burnet. 5 vols. Oxford: Clarendon Press, 1900-07.

————. *The Collected Dialogues of Plato*. Edited by Edith Hamilton and Huntington Cairns. Princeton: Princeton University Press, 1963.

————. *The Republic of Plato*. Translated by Allan Bloom. New York: Basic Books, 1968.

Plotinus. *The Essential Plotinus*. Translated by Elmer O'Brien. New York: New American Library, 1964.

Poe, Edgar Allen. *The Complete Works of Edgar Allen Poe*. Edited by James A. Harrison. 17 vols. New York: AMS Press, 1965.

Radhakrishnan, Sarvepalli, and Moore, Charles A. *A Source Book in Indian Philosophy*. Princeton: Princeton University Press, 1957.

Sartre, Jean-Paul. *Search for a Method*. Translated by Hazel E. Barnes. New York: Vintage Books, 1968.

———. *Existentialism*. Translated by Bernard Frechtman. New York: Philosophical Library, 1947.

Saunders, Jason L. *Greek and Roman Philosophy after Aristotle*. New York: Free Press, 1966.

Sextus Empiricus. *Outlines of Pyrrhonism*. Translated by R. G. Bury. In *Sextus Empiricus*, Vol. I. (Loeb Classical Library.) London: William Heinemann, 1933.

Shakespeare, William. *Twenty-Three Plays and the Sonnets*. Edited by Thomas Marc Parrott. New York: Charles Scribner's Sons, 1938.

Smith, Adam. *An Inquiry into the Nature and Causes of the Wealth of Nations*. Edited by Edwin Cannan. 2 vols. London: Methuen and Co., 1904; reprinted Chicago: University of Chicago Press, 1976.

Smith, T. V., and Grene, Marjorie. *From Descartes to Kant*. Chicago: University of Chicago Press, 1933.

Sophocles. *Oedipus the King*. Translated by David Grene. In *Sophocles I*. Chicago: University of Chicago Press, 1954.

Spinoza, Benedict de. *Ethics* preceded by *On the Improvement of the Understanding*. Edited by James Gutmann. New York: Hafner Publishing Co., 1949.

Sprague, Rosamond Kent. *The Older Sophists*. Columbia, South Carolina: University of South Carolina Press, 1972.

Stoicorum veterum fragmenta. Edited by J. von Arnim. 4 vols. Leipzig, 1905-24.

The Ten Principal Upanishads. Translated by Shree Purohit and W. B. Yeats. London: Faber and Faber, 1937.

Thomas Aquinas, Saint. *On Being and Essence*. Translated by Armand Augustine Maurer. Toronto: Pontifical Institute of Medieval Studies, 1949.

———. *Introduction to Saint Thomas Aquinas*. Edited by A. C. Pegis. New York: Modern Library, 1948.

Tolstoy, Leo. *The Death of Ivan Ilych and Other Stories*. Translated by Aylmer Maude. New York: New American Library, 1960.

———. *War and Peace*. Translated by Louise and Aylmer Maude. New York: Simon and Schuster, 1942.

———. *Selected Essays*. Translated by Aylmer Maude. Selected and introduced by Ernest J. Simmons. New York: Modern Library, 1946.

Voltaire. *Candide*. In *The Complete Romances of Voltaire*. New York: Walter J. Black, 1927.

Warren, Henry Clarke. *Buddhism in Translations*. New York: Atheneum, 1974.

Watson, Walter. *Nature and Action*. Ann Arbor, Michigan: University Microfilms, 1958.

———. "Chu Hsi, Plato, and Aristotle." *Journal of Chinese Philosophy*, V (1978), 149-74.

———. "Principles for Dealing with Disorder." *Journal of Chinese Philosophy*, VIII (1981), 349-70.

———. "The Existentializing of Psychoanalysis." *Cross Currents*, XXX (1980-81), 461-63.

———. "The Voices of the God." In *New Essays on Socrates*, edited by Eugene Kelly. Lanham, Maryland: University Press of America, 1984.

Weber, Max. *The Protestant Ethic and the Spirit of Capitalism*. Translated by Talcott Parsons. New York: Charles Scribner's Sons, 1958.

———. *Max Weber on the Methodology of the Social Sciences*. Translated and edited by Edward A. Shils and Henry A. Finch. Glencoe, Ill.: Free Press, 1949.

———. *The Theory of Social and Economic Organization*. Translated by A. M. Henderson and Talcott Parsons. New York: Free Press, 1964.

Wheelwright, Philip. *The Presocratics*. New York: Odyssey Press, 1966.

Whewell, William. *The History of the Inductive Sciences*. 3d ed. 3 vols. London: John W. Parker and Son, 1857.

———. *The Philosophy of the Inductive Sciences*. 2d ed. 2 vols. London: John W. Parker, 1847.

———. *Novum Organum Renovatum*. 3d ed. London: John W. Parker and Son, 1858.

Whitehead, Alfred North. *Process and Reality*. New York: Macmillan Co., 1929.

———. *Adventures of Ideas*. New York: Macmillan Co., 1933.

———. *Modes of Thought*. New York: Macmillan Co., 1938.

Whitehead, Alfred North, and Russell, Bertrand. *Principia Mathematica*. 2d ed. Cambridge: University Press, 1927.

Whitman, Walt. *Leaves of Grass*. Edited by Harold W. Blodgett and Sully Bradley. New York: New York University Press, 1965.

Wittgenstein, Ludwig. *Philosophical Investigations*. Translated by G. E. M. Anscombe. Oxford: Basil Blackwell, 1953.

Index